Christian Perfection

AND

American Methodism

JOHN LELAND PETERS

ISBN 0-88019-341-7

 Schmul Publishing Co., Inc.
Wesleyan Book Club   1995   Salem, Ohio

Printed by
Old Paths Tract Society
Route 2, Box 43
Shoals, IN 47581

Preface

THIS STUDY IS the result of a desire to discover certain facts about John Wesley's doctrine of Christian perfection and in particular to learn what happened to it in the years following Wesley's death. For even a cursory examination of his works makes evident that this doctrine was a distinctive feature of Wesley's thought and teachings. It appears in the early phases of his ministry and continues in undiminished emphasis to its close. Yet W. W. Sweet in his *Methodism in American History* states that in less than a century after Wesley's death the doctrine had become "little more than a creedal matter among the main Methodist bodies."

What brought about this difference of evaluation between John Wesley and the church which regards him as its founder? Had the doctrine been a mere Wesleyan foible? Was it a curious theological anachronism which an increasingly intelligent generation had relegated to its doctrinal attic? Whence was it derived? What had been its historic development? And is its specialized proclamation today the same as when Wesley presented it? The search was encouraged, and this study ensued.

I am particularly indebted to Professor Albert C. Outler and to Dean Emeritus Luther A. Weigle of the Yale Divinity School for the inspiration provided, both in classroom discussion and in personal consultation, to attempt this project. Their suggestions concerning the general outline of the work and their guidance in its development are deeply appreciated. Dr. Richard C. Wolf of Yale has similarly aided in valued criticism and direction.

For assistance in the location and evaluation of relevant sources I am sincerely grateful to Dr. Raymond P. Morris of the Divinity School Library at Yale, to Dr. James R. Joy of the Methodist Historical Society Library in New York, to the Rev. C. H. Stackpole of the New England Methodist Historical Association Library in Boston, and to Miss Isabel Howell formerly of the Methodist Publishing House Library in Nashville.

I have been given every assistance in this task by the personnel of the Sterling Memorial Library at Yale, the Widener Memorial Library at Harvard, and the library of the Boston School of Theology. I acknowledge with deep thanks that consideration.

Finally, to my wife and son, but for whose understanding and patience this venture would never have been possible, I am more deeply indebted than I can possibly acknowledge.

JOHN LELAND PETERS

Foreword

THIS LITTLE BOOK was born out of due time, before there was much interest in John Wesley as a theologian and when interest in the story of the descending fortunes of his ideas among his American followers was limited. Neo-orthodoxy had made its point about the depths and pervasiveness of sin, and Freud's analyses of a libidinous unconscious had made Wesley's definition of sin as the " willful violation of a known law of God" seem quite superficial. In the still bouyant liberal culture of the late 1940s, after victory in war, there was a rekindled optimism, a still unshaken faith in the dogmas of progress and perfectibility. Civil religion and the social gospel had raised the hopes for human self-fulfillment, along with a lively faith in the efficacy of social engineering. It was before the Bay of Pigs, Vietnam, and Watergate. Why, then, a detour of exploration into the ideas of an eighteenth-century Anglican priest about *Christian* perfection—and into the divagations of an unholy war about holiness in nineteenth-century American, in a tradition better known for its enthusiasm than for its reflective temper?

In New Haven, at the Yale Graduate School, young John Peters saw the matter in a different light. At stake, he thought, was a clarification of a crucial issue in at least a couple of chapters in the long story of Christian bafflement about Matthew 5:48: What *is* God's design for the human family, in this life? What is the utmost reach of divine grace and of human participation in the divine life?

Peters was a Wesleyan by upbringing, and so it seemed natural for him to address these questions first to Wesley and then to his putative heirs in America, where the Wesleyan theology had suffered a sea-change in the course of its transplantation and Americanization. Then there was the need for a plausible explanation of the subsequent history of a violent and protracted contention over the question of "entire sanctification" as "a second and separate work of grace, following after justification."

It was characteristic of a good graduate school that such a project was accepted as a suitable dissertation topic; it was a tribute to Peters that he completed the task with honors. This required an uncommon measure of diligence and self-direction, for we who were his supervisors knew enough to hold him to Yale standards but not enough to guide him step-by-step. We could insist on firsthand contact with primary sources, but we could not always foresee what the results might be. I still remember how much I learned over the course of having to verify Peters' references. (At the time, I was still chiefly a patrologist, my acquaintance with Wesley was nominal, and my knowledge of American Methodist history was still dominated by the reigning stereotypes.)

The resulting dissertation was published in 1956 and was received with more respect than excitement. Its impact was limited, partly because of the times and partly because there was no comparable follow-up. The book invited a filling out of its rich number of "opening insights," but Dr. Peters had gone to launch a distinguished career of global Christian philanthrophy, as if he had learned from Wesley that Christian love in praxis is even more fruitful than its academic study and analysis. Even so, the book became a standard reference (it has been cited in all of the essays I have seen on the history of the "holiness movement"—sometimes by authors who seem not to have read it entirely and who certainly did not check out its footnotes and bibliography). Moreover, it exerted a quiet but potent influence in the "rediscoveries" of Wesley that were even then beginning, just as it challenged a newer generation to more critical analyses of American Pentecostalism.

In the ensuing three decades, the atmospheric changes in

Christian theology have included a new focus on Wesley and new perspectives on American Methodism, not to mention the attention lavished on secular developments in the Wesley-inspired "human potential movement." Early in the 1960s, Wesley got a volume of his own in *A Library of Protestant Thought,* which has had a wider circulation than any other volume in that series. A new edition of Wesley's *Works* has been inaugurated and, currently, five volumes of it are in print with four more in the immediate offing. Sophisticated topical studies of Wesley have been multiplying—and not just among Methodists. (Last spring a dissertation on *The Perceptibility of Grace in the Theology of John Wesley: A Roman Catholic Consideration* was submitted to Rome's Angelicum by Daniel J. Luby—and approved!)

Meanwhile, the general situation in American Christianity has been in the throes of drastic change, with the impact of the Second Vatican Council on Roman Catholics and Protestants alike, with most mainline Protestant churches in decline, and with major reversals in the ecumenical movement (faltering at the top, though flourishing at the grassroots). We have seen a tipping of the balance from an effortless domination of the theological scene by old-fashioned "liberals" to a resurgence of the "new evangelicals," who are in the process of discovering their own versions of the social gospel. The tangled web of the holiness controversies has begun to be untangled by a new generation of evangelical scholars. There are, for example, Donald W. Dayton (with his brief study entitled, *The American Holiness Movement: A Bibliographic Introduction,* 1971, and his *Discovering an Evangelical Heritage,* 1976), Vinson Synan (*The Holiness-Pentecostal Movement in the U.S.,* 1971), R.M. Anderson (*Vision of the Disinherited: The Making of American Pentecostalism,* 1979), and George M. Marsden (*Fundamentalism and American Culture,* 1980). And there is preeminently the wide range of studies by Timothy L. Smith, such as his *Called unto Holiness* (1962) and *Revivalism and Social Reform* (1965).

Professor Marsden has expanded our understanding of the

influences of the Keswick Convention on American holiness thought; but no one has gone much farther than Peters in linking the American Methodists with Wesley and his sources. Indeed, save in the case of Professor Smith, it is not clear that other historians of American Pentecostalism have taken Wesley seriously, and certainly they have not probed his sources in the longer Christian tradition. This is important, for it reminds us that the stereotype of Wesley as the effectual tutor to American Methodists was never more than that: a stereotype. While most of the Methodists reverenced his name, they did not trouble themselves with critical studies of his texts and sources.

Recent general surveys of American church history have taken due notice of the holiness controversies (tipping the hat to Peters, by the way); but they have tended to regard it as a species of clan warfare, rather than a parochial conflict about a universal issue. A partial exception to this trend may be seen in Charles Ferguson's *Methodists and the Making of America* (1983), where a vivid chapter on "The Second Blessing" devotes as much space to John Humphrey Noyes as to Phoebe Palmer!

This is to say, then, that the reissue of *Christian Perfection and American Methodism* is by no means a redundancy; it still has much to teach us about the extent of the unfinished business in the field of Wesley studies. It may have even more to teach us about the gaps in the American story. Interpreters of Wesley need to discover what happened to his ideas when they were hybridized with others in the American setting that he was never able to comprehend. American church historians, thus led back to Wesley, might be encouraged to look more deeply into the total tradition in which Wesley (and Jonathan Edwards) were immersed.

There is still more light to be shed on the unhappy tendencies of American Methodists to swirl off into bitter and barren polarities (saved *or* damned; faith alone *or* faith and good works; fideism *or* moralism; "imputation" *or* "impartation"; "gradual" *or* "instantaneous" pefection). Such polarities persist, as if Wesley had struggled in vain to avoid the traditional forensic images of classic Protestantism and to revive the Eastern notion of *teleosis* (perfecting perfection) in the place of a static view of *perfectus est* (perfected perfection). Lastly, and most importantly, we need more clarity as to Wesley's understanding of the person and work of the Holy Spirit as the divine agent of perfecting grace (as indeed of all grace).

It occurs to me that some readers will find it helpful to read this book backwards—that is, to start with the appendices, in which Dr. Peters has collected almost all that Wesley, Fletcher, and Asbury had to say about their experiences of "sanctification." Against so lively a background, the reader might turn to the summary, where Peters's whole thesis is lucidly compacted. After this, the longer expository sections might make more sense when they are read in normal sequence. I suppose, though, that it would be asking too much to suggest that the whole book will make even more sense if Peters's footnotes are examined and the questions that they raise are pursued in their own right.

Here then is a thirty-year-old book that, for all its datedness, still has much to teach at least three audiences: (1) students of Wesley who no longer recognize the intimate connections between the idea of "perfection" and the whole conspectus of his "order of salvation"; (2) American church historians who realize what it was, besides contentiousness, that energized the advocates of "entire sanctification"; and (3) Christians of all sorts and serious inquirers after the truth who can understand anew how the question of sanctification is really a question about the power of God in human life—a question of whether faith is trust more than assent.

Here is a needful reminder to evangelicals that holiness, in the Wesleyan tradition, was never meant to excuse loving their human fellows any less in order to love God more. Here is a useful warning to liberals against twin dangers: the final lassitudes that come with Pelagianism and the final futilities of misplaced prophetic zeal, when it allows trendy rhetoric and token actions to become substitutes for authentic Christian martyrdom.

Most of all, I hope the book will be read for its deepest insights, for then it will spark further reflections on new possibilities in the Christian dialogue about grace. It is significant that other Christians in the current scene—Reformed, Roman Catholic, Lutheran, even Orthodox—are, without abandoning their old convictions, seeking new ways to speak of God's sovereignty. Can Methodists (and Anglicans in the same tradition as Wesley) find new ways of celebrating the triumphs of grace *in this life and this world*, without fixating upon those cultural polarizations that Wesley deplored as "opinions?"

What is left of Latin Christendom is being nudged forward into a postliberal age, in which the soaring hopes of the Enlightenment in "what people can make of people" have lost their bouyancy. In such a situation, nostalgia for whatever is still remembered as the "good old days" is not so harmless a self-deception as it may seem, since it drains the energies needed for pushing across the difficult frontiers of the spirit. Coterie-theologians complain and threaten—and promise more than they have yet delivered. And yet, on this account, to fall in with the world's optimism or pessimism is a form of treason to the Christian's core belief in the assured lordship of Christ, now and whenever. Over the long haul, Christians have found God's good gifts sufficient for their fortitude in troubled times.

Church history has been a sort of relay race in which many septs of the Christian family have taken their turns. Wesley and the American Methodists belong to that succession. Dr. Peters's book has something to teach all of us about how the Christian baton of faith can be picked up and passed on.

Albert C. Outler
Professor of Theology, Emeritus
Southern Methodist University

Introduction

THE WESLEYAN DOCTRINE of Christian perfection has enjoyed widely varying regard in the church whose standards embody it. It has been in certain periods valued and proclaimed. In other periods it has been suspected and ignored. Its status remains uncertain. There is genuine need, however, of understanding and evaluating this facet of Methodist theology since many commentators on that theology have considered "perfection" its distinguishing doctrinal feature.

Any attempt to chart the fortunes of this doctrine must accept at least two tasks. In the first place, what *did* Wesley teach concerning perfection? And do his teachings in one period vary from his teachings in another? If so, did he finally arrive at what may be considered a mature view? This point must be established, for without it all further comments on the doctrine as Wesleyan are remarks at random. And much of the discussion on this subject has been exactly that. In the second place, it is necessary to determine the actual historical record of the proclamation, neglect, modification, or rejection of this doctrine in later Methodism. Only then can evaluating conclusions be drawn.

In the search for needed data it was found that the works which dealt with Wesley's doctrine of perfection were primarily concerned with two major points: (1) to determine its relationship to Roman Catholic and Protestant traditions, and (2) to weigh its ethical, empirical, and sacramental elements.

Some of the most significant of these studies have stressed the dependence of Wesley's doctrinal system upon the Catholic tradition, either directly or as mediated through Arminian Anglicanism. These include J. E. Rattenbury's *Wesley's Legacy to the World*, Umphrey Lee's *John Wesley and Modern Religion*, and R. N.

Flew's *The Idea of Perfection in Christian Theology*. Augustin Leger, who places Wesley well within this tradition, does not, however, deal at any length with his doctrine of perfection since Leger has limited himself to *"la jeunesse de* Wesley." Maximin Piette's *John Wesley in the Evolution of Protestantism* finds his formulation of Christian perfection of little consequence to his general theological system—a "pet theory."

George Croft Cell is the outstanding example of those who view Wesley as primarily within the Reformation tradition. And while the doctrine of perfection, embodying the Catholic ethic of holiness, illustrates Wesley's genius for synthesis, Cell sees it primarily as the high point in Wesley's religious reaction againt the humanism of his day. It was simply the rounding out of Wesley's doctrine of the "entire work of God."

The most characteristic interpretation of Wesley's theology, however, maintains that it was empirically determined. It was Wesley's intense concern with experience which, it is held, shaped his doctrine far more than his dependence upon any particular tradition. H. B. Workman and Henry Bett explain the rise and nature of the doctrine in this fashion. They are joined by S. G. Dimond and George Eayrs, who recognize and report more fully the considerable influence of sacramental nurture on Wesley's developing doctrinal ideas.

Two comprehensive studies of Wesley's theology have been recently published. The first, W. R. Cannon's *The Theology of John Wesley*, is more accurately described by its subtitle: "With Special Reference to the Doctrine of Justification." Cannon holds that "Wesley's doctrine of justification was the measure and determinant of all else." In consequence the doctrine of Christian perfection receives only incidental attention. On the other hand, Harald Lindström's *Wesley and Sanctification* is an exhaustive study attempting a "systematic-theological analysis of the function and significance of sanctification in Wesley's conception of salvation." Lindström feels that "Wesley is primarily concerned with justification and sanctification as the two fundamental doctrines."

But he is also convinced that "of these it is undoubtedly sanctification that receives major attention."

A number of writers stress the practical difficulties which have arisen in connection with the historic preaching of the doctrine. Of these Francis J. McConnell in his *John Wesley* is inclined to feel that the traditional formulation has been a source of "difficulties and divisions and confusions," though the ideal which it reflects "has been the glory of Methodism." But others, such as W. E. Sangster and R. N. Flew, while recognizing the dangers inherent in unwise exposition, believe that the doctrine embodies a dynamic tradition whose values are needed in the personal and corporate experience of Christians today.

As valuable and valued as were these works, none of them answered in any definitive fashion the original problem of the study—why the vicissitudes in the development of the doctrine of Christian perfection? Since their interpretations differed widely, Wesley's own works came to be almost exclusively relied upon. The fourteen-volume collection of his *Works* (1856 edition) was a major source. His *Journal* (Curnock's edition), his *Sermons* (Sugden's edition and the 1857 edition of *Sermons on Several Occasions*), his *Explanatory Notes upon the New Testament,* and particularly his *Letters* (Telford's edition) were constantly consulted primary sources. Such other works of Wesley's as were available were examined to discover qualities which might further illuminate his doctrinal conclusions. George Osborn's *Outlines of Wesleyan Bibliography* and Richard Green's *The Works of John and Charles Wesley—A Bibliography* were used for relevant chronological data. The judgment of Wesley's contemporaries at any point affecting his theological views was given critical attention. And the literary sources to which he was indebted were also considered of primary importance.

The report of this survey of Wesleyana has been given in considerable detail and may appear to consume disproportionate space in a study devoted to one aspect of *American* Methodism. It was felt, however, that any statement purporting to describe Wesley's views concerning Christian perfection was obligated to present an adequate account of the data from which that statement was derived. Further brevity could be had only at the sacrifice of clarity.

In pursuing the study of the development of the doctrine, it was necessary to examine its treatment at the hands of those theologians whose work was considered from time to time standard in Methodism. Thus the works of such men as John Fletcher, Adam Clarke, Richard Watson, Miner Raymond, W. B. Pope, John Miley, T. O. Summers, and that host of writers who chose to defend or attack certain features of the doctrine during the days of high controversy in nineteenth-century American Methodism were examined at relevant points.

The historic fact of the proclamation or neglect of the doctrine was noted, and effort was made to discover the causes which brought about such changes. Records, diaries, conference journals, representative religious periodicals, and reliable secondary sources have been sought out and used wherever possible. In particular the *Methodist Quarterly Review* from 1818 to 1900, the *Quarterly Review of the Methodist Episcopal Church, South,* from 1847 to 1900, the New York *Christian Advocate* and Nashville *Christian Advocate* covering most of the century, and the General Conference journals were comprehensive general indexes of the changing status of the doctrine.

Reliable data concerning the nineteenth-century Holiness Movement were considered of compelling importance. Fortunately the complete edition of the *Guide to Holiness,* from 1839 to 1903, was available, and thoroughly explored. Other publications of the movement were similarly used.

The only really careful effort to trace the history of Wesley's doctrine of Christian perfection in American Methodism through the nineteenth century is M. E. Gaddis' *Christian Perfectionism in America,* a Ph.D. dissertation completed at Chicago University in 1929. Dr. Gaddis attempts a study of all groups who reflect any sort of perfectionism in their doctrinal views. His work is an excellent index to the multitude of American sects which may be so identified. In covering so broad a field, Gaddis necessarily paints with a wide brush. He fails to give, therefore, detailed attention to critical areas of tension within American Methodism. Moreover, he tends to identify perfectionism with sectarian puritanism. He gives relatively little attention to the qualified perfectionism of the Catholic tradition and does not indicate, therefore, how large is the sacramental element in Wesley's own formulation of the doctrine.

It is consequently felt that a more thorough study both of Wesley's doctrine and of nineteenth-century American Methodism is not only justified but needed. For Wesley's doctrine has been too often judged on partial evidence and too often fractionally taught. Moreover, many of the influences upon the theological thought of American Methodism remain to be described. This study, it is hoped, will add to an understanding of the doctrine and of the circumstances which shaped its history in the American denominations which espoused it.

It should be remembered that the purpose of this work is primarily historical, and readers interested in the further study of the doctrine are referred to such works as R. N. Flew's *The Idea of Perfection in Christian Theology,* Harald Lindström's *Wesley and Sanctification,* and W. E. Sangster's *The Path of Perfection.*

Contents

CHAPTER I

The Doctrine in Process of Formation, 1725-64

WHEN JOHN WESLEY prepared his official account of the genesis of his doctrinal views, he simply said: "In 1729, two young men, reading the Bible, saw they could not be saved without holiness, followed after it, and incited others so to do." The statement has the power and the poverty of conciseness.

On the one hand, it would be difficult to exaggerate the influence of the Bible on Wesley's life and thought. He was ready, in fact, to be considered a "Bible bigot," insisting on more than one occasion that the Scriptures alone had been his mentor and guide. On the other hand, Wesley was far from being the "man of one book" he sometimes considered himself. And his opinions and doctrines were shaped by his literary and cultural environment to a considerably greater degree than he appeared to recognize. The manner and measure of that influence is worthy of note.

At the beginning of the eighteenth century the Church of England more nearly resembled a political instrument than a spiritual force. Its policy had been defined by the Bishop of London as the "maintenance of the Protestant Succession, the Church Establishment and the Toleration Act of 1689." It was a policy whose keynote was stability and whose purpose was to obviate a return to the partisan and profitless conflicts of the Commonwealth and Restoration periods. It was designed to satisfy most, palliate some, and offend none too grievously. As such it called for careful restraint. Enthusiasm, that volatile threat to order and discipline, came consequently to be considered not only uncouth but also dangerous. The church, naturally conservative, had become almost entirely subservient to the purposes of civil government.

Nevertheless, there was vitality in both church and chapel. Humanitarian movements budded and flourished. An increasing concern for the welfare of the poor was manifested. There was agitation for prison reform and for the founding of charity schools and hospitals. All this was indicative of a real and socially conscious piety.

In most instances these early reforms were the result of the activity of single individuals or of small, and often obscure, groups. But there was an increasing tendency toward the organization of church-related societies for the accomplishment of religious ends. The aim of these societies was the deliberate encouragement of personal piety. They had their genesis during the reign of Charles II, suffered a partial eclipse under James II, were revived under William and Mary, and prospered greatly during the reign of Queen Anne. A report from one of them states their typical objective: "That the sole design of this Society being to promote real holiness of heart and life, it is absolutely necessary that the persons who enter into it do seriously resolve, by the grace of God, to apply themselves to all means proper to accomplish these blessed ends." [1]

The pursuit of holiness was not, in fact, an uncommon theme in the religious literature at the turn of the century. A sermon preached in 1647 before the House of Commons by Ralph Cudworth, Regius professor of Hebrew at Cambridge, was in general circulation. Its tone was strongly evangelical. Said Cudworth:

The great mystery of the Gospel, is to establish a *God-like* frame and disposition of spirit, which consists in Righteousnesse and true

Holinesse, in the hearts of men. . . . The end of the whole Gospel . . . is, not onely to *cover sinne*, by spreading the Purple Robe of Christ's death and sufferings over it, whilst it still remaineth in us with all its filth and noisomnesse unremoved; but also to convey a powerfull and mighty spirit of holinesse, to *cleanse* us and *free* us from it. And this is a greater grace of God's to us, then [*sic*] the former, which still go both together in the Gospel; besides the free remission and pardon of sinne in the *blood of Christ*, the delivering of us from the power of sinne, by the *Spirit of Christ*, dwelling in our hearts.

And he adds:

The end of the Gospel is *Life* and *Perfection*, 'tis a *Divine Nature*, 'tis a Godlike frame and disposition of spirit; 'tis to make us partakers of the *Image of God* in Righteousnesse and true Holinesse, without which, Salvation itself were but a notion. . . . Grace is *Holinesse Militant* . . . and Glory is nothing else but *Holinesse Triumphant*. . . . Happinesse is nothing, but the releasing and unfettering of our souls, from all these narrow, scant, and particular good things; and espousing them to the Highest and most Universall Good . . . *goodnesse* itself: and this is the same thing that we call Holinesse. . . . I mean by Holinesse, nothing else but God *stamped* & *printed* upon the soul.[2]

A thick volume of fifty-eight sermons on *Holiness the only Way to Happiness*, by Thomas Brooks, a "Congregational Divine," was likewise widely read. The purpose of his treatise, said Brooks, was to encourage his readers

. . . to study holinesse, to love holinesse, to promote holinesse, and to be restlesse till you have experienced the power, and the life, and the sweet of holinesse in your own lives and heart.

His work continues to set forth the "Necessity, Excellency, Rarity, Beauty and Glory of Holiness," warning that

hee that is more affected with that holinesse hee hath, than hee is afflicted about those great measures of holinesse that hee needs, will never bee but a Puny, a Dwarf in holinesse.[3]

Brooks's works were especially well received in dissenting circles, some of his books going into fifty editions.

Better known to churchmen was Richard Lucas' *An Enquiry after Happiness,* a three-volume work which reached its tenth edition in 1764. In Lucas' exposition religious perfection represents a second perceptible stage in the Christian life. He explains it thus:

> The *first change* of a Sinner from Darkness to Light, from Vice to Virtue, and from an aversion for God and Goodness, to a *Sincere,* though not a *Perfect* Love of both, is very palpable: *So again, the* change from a state of weakness and inconstancy, to one of strength; of conflict and difficulty, to one of ease and liberty; of fear and doubt, to one of confidence and pleasure, is little less evident than sensible. *But* the several degrees of growth *afterwards,* the improvements, whatever they be, of a mature state, are of *another* nature, not consisting in a *change,* but *addition;* and that made insensibly.[4]

This perfection is, in brief, the divinely aided attainment of a "well settled and established *Habit* of Goodness." Despite the fact that such a "Habit of Goodness" may be actually attained, Lucas is insistent that such perfection was an ever-developing maturity.

Wesley never specifically acknowledged any doctrinal indebtedness to Lucas; but Alexander Knox, eminent Anglican and Wesley's personal friend, points out that one of Wesley's early hymns, called "Zeal," is "from beginning to end, a close versification of a passage in Lucas."

The most influential churchman of the time was Archbishop John Tillotson, silver-tongued and highly regarded. Tillotson had been strongly influenced by the Cambridge Platonists, that thoughtful and devout group who sought to maintain religion and philosophy as allies rather than as aliens. He joined them in affirming that "holiness is an essential and principal ingredient of happiness." He further declared that holiness had both negative and positive aspects: the absence of sin and the presence of grace—"Whenever we are made holy, every lust and corruption in us is supplemented by the contrary grace."

However, the burden of Tillotson's teaching was that holiness was principally a "course of good works." In a typical discourse he says:

> And what an encouragement is this to holiness . . . Let us then do all the good that possibly we can . . . let us serve God industriously . . . knowing that no good action . . . shall lose [its] reward.[5]

Wesley was acquainted with Tillotson's views and strongly opposed the tendency to reduce holiness to the level of a mere prudential morality.

For the development of his own views on this subject Wesley gives explicit credit to three authors of devotional classics: Jeremy Taylor, Thomas à Kempis, and William Law. He first read Taylor's *Rule and Exercises of Holy Living and Dying* in 1725, "being," as he said, "in the twenty-third year of my age." He was "exceedingly affected" by those portions of the work which dealt with purity of intention and "instantly resolved to dedicate all my life to God, all my thoughts and words, and actions."[6] When, not long thereafter, he read the *Imitation of Christ*, this impulse to "give God all my heart" was reinforced.

But it was Law's *Treatise on Christian Perfection* and *Serious Call to a Devout and Holy Life* that shaped Wesley's developing doctrinal views. Few books have had the influence which these volumes, especially the latter, exerted upon their day. Written in a sparkling style and illuminating by homely illustrations the author's contention that a holy life is dependent upon a new principle of spirit and practice, the *Serious Call* was a powerful instrument against the current Deism. So influential were these volumes that their publication has been called the spark which kindled the flame of the Evangelical Revival.

Wesley began reading Law's works shortly after his election as Fellow of Lincoln College, Oxford, in March, 1726. He had only six months before been ordained deacon, having chosen to accept his father's recommendation that he enter holy orders. He had acted, it would appear, out of sincere motives but with no moving sense of vocation. As he read Law, however, he was deeply affected. He reported:

> Meeting now with Mr. Law's *Christian Perfection* and *Serious Call*, although I was much offended at many parts of both, yet they convinced me more than ever of the exceeding height and breadth and depth of the law of God. The light flowed in so mightily upon my soul, that everything appeared in a new view. I cried to God for help, and resolved not to prolong the time of obeying Him as I had never done before. And by continued endeavour to keep His whole law, inward and outward, to the utmost of my power, I was persuaded that I should be accepted of Him, and that I was even then in a state of salvation.[7]

Turning to the Bible to check there his newly acquired views, Wesley found only confirmation. He said:

> I then saw in a stronger light than ever before that only *one thing is needful,* even *faith that worketh by the love* of God and man, all inward and outward holiness.[8]

Out of such insights, not yet fully comprehended, grew the doctrines of Methodism, in particular the Wesleyan doctrine of Christian perfection. It was John Wesley's most distinctive doctrinal contribution, and its development extended over the greater portion of his life.

To this development as a result of his wide-ranging literary taste Wesley brought the contributions not only of Taylor, Law, and à Kempis, but also of Clement of Alexandria, Plotinus, Augustine, Tauler, the Cambridge Platonists, Molinos, Antoinette Bourignon, Madame Guyon, Macarius the Egyptian, François de Sales, Juan de Castaniza, Fénelon, and Pascal. From among these writers, representing as they do the mystical tradition of the Church, it is obvious that Wesley was most influenced by that distinctively practical type exemplified in Law and Taylor.

When George Croft Cell says that Wesley's theology was a "necessary synthesis of the Protestant ethic of grace with the

Catholic ethic of holiness,"[9] it is this rich field of sources which illuminates and justifies his characterization. It would be difficult to arrive at a more apt description than Cell gives, though it may be added that, while the Catholic tradition indicated the goal, the Protestant emphasis provided the dynamic.

The ideal of Christian perfection, then, was almost wholly derived by Wesley from the devotional literature in which he was steeped—plus the Bible. The outline of that ideal was to be clearly discerned by 1733. On the first day of that year Wesley preached before the University at St. Mary's, Oxford, his sermon on "The Circumcision of the Heart." In that sermon the influence of his study in the devotional classics stands clearly revealed. The sermon has much to say about love as the epitome of perfection, and the Christian goal is described as

that habitual disposition of soul which, in the sacred writings, is termed holiness; and which directly implies, the being cleansed from sin, . . . and, by consequence, the being endued with those virtues which were also in Christ Jesus; the being so "renewed in the spirit of our mind," as to be "perfect as our Father in heaven is perfect."[10]

The Anglo-Catholic tradition could scarcely have been more explicitly represented. This sermon was a definitive expression about which Wesley was fifty years later to say: "This is the view of religion I then had, which, even then I scrupled not to term 'perfection.' This is the view I have of it now, without any material addition or diminution."[11] Thus early the ideal was fully "onstage." Such refinements as later developed were to be more a reconsideration of paths toward the goal than any significant alteration in the concept of the goal itself.

Although the *content* was adequately defined by 1733, the *method* of attainment was evolved only through successive periods of empirically determined judgments. It is in the development of this latter area, the study of the religious experience of individual Christians, that Wesley reflects his most characteristic approach to the problems of theology and religion. Hereafter, religious experience—his own and others—would be for Wesley an authoritative criterion of theology.

Wesley as a "religious" man was not satisfied merely to define the goal. Once glimpsing it he says, "I sought after it from that hour." He began by an assiduous cultivation of all the precepts learned from Taylor, Law, and à Kempis—enforcing where he could this regimen on others. He won opprobrium and drew grim satisfaction from it. To his brother Samuel he wrote:

> To the objection, you are despised at Oxford . . . I answer: (1) A Christian will be despised anywhere. (2) No one is a Christian till he is despised.

Yet his principal confession during this period was one of frustration. To his mother he wrote: "What shall I do . . . to gain . . . the mind which was also in Jesus Christ? . . . This is the very thing I want to do . . . but how?"

It was this pursuit of perfection which led him to leave England for Georgia. In a letter to a friend he said:

> I have been hitherto unwilling to mention the grounds of my design of embarking for Georgia. . . . My chief motive, to which all the rest are subordinate, is the hope of saving my own soul. . . . But you will perhaps ask: "Cannot you save your own soul in England as well as in Georgia?" I answer,—No; neither can I hope to attain the same degree of holiness here which I may there.[12]

He expected to find in Oglethorpe's new colony that which always seemed to elude him at home. But whatever else Georgia may have had to give to Wesley, and it was much, the principal contribution at this point was a shattering but indispensable disillusionment. He did not discover among the "noble savages" of the New World that pristine purity so romantically attributed to them. He did discover new areas of his own inadequacy.

It was the Georgian interlude, in fact, which opened the door to an aspect of religion with which Wesley was in large measure unacquainted. On the stormy outward journey Wesley had been much impressed by the calmness of a group of Moravians who were his fellow travelers. Since he did not share their equanimity, Wesley came to feel that they were in possession of spiritual resources to which he was a stranger. He had an opportunity later to discuss the matter with their leader, Bishop Spangenberg. The conversation did not reassure him. Wesley reported it as follows:

[Spangenberg]: "Does the Spirit of God bear witness with your spirit that you are a child of God," . . . I paused, and said, "I know He is the Saviour of the world." "True," replied he; "but do you know He has saved you?" . . . I said, "I do." But I fear they were vain words.[13]

Tyerman reports this as "an odd conversation . . . leading Wesley to think of doctrines which took the next two years to understand."

Further stay in Georgia brought him no closer to the goal he was seeking. Indeed, he returned to England in greater dissatisfaction than when he had embarked.

Early in 1738, however, Peter Böhler, an ordained Moravian missionary on his way to the Carolinas, stopped for about three months in London. John and Charles Wesley, at that time in close association with the Moravians, were his frequent companions. Their conversations revolved around the meaning of faith, and Böhler was insistent that saving faith brought with it both dominion over sin and true peace of mind—both holiness and happiness. He urged them to seek this "free gift of God"; and John, convinced, began not only to seek but to preach it.

The particular element in Böhler's teaching which seemed to impress Wesley most strongly was the instantaneous character of the faith described. On April 22, 1738, he wrote:

I met Peter Böhler once more. I had now no objection to what he said of the nature of faith. . . . Neither could I deny either the happiness or holiness which he described as fruits of this living faith. . . . But . . . I could not understand how this faith should be given in a moment: how a man could *at once* be thus turned from darkness to

light. . . . I searched the Scriptures again: . . . but, to my utter aston-
ishment, found scarce any instances there of other than *instantaneous*
conversions. . . . I had but one retreat left; namely, *"Thus,* I grant,
God wrought in the *first* ages of Christianity; but the times are
changed. . . ." But on *Sunday,* the 23rd, I was beat out of this retreat
too, by the concurring evidence of several living witnesses; who testified
God had thus wrought in themselves. . . . Here ended my disputing.
I could now only cry out, "Lord, help Thou my unbelief!" [14]

At this point, as in subsequent doctrinal issues, it was the concurrence of "living witnesses" which was the decisive factor in
shaping Wesley's conclusions.

The events of the following month, during which Wesley continued to seek for the faith that Böhler had described—"though
with strange indifference, dullness, and coldness, and unusually
frequent lapses into sin"—are too well known to require reiteration. The climax came on the evening of May 24 when "very
unwillingly" Wesley attended a meeting of a religious society in
Aldersgate Street. There while he listened to a reading of Luther's
preface to Romans, he entered into his famous "heart-warming"
experience.

Exactly what was the significance of this experience? There are
those who insist that the character of the May 24th event has
been generally misread. In support of that claim Wesley's amendments to some of his pre-Aldersgate assertions are cited to show
that he came to see this experience as a stage rather than as a
crisis. Certainly these are pertinent. In 1738, for instance, he
wrote: "I who went to America to convert others was never converted myself." But thirty-three years later he added to this
record, "I am not so sure of this."

Again in 1738 he wrote: "Does all this [strenuous religious
activity] give me a claim to the holy, heavenly, divine character
of a Christian? By no means." And again he later added, "I had
even then the faith of a *servant,* though not that of a *son.*" [15]

It seems sufficient to observe that the controversy arises principally out of a differing definition of terms. On the one hand there

are those who think of conversion in the more general sense of the "turning of a man of the world to God." For them Wesley's decision in 1725 is a sufficiently clear point of departure—a conversion. On the other hand there are those who consider conversion as an evangelical experience by which one receives the "consciousness of being saved by faith in Christ." To them the spiritual bench mark is May 24, 1738.

This very issue had perplexed Wesley's older brother Samuel. His bewilderment is reflected in the following letter:

What Jack means by his not being a Christian till last month I understand not. . . . I do not hold it at all unlikely, that a perpetual intenseness of thought, and want of sleep, may have disordered my brother.[16]

But John answers the question in this fashion:

By a Christian, I mean one who believes in Christ, as that sin has no more dominion over him, and in this obvious sense of the word, I was not a Christian until May 24 last past. For till then sin had the dominion over me, although I fought with it continually; but surely then from that time to this it hath not.[17]

This, it should be remembered, was in 1738. Before many years had passed, Wesley arrived at a doctrine of "degrees" of faith. By 1745 he was saying:

We allow there may be infinite degrees in seeing God: even as many as there are between him who sees the sun when it shines on his eyelids closed, and him who stands with his eyes wide open in the full blaze of his beams.[18]

As a consequence he increasingly hesitated to make hard and fast distinctions with regard to spiritual states. The qualifying amendments which he added to his *Journal* in 1771 are, therefore, but an expression of this developing attitude.

Whatever the judgment upon the Aldersgate Street experience, the relevance of the event for this study is its effect upon Wesley's doctrine of Christian perfection. It is apparent that he was fully prepared by Böhler's counsel and Moravian testimony to expect that this heart-warming experience was to bring him not only the assurance which he sought, "that faith which none can have without knowing that he hath it," but the "inward holiness" which for some years had been his goal. In both instances he was to suffer a measure of disappointment.

First, and despite Böhler's avowals, Wesley's tide of joyful assurance began to ebb. Now he recalled what another Moravian, Arvid Gradin, had told him concerning a second crisis subsequent to initial regeneration which brings "deliverance from every fleshly desire, and from every outward and inward sin." This, he had been told, is the "witness of the spirit." Thus in a letter to his brother Samuel he says:

> This witness of the spirit I have not, but I patiently wait for it. I know many who have already received it, more than one or two in the very hour we were praying for it.[19]

But apparently it did not come to Wesley. By late November he was declaring that his heart was "cold and senseless" with "no love or joy in the Holy Ghost." "I want stirring up," he wrote, "or, rather, I want to be made alive." He was deeply humbled, almost despairing, and finally convinced that he was no Christian at all. These harsh self-condemnations can be and have been variously explained. Wesley, for instance, was still under the strong influence of Peter Böhler, who had taught him that

1. When a man has living faith in Christ, then is he justified:
2. This is always given in a moment;
3. And in that moment he has peace with God;
4. Which he cannot have without knowing that he has it.
5. And being born of God, he sinneth not;
6. Which deliverance from sin he cannot have without knowing that he has it.[20]

Finding himself lacking in sufficient intensity at points four and six, Wesley concluded that he had no saving faith whatsoever. His disavowals followed. With the passing of time, however, he reconsidered his denials.

Again and again throughout his long career by references both direct and indirect Wesley specified 1738 as the beginning of his evangelical insights. Moreover, he directly repudiated his earlier disavowals in a letter to the Bishop of Exeter, who had extracted and printed these self-denunciations of 1738-39. He quotes them in 1751 as proof of Wesley's own low spiritual state. Wesley, charging the bishop with no regard for "mercy, justice nor truth," reminds him in reply that these citations were from a particularly trying period in Wesley's own early spiritual development. He adds:

> To any who knew something of inward religion I should have observed that this is what serious divines mean by desertion. . . . Sir, I do not tell you or any man else that "I cannot now find the love of God in myself." [21]

The fact remains that the heart-warming experience at Aldersgate Street Chapel did not do for Wesley all that he had been led to expect. For him the goal of Christian perfection was still ahead.

But Wesley was not content to form his doctrinal conclusions from his own experience alone. As early as August of 1738 he had started collecting and tabulating accounts of those acquaintances whose spiritual histories he considered significant. He was at first strongly attracted to the Moravians and in a visit to Frankfort reported to his brother Charles that

> here I continually met with what I sought for . . . : persons saved from inward as well as outward sin . . . and from all doubt and fear by the abiding witness of "the Holy Ghost given unto them." [22]

It was the myopic ecstacy of a fresh and fervent love. Before many weeks had passed, he revised his judgment. He was repelled by what he considered their quietism and antinomianism, neither of which had any place in his conception of holiness.

By December of 1738 he turned his attention increasingly toward his fellow "Methodists." He wrote to many of them "concerning the state of their souls," and it was their answers which began that clinical collection of personal testimony which with its emphasis on experience was increasingly to affect Wesley's doctrine of Christian perfection.

The earliest result of this attention to the claims of experience was confusion. For instance, Wesley, seeking to transmit a systematic account of what he had heard on his visit to Herrnhut, wrote to Charles as follows concerning the Moravian opinion then prevailing:

> That we ought to distinguish carefully, both in thinking and speaking, between faith (absolutely speaking), which is one thing; justifying or saving faith, which is a second thing (and ought to be called, not faith absolutely, but always justifying or saving faith); the assurance of faith, where we know and feel that we are justified; and the being born again, which they say is a fourth thing, and often distant in time (as well as in the notion of it) from all the rest.[23]

But such careful refinements of principles so subjectively derived made neither for clarity nor for peace. Wesley was unable to make personal application of such counsel. He was certain only of his dissatisfaction.

In early December of 1744, however, he began to meet with witnesses who testified that they had by faith already come into possession of the perfection which he sought and which he had been tentatively preaching. Of these witnesses he said:

> Dec. 2, *Sun.*—I was with two persons who believe they are saved from all sin. Be it so, or not, why should we not rejoice in the work of God, so far as it is unquestionably wrought in them? For instance, I ask John C., "Do you pray always? Do you rejoice in God every moment? Do you in everything give thanks? In loss? In pain? In sickness, weariness, disappointments? Do you desire nothing? Do you fear nothing? Do you feel the love of God continually in your heart? Have you a witness, in whatever you speak or do, that it is pleasing to God?" If he can solemnly and deliberately answer in the affirma-

tive, why do I not rejoice and praise God in his behalf? Perhaps because I have an exceeding complex idea of sanctification or a sanctified man. And so, for fear he should not have attained all I include in that idea, I cannot rejoice in what he has attained.[24]

At this early date Wesley seemed reluctant to receive such testimonials. Other and improper claims had previously been made which the Calvinistic "Methodists" had seized upon to discredit the entire doctrine. However, these two in 1744 were only the vanguard of many who came before him. And as they continued to come, Wesley put them under the "most searching questions we could devise."

It is possible to trace Wesley's changing reactions to these claims of attainment. In 1744 he seemed inclined to discount them. Gradually, however, he came to concede that such witnesses may, possibly, be not self-deceived. Even so he counseled restraint and reticence in making such claims. His advice was as follows:

Q. 13. Suppose one had attained to this, would you advise him to speak of it? A. Not to them who know not God. It would only provoke them to contradict and blaspheme. Nor to any without some particular good in view. And then they should have an especial care to avoid all appearance of boasting.[25]

This was in 1747. In the ten succeeding years his opinion was greatly modified. Many of his writings reflect a conviction of the validity of an instantaneous attainment. But in a letter to Thomas Olivers, written in March of 1757, he cautioned, "We should neither be forward nor backward in believing those who think they have attained the second blessing. Of those in Courtmatrix and Ballingarrane I can form no judgment yet." And as late as 1759 he was at times still reflecting that mood.

In February of the following year, however, a revival broke out in Yorkshire. Of it Wesley said, "Here began that glorious work of sanctification which had been nearly at a stand for twenty years."

The Yorkshire revival spread; and with its spread—and the increasing testimonies to "salvation from all sin"—Wesley's long-ebbing dubiety disappeared. He was particularly impressed that these witnesses "answered every one without hesitation, and with the utmost simplicity." Moreover, they seemed to agree in that they regularly declared that "constant communion with God the Father and the Son fill[ed] their hearts with humble love." As a consequence of these repeated claims which, though coming from widely scattered areas, reflected what he considered to be a spontaneous unanimity, Wesley laid aside all tendency to qualify his endorsement and roundly affirmed:

Now this is what I always did, and do now, mean by perfection. And this I believe many have attained, on the same evidence that I believe many are justified. May God increase their number a thousandfold.[26]

Soon the trickle of witnesses to Christian perfection had become a stream, and Wesley made a conscientious effort to examine them all. The result was that he came to say:

Many think they are justified, and are not; but we cannot infer that none are justified. So neither, if many think they are "perfected in love," and are not, will it follow that none are so. Blessed be God, though we set an hundred enthusiasts aside, we are still "encompassed with a cloud of witnesses," who have testified, and do testify, in life and in death, that perfection which I have taught these forty years! [27]

From 1759 on witnesses to the instantaneous attainment of entire sanctification were never lacking. By 1762 Wesley considered that a "day of Pentecost" was "fully come," for

we did hear of persons sanctified, in London, and most other parts of England, and in Dublin, and many other parts of Ireland, as frequently as of persons justified, although instances of the latter were far more frequent than they had been for twenty years before.[28]

Even after these surging revival years witnesses still appeared in abundance. In 1770 the Whitby Society reported "sixty-five professed to be entirely sanctified." And three years later Wesley wrote: "In most places in the kingdom there is such a thirst after holiness as I scarce ever knew before." As late as 1788 Wesley was saying: "I believe no year has passed since that time [1760-62] wherein God has not wrought the same work in many others." [29]

It was this continuing and consistent evidence of experience which caused Wesley *finally* to orient his doctrine around the concept of an instantaneous act of the Holy Spirit receivable *now* and *by faith*. He had been moving toward it since 1738, but almost twenty years elapsed before he gave it unreserved emphasis. The revival of 1759-63 furnished him with data in such quantity as to demand explanation—and for which he could find but one. It was the final precipitant in a hitherto unstable solution. He halted no longer between two opinions. Entire sanctification henceforth was a gift of God, who "is able and willing to do it now. And why not? Is not a moment to Him the same as a thousand years?"

CHAPTER II

The Doctrine
Stated and Qualified

IN THE LATE 1760's Wesley's doctrine of Christian perfection came to its full-orbed presentation. There had been a quarter-century of uncertainty and confusion—of claims made and withdrawn, of affirmation and qualification, of conclusion and amendment. In his early post-Aldersgate sermons Wesley had confounded results which he later distinguished as belonging to (1) the new birth and (2) entire sanctification. At a much later date he readily admitted that his views "at first" were neither clear nor distinct. In 1740 he had advanced a belief in "mental perfection"—those possessed of the "great salvation" would "see the way straight before them" and be untroubled by temptation. These extreme views had, however, an early mortality.

In 1766 there appeared the *Plain Account of Christian Perfection*. It was Wesley's most comprehensive exposition of his doctrine. And its fourth edition, in 1777, remained Wesley's definitive statement of his position. He' included it without further revision in the *Discipline* of 1789.

The *Plain Account* contains in full quotation or in summary almost everything Wesley had written on the subject prior to its publication. Here was his official view. Here was the doctrine as he proclaimed and defended it. One word of caution is needed for its interpretation: the *Plain Account* delineates the *progress* of Wesley's thought, and quotations from its earlier sections do not necessarily represent his final judgment. This rather obvious fact is frequently forgotten or ignored.

His own eleven-point summary, which was written in 1764 and which he included in the closing pages of the *Plain Account,* is a succinct presentation of the doctrine. The following analysis is based upon it.

First of all, Christian perfection is of such a character that it may be experienced in this life. Said Wesley:

1. There is such a thing as perfection; for it is again and again mentioned in Scripture.
2. It is not so early as justification; for justified persons are to "go on unto perfection."
3. It is not so late as death; for St. Paul speaks of living men that were perfect.

Here the entire argument rests upon certain passages of scripure. To support his first claim Wesley refers chiefly to Matt. 5:48 (which he translates as "Therefore ye shall be perfect, as your father in heaven is perfect."); II Cor. 7:1; Phil. 3:15; Heb. 6:1; 10:14; and Jas. 1:4. For his second and third statements Wesley depends upon Heb. 6:1 and Phil. 3:15. It is evident that he is thinking of perfection as an event in time—not a development but the culminating of a development, not sanctification but entire sanctification. He sets a point after justification as a *terminus a quo* and a point, however indefinite, sometime before death as a *terminus ad quem.*

There had been a time when Wesley had believed that perfection was the immediate result of justification by faith; and though he soon abandoned that view, he found it necessary to combat its frequent reappearance among his followers. In 1750 he strove to make this distinction clear by pointing out that such identification was Moravian and not Methodist. But the contrary opinion did not easily go down. As late as 1772 he writes thus to the sister of one of his local preachers:

You seemed a little inclined to that new opinion which lately sprung up among you—that we are (properly) *sanctified* when we are justified. You did not observe that this strikes at the root of perfection; it leaves no room for it at all. If we are never sanctified in any other sense than we are sanctified then, Christian perfection has no being.[1]

Wesley is here dealing with a situation which arose out of his failure to maintain and insist on the original distinction enjoined between sanctification and entire sanctification. More and more frequently the former was used when the latter was intended. Consequently, in time the statement, which Wesley held to be entirely Pauline, that when a man is justified, he is also sanctified (in the more restricted sense which did not include entire sanctification), came to mean that a justified person is sanctified in the more popular sense, which included entire sanctification. Thus in the societies there had grown up this identification of justification (or properly its subjective counterpart, regeneration) and sanctification in its complete sense. Wesley sought to clarify this. He cried out against the "mischievousness of that opinion,—that we are *wholly* sanctified when we are justified. . . . It does immense harm: it entirely blocks up the way to any farther change."[2] But he was not always heeded nor understood.

The confusion roots, of course, in the ease with which in Wesley's system regeneration may be identified with sanctification. They both have to do with that "real, inward change" which is concomitant with justification and are at that point indistinguishable in practical result. But Wesley maintains further that sanctification is a process, generally long, whereby the believer is brought into that "holiness without which no man shall see the Lord." Regeneration, a complete work in itself, is the beginning of sanctification. It is the primary and basic change which continues in that process of development called sanctification.

Regeneration according to Wesley is not sanctification; it "is

only the threshold of sanctification, the first entrance upon it." [3]
And wholly to identify these two was not only to cancel out the
concept of entire sanctification but to make the "threshold" the
full extent of the spiritual journey. Therefore in this summary
Wesley says, "It it not so early as justification."

As for the lapse of time necessary to the attainment of Christian perfection, Wesley still believed that such attainment was
possible only after a long and gradual period of development—
though he was more and more inclined to recognize as valid the
instances which seemed to violate the rule.

Just as he was at one time inclined to believe that perfection
followed immediately upon justification, so there had been a time
(before Aldersgate) when Wesley was certain that sanctification
was accomplished in the "hour and article" of death and by its
instrumentality. Even in 1767 he seems still to be of the opinion
that the moment before death is for many the moment of their
entire santification. He writes thus to Charles, "As to the time,
I believe this instant generally is the instant of death, the moment
before the soul leaves the body. But," he adds, "I believe it may
be ten, twenty, or forty years before death." All that he maintains
here, however, is that "it is not so late as death."

*In the second place, since it is an affair of this life, Christian
perfection is a necessarily limited perfection.*

4. It is not absolute. Absolute perfection belongs not to man, nor
to angels, but to God alone.

5. It does not make a man infallible: None is infallible, while he
remains in the body.

Here are the points at which perfection is not perfection. And
unless the term itself be ruled out as altogether inapplicable, the
first qualification needs little by way of explication. As Wesley
sees them, angels are

those glorious beings [who] never *left their first estate,* never declined
from their original perfection, all their native faculties are unimpaired,

their understanding in particular is still a lamp of light, their apprehension of all things clear and distinct, and their judgment always true.[4]

Man, on the other hand, having fallen, is unable to think at all "but by the mediation of organs which are weakened and depraved." Perfection in the angelic sense is in consequence not possible to him. Absolute perfection, which is not possible even to unfallen angels, would therefore be even further removed.

As to the second qualification, Wesley had at one time seemed to teach that Christian perfection did bring infallibility to its recipients. In his preface to the 1740 edition of *Hymns and Sacred Poems*, Wesley had stated that the sanctified would be freed from fear or doubt "either as to their state in general or as to any particular action." This position he was not long in correcting. But he continued to maintain that in certain distinctive spiritual realms such Christians were possessed of an insight and an awareness not given to the "natural" man. Even here, however, definite limitations were recognized. To understand the nature of the Trinity, to explain the Incarnation, accurately to foretell the "times and seasons when God will work His great works upon the earth"— all this is beyond the power even of him "made perfect in love."

Moreover, "the highest perfection which man can attain, while the soul dwells in the body, does not exclude ignorance and error, and a thousand other infirmities."[5] This ignorance and error does not extend to "things essential to salvation" but "in things unessential to salvation they do err, and that frequently." In his sermon "On Perfection," which is about forty years later than his standard sermon "On Christian Perfection," Wesley readily admits that

from wrong judgments, wrong words and actions will necessarily flow. And in some cases, wrong affections also may spring from the same source. I may judge wrong of you; I may think more or less highly of you than I ought to think. And this mistake in my judgment may not only occasion something wrong in my behaviour, but it may have a still deeper effect; it may occasion something wrong in my affection.

From a wrong apprehension, I may love and esteem you either more or less than I ought.

There may be errors, then, not only of behavior but of attitude. This represents Wesley's general tendency, as he grew older, toward a flexible application of the details of his doctrine of perfection. For to be mortal and yet perfect was no simple matter. And so, as he counseled with sensitive souls who sought to determine their own spiritual status, Wesley took pains to point out that, while the Christian "need never more feel pride, anger, or any other evil temper," is was also true that

there is an anger which is not sinful, a disgust at sin which is often attended with much commotion of the animal spirits: and I doubt whether we can well distinguish this from sinful anger but by that light from heaven.[6]

He goes even further and declares that "anger at sin, accompanied with love and compassion to the sinner, is so far from being itself a sin, that it is rather a duty." He sums up the matter thus: "Truth and falsehood, and so right and wrong tempers, are often divided by an almost imperceptible line. . . . In many cases we cannot distinguish them but by the unction of the Holy One."[7]

The fact is that Wesley neither expected nor desired that entire sanctification should equate the destruction of those impulses which go to make up the complex constituents of human personality. In his more mature years he wrote, with some injustice to Clement's Christian "Gnostic":

Many years ago I might have said, but I do not now,
    Give me a woman made of stone
    A widow of Pygmalion.
And just such a Christian one of the Fathers, Clemens Alexandrinus, describes; but I do not admire that description now as I did formerly. I now see a Stoic and a Christian are different characters.[8]

A month later he said in similar vein, "I want more of human mingled with the divine. . . . I desire no apathy in religion; a Christian is very far from a Stoic."

As Wesley completes his picture, the perfect Christian is still robustly human. His judgment is affected by the limitations of his knowledge—and his actions and affections, based on that judgment, are accordingly faulty. He does, and should, possess impulses which, though refined, require the constant guidance of the Holy Spirit lest they cross the well-nigh indistinguishable line between right and wrong expression. He is not only liable to error; he does err. For this reason Wesley was convinced

that a truly sanctified person does involuntarily fall short in divers instances of the rule marked out in the 13th chapter to the Corinthians. And that on *this* account, they continually need their Advocate with the Father. And I never talked with one person who denied it.[9]

It would be an egregious error to conclude that, because he readily admitted these limitations, Wesley was ever tolerant of antinomianism. It was his aversion to this facet of their teaching that led to the early, and painful, break with the Moravians. It was a similar aversion that led to his later, and equally painful, separation from the Calvinistic Methodists. For Wesley, Christian perfection had been from the very first a concept intensely ethical in its stress. The Minutes of his early conferences are specific in their attack upon antinomianism. He refused to be forced by this aversion into an endorsement of work-righteousness, but he did not hesitate to describe antinomianism as an instrument of Satan "which strikes directly at the root of all holiness."

To the charge that he had taught "that good works are not only not necessary, but also dangerous," Wesley replied:

The truth is, we have been these thirty years continually reproached for just the contrary to what you dream of: with making the way to heaven too strait, with being ourselves "righteous overmuch," and teaching others they could not be saved without so many works as it was impossible for them to perform. And to this day, instead of teaching men that they may be saved by a faith which is without good works, . . . we teach exactly the reverse, continually insisting on all outward as well as all inward holiness.[10]

In the flush of his early evangelical experience Wesley had yet written:

The Gospel of Christ knows of no religion, but social; no holiness, but social holiness. *Faith working by love* is the length and breadth and depth and height of Christian perfection.[11]

And nothing in his later works indicates a changed point of view. Good works, Wesley held, "are a condition (though not the meritorious cause) of final salvation." [12]

Christian perfection, moreover, may or may not be sinless, depending upon the interpretation of the term.

6. Is it sinless? It is not worth while to contend for a term. It is "salvation from sin."

It may not be worth while to "contend for," but it is of value to examine further the term "sinless" as it relates to Christian perfection. What, for instance, did Wesley mean by sin? And in what sense, if any, is perfection "sinless"?

In an effort to leave no loophole for Calvinism, Wesley had said:

Nothing is sin, strictly speaking, but a voluntary transgression of a known law of God. Therefore every voluntary breach of the law of love is sin; and nothing else, if we speak properly. To strain the matter farther is only to make way for Calvinism. There may be ten thousand wandering thoughts and forgetful intervals without any breach of love, though not without transgressing the Adamic law. But Calvinists would fain confound these together.[13]

This was his standard definition. It stemmed from his Arminianism and from that azimuth clearly marked off as sin that only for which personal guilt could be ascribed. Sin, "properly so called," was only that for which man might be held directly responsible. And Wesley would say that man, limited as he was, could be held responsible only for those moral issues of which he was aware.

It might be rightly observed that in so limiting his definition,

Wesley was overlooking some plain facts with regard to human nature. Had he forgotten how easily the mind can be clouded by its own rationalizations, how loath to and incompetent for honest self-appraisal man is, and how insensitive to social issues and to their own shortcomings the most saintly have often been? Perhaps he had.

Confronted with such considerations, however, Wesley would probably have maintained that, even so, his definition was relevant. Any sin which involved guilt, he would reiterate, required intelligent freedom of choice. Where the highest possibility had been presented and choice had been made of anything less, therein was sin, "properly so called."

Reinhold Niebuhr appears to deny that the highest possibility *can* be chosen. "In the Christian interpretation of moral evil," he says, "guilt is attached not only to actions in which the individual is free to choose a higher possibility and fails to do so, but in which higher possibilities, which the individual is not free to choose, reveal the imperfection of the action which he is forced to take." [14] With this Wesley would not agree. By "possibility" he would mean that which the individual is actually able to accomplish. Niebuhr's impossible "higher possibility" is Wesley's impossible "full conformity to the perfect law."

Wesley would insist that guilt was entailed at the point where the uncoerced will turn from moral heroism to compromised good. Again, where righteousness became self-conscious, there was sin. Humility had been bartered for pride. In these instances a recognized issue had been unworthily decided. There had been a "voluntary transgression of a known law." The personal agent had been guilty at the point of deliberate commission or omission— responsible also for the ensuing results. Moreover, in the original Methodist polity, which must be always considered as the proving ground for Wesley's teachings, an individual was not left to his own interior judgment as to the substance or quality of his piety. The society, the bands, the class meetings were specifically devised to bring the critical judgment of the spiritual community to bear upon its members, particularly upon such as might otherwise fail to recognize the fact and nature of their own transgressions. In such a community one's judgment of his own degree of sanctification was subject to constant modification. Such a climate of Christian nurture and mutual counsel was designed to inform benevolent ignorance and to detect malevolent intention. It must be admitted that this design was not always achieved, nor was the ever-insinuating "self-righteousness of the righteous" always excluded.

From yet another point of view this Wesleyan notion of sanctification might be criticized particularly by moderns who feel deeply the solidarity of sinful man in his social, political, and economic dealings. Thus Reinhold Niebuhr can speak of a "sense of religious guilt which feels a general responsibility for that for which the individual agent cannot be immediately responsible." And J. Brazier Green declares that

there is no evidence that he [Wesley] recognized that the most holy and blameless character shares the life of the state, and with it, the moral responsibility for its collective evils.[15]

In that sense, of course, it could never be said even of Jesus that he lived a sinless life. The criticism has value, however, in that it seeks to prevent moral complacency and to enforce the idea of a limited, relative perfection—something Wesley was concerned also to do.

There is, Wesley would say, none so saintly but that the moral ideal does not lie somewhere ahead. "How much soever any man has attained, . . . he hath still need . . . daily to advance in the knowledge and love of God his Saviour." It is obvious that man should be alert to and ready to act upon increasingly higher ethical standards. To maintain, however, that despite his best efforts man sins so long as evil remains within his social context is to identify personal sin with social imperfection. This Wesley was not willing to do. Furthermore, he felt it unjust to consider an individual guilty for failure to act upon standards not apparent to him. Tomorrow's insights could not be held in judgment over him today.

Much of the criticism at this point seems to reflect a forced identification of right motive with infallible judgment. It was Wesley's contention that by the grace of God man could come wholly into possession of the former. The latter, he was equally sure, was a status never perfectly realized in this life. Sin, properly so called, could be ascribed only to those volitional acts or attitudes in which less-than-right motives were operative.

However, Wesley freely used the term "sin" in still another sense. He profoundly believed, that is, in original sin. It was to him such a basic doctrine that he quoted with approval:

Nor, indeed, can we let this doctrine go without giving up, at the same time, the greater part, if not all, of the essential articles of the Christian faith.[16]

Here he reveals that his full concept of sin goes considerably beyond his oft-quoted limitations. For original sin despite its non-volitional character is not only sin but the very essence of sin. It is the inherent force, the root stock, from which sins as "voluntary transgressions" spring. It is distinguishable as sin without specific guilt—for Wesley held that "by the merits of Christ, all men are cleared from the guilt of Adam's actual sin"—yet with universal consequences—which needs and requires the grace of God in no less measure, though in differing relationship, than "deliberate violations of a known law of God."

It is easy to underestimate the strength of this concept in Wesley's thought. For instance, it has been stated that Wesley's doctrine of prevenient grace made his concept of the "natural" man a "logical abstraction." The statement, while perceptive, tends to suggest inferences that are invalid. It cannot be inferred, that is, that Wesley thus looked upon man with the optimistic eye of nineteenth- and twentieth-century humanism. Nor is he Pelagian. His view was far more realistic. While Wesley taught that prevenient grace might free man from his "total inability," he still pictured him as the corrupted and impaired creature of the semi-Augustinian tradition. Wesley did have a doctrine of total depravity. He also had a doctrine of grace.

Under his doctrine of depravity Wesley viewed man as an invalid, sick unto death but not yet a corpse. In a letter on this subject Wesley wrote:

One of Mr. Fletcher's *Checks* considers at large the Calvinist supposition "that a natural man is *as dead as a stone*"; and shows the utter falseness and absurdity of it, seeing no man living is without some preventing grace, and every degree of grace is a degree of life.[17]

Wesley's concept of total depravity is a qualified concept. It is a depravity total in extent, "leaving no part uninfected"—but not in degree, since "no man living is destitute of preventing grace." He believed that all men as recipients of prevenient grace possessed thereby spiritual capacities congruent with further, redeeming, grace. Wesley insists, however, that man has no power in and of himself to do other than evil. When he turns to God, it is grace (prevenient) co-operating with grace (redemptive). And this redemptive grace is conceived of as infused rather than imputed. It effects not simply a changed relationship but a changed nature. And it is sufficient to effect man's complete salvation. It is this high doctrine of grace which makes possible in a single system a synthesis of total depravity and Christian perfection. It is by the grace of God that man can find the power to move from extended depravity to limited perfection.

This concept of original sin, modified by a doctrine of congruent grace, is an indispensable component of Wesley's system of theology. It underlies and requires the doctrine of sanctification. "Indeed," wrote Wesley, "if man were not thus fallen, there would be no need of all . . . this work in the heart, this renewal in the spirit of our mind."[18] And Wesley was convinced that such renewal could be accomplished. When he spoke of "salvation from all sin," it was with particular reference to this inherent, original sin. To stop short of this sense of "freedom from sin" is

43

to fail to recognize one of the basic premises of Wesley's doctrine of sanctification.

In sum Wesley's idea of salvation from sin would include the following: (1) that sins, properly so called, have been forgiven in justification and that he who is justified is thereby delivered from resultant guilt; (2) that the believer, as long as he "keepeth himself," does not commit further sin and is delivered from the "power" though not the "being" of sin; (3) that, finally, deliverance from "inbred sin"—its "being" and "corruption"—is accomplished through entire sanctification. It is in such fashion that Wesley indicates the two aspects under which he considers the extended category of sin. Lindström chooses to label the distinction the "objective-judicial" and the "subjective-medical." The first of these refers to the relationships dealt with in justification; the second, to the results effected in sanctification.

It has been occasionally intimated that Wesley found himself embarrassed by his contention that man could actually be freed from inbred sin. He had, for instance, a correspondent who raised the point that

if two persons absolutely free from the corruption of human nature should marry and have children, these children would have no corruption of nature and would stand in no need of a Saviour.

In his immediate reply Wesley did not deal with this query. But in the conference of 1759 that same question was thus answered:

I answer, Sin is entailed upon me, not by immediate generation, but by my first parent. "In Adam all died; by the disobedience of one, all men were made sinners;" all men, without exception, who were in his loins when he ate the forbidden fruit. We have a remarkable illustration of this in gardening: grafts on a crab-stock bear excellent fruit; but sow the kernels of this fruit, and what will be the event? They produce as mere crabs as ever were eaten.[19]

There is something, then, native to man as man. And Wesley viewed original sin as that common endowment, rather than the specific and individual inheritance, of all men.

But such a doctrine raises other logical difficulties. How, for instance, could one whose original sin was gone be ever again so corrupted? Two answers are possible: (1) he could not, and (2) he could because of the nature of sin and grace. The first after 1758-59 Wesley rejected. The second may be found implicit in his concept of the nature of original sin.

It is frequently said that Wesley thought of original sin as a thing, a near-physical entity which could be removed much as a diseased tooth is extracted. It is true that Wesley repeatedly used such Pauline expressions as the "root of bitterness," which must be destroyed, and the "old man," which must be crucified. But when he placed his view of original sin in a soteriological context, he presented it generally as a disease which it is the primary business of religion to heal. It is a virus, or "yeast," infecting the total person. It is a "leprosy" corrupting "every power and faculty." Man was not naturally "healthy" and injured only by untoward circumstance and his own occasional lapses of judgment. He was instead naturally "diseased" and tending toward an increase of moral wounds and death. Said Wesley:

> The whole world is, indeed, in its present state, only one great infirmary. All that are therein are sick of sin; and their one business is to be healed.[20]

To this view of sin he joined his doctrine of grace. For he says that the very essence, the "proper nature," of Christianity is the

> *healing a soul* which is thus diseased. Hereby the great Physician of souls applies medicines to heal this sickness; to restore human nature, totally corrupted in all it faculties. . . . Know your disease! Know your cure! . . . By nature ye are wholly corrupted: by grace ye shall be wholly renewed.

Entire sanctification is spiritual health—fully restored. But such restoration is maintained on a "moment-by-moment" basis. The grace whose sufficiency alone makes such moral health possible may be lost; and if and while it is, those capacities once freed from

45

that "infection" native to man—and always congruent with it—may fall again victim to it. In a world in which original sin is ever-present disease, man—once "healed"—may remain so only by giving attention to the maintenance of vigorous health.

As regards sin, then, Wesley taught that man could be delivered both from sin as voluntary transgression and from sin as involuntary principle—both from sin as symptom and from sin as disease. To that extent Wesley would have no objection to the term "sinless perfection."

But in Wesley's thought there was a recognition of that absolute law to which we are still in some measure responsible. And to any falling short of that unremitting obedience thus demanded, he still gave, in a highly refined but nevertheless real sense, the designation "sin." "*All* deviation from perfect holiness *is sin*,"[21] he said. Since even those who are "perfect in love" may still fall short of this law of absolute obedience, Wesley was not ready to distinguish their attainment as "sinless perfection." His remarks at this point appear to be, but actually are not, contradictory. He recognized the issue as primarily terminological. In one of his sermons he said, "To say the truth, this is a mere strife of words. You say, 'None is saved from sin' in *your* sense of the word; but I do not admit of that sense."[22] Consequently he could say: "I do not contend for the term 'sinless,' though I do not object against it." It was not that the matter was of no consequence, for Wesley was repeatedly attacked as preaching "sinless perfection." It was simply that while under one set of definitions (sin is a voluntary transgression of a known law of God) sinless perfection was a defensible concept, under another set (sin is any coming short of the law of love) it was not. "Explain the term one way," he wrote, "and I say, Yes; another, and I say, No." Wesley himself did not use the phrase. But if one who made clear his definitions wished to use it, Wesley would not object—"it is not worth disputing about."

Christian perfection may, but need not, be lost. And if it is lost, it may be recovered.

9. It is amissible, capable of being lost; of which we have numerous instances.

This admission of Wesley's was long in coming. He had early held that "there is a state attainable in this life, from which a man cannot finally fall." [23] And as late as March of 1757 he wrote:

One fruit [of Christian perfection] given at the same instant (at least usually) is a direct, positive testimony of the Spirit that the work is done, that they cannot fall away.[24]

But four years later he reversed his opinion and stated, "I cannot perceive any state mentioned in Scripture from which we may not, in a measure at least, fall." [25]

He therefore reluctantly observes:

Q. Can they fall from it?
A. I am well assured they can. Matter of fact puts this beyond dispute.

This unhappy "matter of fact" was all too obvious. It was the loss by many of the evidence, subjective and objective, held necessary for perfection. Rather than to deny that the "gift of God" was not received by them, Wesley accepted the view that it could be lost. The declension in the societies during the early 1770's confirmed this opinion. But he still maintained:

Two things are certain: the one, that it is possible to lose even the pure love of God; the other, that it is not necessary.[26]

Such loss was to him an unnecessary tragedy, not an anticipated norm.

Christian perfection is both instantaneous and gradual.

10. It is constantly both preceded and followed by a gradual work.
11. But is it in itself instantaneous or not? In examining this, let us go on step by step.

This consideration—instantaneous and gradual—was to become the watershed in the development of Wesley's doctrine.

Down one slope would move the absolutist interpreters until Christian perfection would come to mean an almost exclusive emphasis upon a single climactic experience. Down the other slope would move the accommodative interpreters until Christian perfection would come to mean little more than a dimly remembered tradition. And both in mutual reaction would abandon the synthesis Wesley had labored to establish. The evolving of that synthesis should be noted.

As early as 1729 Wesley had concluded that holiness was necessary to salvation. His debt to Anglo-Catholic sources has already been indicated. As they presented holiness, it meant, in brief, a life of devoted obedience and of diligent attention to works pleasing to God. For a number of years Wesley accepted without question the means proposed by these same sources for the attainment of that goal. For instance, in 1733 he declared that it was vain and blasphemous that one "should ever dream of shaking off his old opinions, passions, tempers, of being 'sanctified throughout in spirit, soul, and body,' without a constant and continued course of general self-denial!" [27] Two years later in the first sermon he ever printed Wesley said:

Who . . . will "deliver" us "from the body of this death?" Death will deliver us. Death will set those free in a moment who "were all their life-time subject to bondage." Death shall destroy at once the whole body of sin . . . in the moment wherein they shake off the flesh, they are delivered . . . from all sin. [28]

This by his own admission was Wesley's pre-Aldersgate view— that a modified asceticism is a requisite discipline and that death is the sole sanctifying agency. Little wonder that Cell says of him: "There was something dynamic, something radically important still lacking in Wesley's preconversion views on holiness or evangelical perfection."

With that series of events centering around Aldersgate, his views changed. It must not be imagined, however, that he leaped at once to any espousal of the instantaneous character of sanctification. Not long after his "heart-warming" experience and while still in its glow, Wesley wrote to a friend that "*if* we continue to watch, strive, and pray, He will gradually become our sanctification here and our full redemption hereafter." [29] Seven years later Wesley was still of the opinion that entire sanctification is rarely given "till a little before death" and that it should meanwhile be waited for

in universal obedience: in keeping all the commandments, in denying ourselves, and taking up our cross daily. These are the general means which God hath ordained for our receiving His sanctifying grace. The particular are, prayer, searching the Scripture, communication, and fasting.[30]

Sanctification was for him that "which implies a continued course of good works." In 1745, then, Wesley still sounded more like Jeremy Taylor and William Law than like Peter Böhler and Arvid Gradin. And as his doctrine developed, the teachings of Law and Taylor kept their place in it. For Wesley had found in those teachings something which his sound eclectic sense recognized as valuable and necessary to any system of Christian perfection. They were therefore never displaced even as his emphasis on the instantaneous became more pronounced.

The fact that he did emphasize the instantaneous is clearly demonstrable. In 1747 Wesley was still of the opinion that entire sanctification was usually received somewhat as a reward for a lifetime of "patient continuance in good works." In that year he had said:

We grant . . . that many of those who have died in the faith, yea, the greater part of those we have known, were not perfected in love till a little before their death.[31]

But ten years later he was saying:

There may be some rare cases wherein God has determined not to bestow His perfect love till a little before death; but this I believe is uncommon: He does not usually put off the fulfilling of His promises. Seek, and you shall find; seek earnestly, and you shall find speedily.[32]

Reasons for the near about-face have been in part already indicated. The abundant testimony of "living witnesses" had again proved determinative. His commitment to the instantaneous character of entire sanctification was emphatic and explicit.

But was this, as it is sometimes thought, but a passing phase to be superseded by more mature views? Two quotations from widely separated periods in Wesley's later ministry may be cited to indicate the continuity of his thought at this point. In 1757 he had written:

A gradual growth in grace precedes, but the gift itself is always given instantaneously. I never knew or heard of any exception; and I believe there never was one.[33]

In 1789 he again wrote in almost identical vein:

Gradual sanctification may increase from the time you was justified; but full deliverance from sin, I believe, is always instantaneous—at least, I never yet knew an exception.[34]

Two such quotations, standing alone, are not necessarily conclusive that this was Wesley's standard and mature conviction. But the corroborating data are abundant and continuous. In his public addresses throughout the period of his maturity, and in his private correspondence,[35] he continued to stress perfection as available "now" and by "simple faith." His exhortations to go on to such perfection continue into the closing months of his life. In fact, if any appreciable change is to be noted, it is that such exhortations become more frequent and explicit.[36] At the point of emphasis, then, the instantaneous view must be recognized as clearly Wesleyan.

Even so, it was not an exclusive emphasis. For coupled with it to the very last was the original idea of gradual sanctification. Thus in 1788 Wesley said: "I cannot but believe that sanctification is commonly, if not always, an *instantaneous* work."[37] But in that same year he was also saying:

And as, in the natural birth, a man is born at once and then grows larger and stronger by degrees; so in the spiritual birth, a man is born at once, and then gradually increases in spiritual stature and strength.[38]

Wesley would insist that he is not in these instances contradictory. Nor does he intend to be deliberately paradoxical. What he affirms according to Lindström is that sanctification is a process beginning in the "sudden supervention of justification and new birth." It continues thereafter as a gradual development which may again be interrupted, though not terminated, by the "higher though analogous experience of full sanctification . . . which in a single instant raises man to a higher plane." [39] Both elements, the gradual and the instantaneous, were, Wesley felt, necessary. Neither was of itself sufficient. He had more and more preached on faith; but he had never intended that such preaching should make less meaningful the holiness to which he had been inspired by Taylor, Law, and à Kempis. Thus in 1790 he said:

I am now on the borders of the grave; but, by the grace of God, I still witness the same confession. Indeed, some have supposed that when I began to declare, "By grace ye are saved through faith," I retracted what I had before maintained: "Without holiness no man shall see the Lord." But it is an entire mistake: these scriptures well consist with each other.[40]

For Wesley the question "Is [it] gradual or instantaneous?" contains an invalid disjunction. His answer is: "It is both the one and the other." And it is this synthesis—the instantaneous *and* the gradual, faith *and* nurture, process *and* crisis—which distinguishes Wesley's system both from those which had preceded him (and from which he had largely drawn) and from those variations, some within his own connection, which were to follow.

Growth in grace, Wesley insists, not only may but must continue beyond entire sanctification.

8. It [Christian perfection] is improvable. It is so far from lying in an indivisible point, from being incapable of increase, that one perfected in love may grow in grace far swifter than he did before.

Here Wesley rejects the idea that Christian perfection is that finished state which the term itself connotes—a rejection he was to make more explicit seven years later at the Conference of 1771. In this statement also Wesley implies a distinction which he generally fails to maintain. This is the distinction between entire sanctification as an event and Christian perfection as a continuing process of which that event is a part. Often Wesley uses the two concepts interchangeably. Usually this is when he is stressing the instantaneous character of perfection. At such times he is very apt to speak of it as though it *were* an "indivisible point." Here, however, he makes it clear that he considers entire sanctification no terminal point in the attainment of Christian perfection. In so doing he displays one of the most significant, *and neglected,* facets of his teaching.

In the first place, according to Wesley there is no point in Christian experience which carries with it the guarantee of a once-and-for-all attainment. Christian perfection or any other grace could be lost and would be lost except as it was maintained by a constant moment-by-moment reliance upon the sustaining grace and power of Christ. Said he:

Our perfection is not like that of a tree, which flourishes by the sap derived from its own root, but . . . like that of a branch which, united to the vine, bears fruit; but severed from it, is dried up and withered.[41]

Such a productive union as this is possible only by faith through which

we feel the power of Christ every moment resting upon us, whereby alone we are what we are; whereby we are enabled to continue in spiritual life, and without which, notwithstanding all our present holiness, we should be devils the next moment.[42]

At this point he is in clear contrast with anything Pelagian. Man according to Wesley begins his spiritual biography with a sense of his need of Christ and never reaches the point where that need ceases to be ever-present.

52

Moreover, Christian perfection was not a state of special grace to be passively enjoyed. In his antipathy to antinomianism and his fear of quietism Wesley rigorously insisted on good works. They were not the decorative fringe but the essential warp and woof of Christian perfection. And just as he held that "going on to perfection" was necessary to the maintenance of a justified state, he also held that a zeal for good works was necessary to the retention of a fully sanctified life.

It was also Wesley's conviction that religious life could never be static—and survive. If one *could* move forward, one must. And in Christian perfection there were always widening horizons. For, maintained Wesley,

> There is no *perfection of degrees*, as it is termed; none which does not admit of a continual increase. So that how much soever any man has attained, or in how high a degree soever he is perfect, he hath still need to "grow in grace," and daily to advance in the knowledge and love of God his Saviour.[43]

Consequently any attempt to maintain the status quo was foredoomed to failure. Spiritual deterioration was its inevitable result. This was particularly true with regard to Christian perfection. In 1789 Wesley wrote:

> You do well strongly to insist that those who do already enjoy it [perfect love] cannot possibly stand still. Unless they continue to watch and pray and aspire after higher degrees of holiness, I cannot conceive not only how they can go forward but how they can keep what they have already received.[44]

Growth in grace, as Wesley insisted throughout his life, is not merely a privilege but an absolute prerequisite to the retention of the "great salvation."

The essence of Christian perfection is perfect love.

7. It is "perfect love." This is the essence of it.

If Wesley had been willing to designate Christian perfection by the term which he now chooses to describe its inherent quality, his path might have been far less thorny. And he might well have done so. He says, in fact, that it was in just such terms that the doctrine first made its impact upon him. And through all the developing sequences of his thought it is this original emphasis of love which recurs unchanged.

Here, stripped of the features which plagued its presentation and clouded its meaning, is the essence of the doctrine—perfect love. The perfection for which Wesley was contending was a perfection of intention and an increasingly improved quality of life and action which he believed would follow therefrom. Here in perfect love he believed he had found the master passion under which man's otherwise unruly motives might be governed. This is why it was the essence of Christian perfection. "All that is necessarily implied," he wrote, "is humble, gentle, patient love: love regulating all the tempers, and governing all the words and actions." [45] Have this love—it mattered not how—and Wesley asked no more.

This love, so needed, is not and cannot be self-initiated. It is, indeed, a gift of divine grace, "shed abroad in the heart by the Holy Ghost." It is the grace-empowered response of man to the extended love of God for man. And that response includes not only the vertical interchange of love between God and man but also, and necessarily, the horizontal expression of one's love to his neighbor. The first initiates and determines the character of the second; the second validates any claim to the first and is requisite to its continuance.

Sanctification thus becomes that process whereby hindrances to man's effective love to God and his neighbor are overcome. In entire sanctification this process is climaxed by the perfecting of love. The increasingly propitious expression of that love thereupon follows. It is toward this end that the processes of salvation move.

Perfect love is the ground on which Wesley elects to take his final stand. He calls this his "exact," his "precise," definition. He insists that nothing short of this pure love is Christian perfection, and he equally deplores any effort to go beyond it. He emphatically declares:

54

There is nothing higher in religion: there is, in effect, nothing else: if you look for anything but more love, you are looking wide of the mark, you are getting out of the royal way. And when you are asking others, "Have you received this or that blessing?" if you mean anything but more love, you mean wrong. . . . Settle it then in your heart, that from the moment God has saved you from all sin, you are to aim at nothing more, but more of that love described in the thirteenth of Corinthians. You can go no higher than this, till you are carried into Abraham's bosom.[46]

In so defining his doctrine Wesley does not, it is true, escape the difficulties which beset the concept of perfection. But he does thus indicate the limited area in which that term is applicable. Perfection, in other words, is limited to intention, to motive. Within that field it is a valid concept; beyond that field, in this life at least it is not. Thus there will remain areas which only education, nurture, and experience can illuminate—and that never fully—yet perfect love may meanwhile have become the mastering affection of the soul. And when love becomes that ruling passion, perfection of intention—never of "degrees"—is attained.

And now Wesley has come around full course. He here defines the goal in terms which he first glimpsed in Taylor and Law and early proclaimed in "The Circumcision of the Heart"—purity of intention, the enthronement of love. But now he says, as in 1733 he did not, that while the goal is won "remotely" by works, it "depends . . . immediately on simple faith." [47]

On the basis of the points just cited, H. C. Sheldon has stated in largely "Wesleyan" terms the following concise definition:

Christian perfection in the Wesleyan sense implies freedom from inbred sin, the complete dominance of love over the voluntary exercises, and such a service of God as is competent to powers which indeed have been given a right direction, but which fail of that ideal measure which they would have had if man had not sinned. It is not, therefore, Adamic or angelic perfection. It does not imply objective faultlessness, since it does not secure from mistakes in judgment and consequent

mistakes in action. It carries with itself immunity neither from temptation nor from apostasy. It is simply loving God with all the heart,
freedom in underlying appetencies and in conscious activities from
anything contrary to love.[48]

The preceding pages have dealt with what Wesley said and
what he seemed to mean in his 1764 summary of his views on
Christian perfection. In concluding this analysis of Wesley's teachings, it may be helpful to point out certain features of his doctrine which sometimes distinguish it from systems which were
in large measure derived from it. For Wesley was that rare soul
who could combine intensity of conviction with liberality of spirit.
Not all who followed him maintained these virtues in equivalence.
Differences of emphasis were consequently inevitable.

Thus while Wesley was insistent on the pursuit of a definite
goal—"holiness of heart and life"—he held no brief for orthodoxy
of method. He found that the great majority of those claiming
perfect love reported its reception as an instantaneous event. And
so he preached it after that fashion. But if it could be realized in
some alternate way, he had no intention of discounting it. As
early as 1745 he had said: "I believe this love is given in a moment. But about this I contend not. Have this love, and it is
enough." Moved by that same spirit, he warned: "We are continually forming general rules from our own particular experience."
To impose a specific and unalterable pattern thus derived was
obviously unwarranted. For while it may be possible to discover
and prescribe certain aids to spiritual progress, Wesley felt that it
was also wise to remember that "God is tied down to no rules." As
time passed, he recognized more clearly that the excellence of a
doctrinal system is not to be found in its unvarying consistency.
He concluded that "there is an irreconcilable variability in the
operations of the Holy Spirit on the souls of men."[50]

This is not to say that Wesley abandoned his rather clear-cut
schematization in the presentation of Christian perfection. He did
not. He felt such a formulation was experimentally sound, peda-
gogically effective, and scripturally defensible. But he did in-

creasingly recognize the validity of variations from it. He was ready to admit, for instance, that one might attain to all the fruits of sanctification in his initial justification, though he added that this must be considered "an exempt case."

And there were exempt cases in other respects as well. Wesley had, that is, been adamant on the doctrine of assurance. It was to him the "very foundation of Christianity." And he wrote concerning it in unequivocal fashion. He believed also that entire sanctification was as self-validating as was regeneration, arguing that "none . . . ought to believe that the work is done, till there is added the testimony of the spirit, witnessing his entire sanctification; as clearly as his justification." [51] These views on the witness of the Spirit Wesley never surrendered. It is occasionally argued that he did, and his words in "A Letter to the Rev. Dr. Rutherford" are quoted in substantiation: "I believe a few, but very few, Christians have an assurance from God of everlasting salvation." The whole emphasis here is upon "everlasting." Wesley continues by saying, "I believe a consciousness of being in the favour of God . . . is the common privilege of Christians." [52]

And yet in 1782 he writes:

It is true that the usual method of our Lord is to purify us by joy in the Holy Ghost and a full consciousness of His love. But I have known several exempt cases. [53]

And so he could speak of entire sanctification as being confirmed "in a gradual and almost insensible manner" and "by almost insensible degrees, like the dawning of the day." [54] With Wesley the *manner* of attaining perfect love was as a ladder the nature and length of which might well vary with the differences which are inescapable in human personality. It was not a Procrustean bed into which all believers must be forced.

In some other respects he differed from certain of his heirs. For instance, he had no outstanding preference for a particular name by which to designate the experience he taught and the life he urged. He had chosen "perfection" because he deemed it scriptural. But he referred to it under various titles. To one of his followers he counseled:

> He has purified your heart. . . . Do not reason one moment what to call it, whether perfection or anything else. You have faith: hold it fast. You have love: let it not go. Above all, you have Christ! Christ is yours! [55]

"I have no time to throw away," he said, "in contending for words, especially where the thing is allowed."

In later holiness history two terms came to be the shibboleths of opposing factions. These were "eradication" and "suppression." The first symbolized the position of the out-and-out perfectionist; the second often characterized his not-so-certain brother. In Wesley's day the issue was between "destroyed" and "suspended." Wesley, though favoring the first as to terminology, was hardly partisan enough in his teachings to give aid and comfort exclusively to either camp. It is true that Wesley, again following Pauline analogy, uses such terms as "eradicate" and "destroy." "I use the word 'destroyed,'" he said, "because St. Paul does; 'suspended' I cannot find in my Bible." [56] But in his immediate context he states, "Indeed, the unclean spirit, though driven out, may return and enter again; nevertheless he was driven out." What Wesley means by "destroyed," then, is "driven out." For Wesley taught, it should be remembered, that whatever it was that happened in entire sanctification (or any other phase of the Christian life) was sustained on a moment-by-moment basis. Consequently, the terms "eradication" and "destruction" may be used, if at all, only in the most qualified fashion. They are not congruous with a teaching which calls for such a sense of momentary reliance nor which allows the possibility of backsliding and restoration. A term far more appropriate to Wesley's thought is the term "expulsion." "Entire sanctification," he said, ". . . is neither more nor less than pure love—love expelling sin and governing both the heart and life." And this is what he preached:

It is love excluding sin; love filling the heart, taking up the whole capacity of the soul. . . . For as long as love takes up the whole heart, what room is there for sin therein? [57]

Here in Wesley is the explicit teaching of the "expulsive power of a new affection." But again Wesley does not contend for a term: "Call this the destruction or suspension of sin, it is a glorious work." [58]

The strenuous vitality of certain later sectors of Wesleyan perfectionism was based in part upon the scriptural watchword "Without holiness no man shall see the Lord," which was then understood to mean: "Without having experienced entire sanctification as a second definite work of grace no man shall see the Lord." What was Wesley's position at this point? Frankly, it is not easy to determine. Certainly in his earlier years he is considerably more dogmatic than at a later period. In 1745 he stated without qualification:

Is it not written, . . . "Without holiness no man shall see the Lord"? And how then, without fighting about words, can we deny that holiness is a condition of final acceptance? [59]

He points out that all Christians "(the Romish themselves not excepted) agree that we must be 'fully cleansed from all sin' before we can enter into glory." And since he rejects purgatory, he at one time said, "Unless we have clean hearts before we die, it had been good we had never been born." However, he is willing to make certain concessions, as the Minutes of August 2, 1745, show:

Q. 2. What will become of a Heathen, a Papist, a Church of England man, if he dies without being thus sanctified?
A. He cannot see the Lord. But none who seeks it sincerely shall or can die without it; though possibly he may not attain it, till the very article of death.

And he later urges his preachers to "speak very tenderly on this head, for it is far better to *lead* men than to *drive*." Wesley occasionally seems to be suggesting the possibility of some sort of posthumous cleansing. He tells Elizabeth Hardy that he will not say, "If you die without it, you will perish," but instead, "Till you are saved from unholy tempers, you are not ripe for glory." In consequence, he adds, "there will . . . more promises be fulfilled in your soul before God takes you to himself." [60] He speaks also of being "entitled" to heaven by justification and "qualified" for heaven by sanctification. Just what happens to one entitled but not qualified who suddenly dies, Wesley does not say.

Wesley was never able, in fact, to be dogmatic at this point. He could not escape the broad inference of Acts 10:35—"But in every nation he that feareth [God], and worketh righteousness, is accepted with him." This, said Wesley, "is express and admits of no exception." Thus when he came to preach his sermon on "The More Excellent Way," his convictions were as follows:

I would be far from . . . discouraging those that serve God in a low degree. But I could not wish them to stop here: I would encourage them to come up higher, without thundering hell and damnation in their ears. . . . I do not affirm, that all who do not walk in this ["more excellent"] way are in the high road to hell. But this much I must affirm, they will not have so high a place in heaven, . . . and will this be a small loss? [61]

As he exhorted to Christian perfection, Wesley chose to make his appeal to aspiration prompted by love rather than to desperation elicited by fear.

To the absolutist temper characteristic of some phases of later perfectionism, such concessions would appear as inexcusable compromise on Wesley's part. This reaction would be due to the very common failure to remember Wesley's high churchmanship, his broad catholic spirit, and his willingness to sacrifice an inflexible consistency to considerations of charity and "matter of fact." Like Paul he held without deviation to certain central convictions and assurances. Also like Paul he was willing to concede issues which he came to see as peripheral.

Recapitulation

1. ORIGINS

It can scarcely be doubted that in his doctrine of Christian perfection Wesley had proceeded to develop a concept enunciated in the New Testament and by the Fathers of the early Church. That he was justified in the full extent of his development is, of course, open to question. But that calls to perfection and affirmations of its possibility are present in those traditions can neither be denied nor ignored. There is in the teachings of the Church a never-relinquished perfectionism, mystical and practical, stemming from Pauline, Johannine, and Petrine sources. It is clearly reflected, though in varying degree, in such Fathers as Clement of Rome, Ignatius of Antioch,[62] Polycarp of Smyrna,[63] and particularly Irenaeus of Lyons[64] and Clement of Alexandria.[65] Even Augustine's remarks in his attack upon Pelagian perfectionism are at times so phrased as to sound almost Wesleyan.[66] The later mystics present the teaching in such terms as anticipate Wesley in striking particular.[67] Finally, the Council of Trent gave dogmatic affirmation to the possibility of this relative perfection.[68] There are qualifications that approach contradictions, but there is also a persistent unanimity upon the possibility of and the obligation to pursue Christian perfection.

In Protestantism this emphasis is most clearly reflected in certain phases of the Arminian remonstrance against ultra-Calvinism and in the Pietistic reaction to "Gnesio-Lutheranism." In the Anglo-Catholic tradition it was a cardinal teaching of the English mystics and the Cambridge Platonists.

There is no attempt here to argue that the Wesleyan doctrine can be fully reproduced from any one of the sources just noted. But they did inspire and contribute to it. The genesis of his doctrine was derived from the tradition to which Wesley was as an Anglican constantly exposed. And that tradition had been always alive in, though often neglected by, the Christian community. It was Wesley's concern to revitalize this tradition and to make exoteric a doctrine which had sometimes appeared esoteric in concept and application.

For this evangelistic impulse Wesley was in large degree debtor to a second great tradition. This was the dynamic Lutheran emphasis on salvation by faith. Under Moravian teaching it had been for him a disturbing compulsion. As a result he felt himself "thrust out"—to raise a people whose passion would be to "spread scriptural holiness over these lands."

Wesley is debtor to the Moravians also for his schematization of salvation into two successive stages: conversion and entire sanctification, although James Arminius had similarly taught two "degrees" of Christian liberty. Moreover, it was principally from the Moravians also that the disciplinary nurture of the bands was derived. Thus the Wesleyan doctrine is a synthesis of elements from systems often regarded as antithetical. It was a synthesis, said George Croft Cell, to which Wesley's disciples were unequal.

Perhaps this failure was not wholly due either to later Methodist perversity or to general human frailty. It must be admitted that Wesley's doctrinal system lacks the close-knit logical unity of such a work as Calvin's *Institutes*. Wesley's rare and very real genius is revealed in his work as an evangelist and administrator. As such his passionate advocacy of holiness was designed to obviate antinomianism and to check the constant tendency to rest in a relative spiritual impotency. His goal was perfection, not mediocrity. Practical and active as he was, he lacked the inclination and did not spare himself the time to weave a doctrinal system of real consistency. If the immediate need required it, he freely used doctrinal materials whose premises were, or seemed to be, contradictory. Tyerman has rightly said of him:

> He was a man of one idea: his sole aim was to save souls. This was the philosophy of his life. . . . The man is best known by what he *did;* not by what philosophers may suspect he *thought.*[69]

In consequence, devoted to this single ideal and absorbed in the task of its practical promotion, he was impatient of fine theoretical distinctions. "I have no time," he said, "to throw away in contending for words." His loose terminology was an inevitable result. It is not surprising that his doctrinal structure was not always strong enough to withstand the tensions of his synthesis.

2. TERMINOLOGY

In developing his doctrine Wesley's choice and use of terms was unfortunate. "Perfection," for instance, inevitably suggests some sort of absolute status—no matter how much the relative character of a particular usage may be insisted upon. It was against this inescapable connotation that opposition always arose. Moreover, Wesley was not consistent in his usage of the term. He defined perfection variously and frequently disregarded even those definitions. For instance, it is obvious that Wesley meant Christian perfection to be the general designation of the fully matured Christian life—the life where perfect love was truly the reigning motive. Perfection was the accomplishment of a journey comprising many stages. Yet Wesley again and again used the term as completely synonymous with entire sanctification—one of the stages of that journey. He warned that Christian perfection must not be considered as "lying in an indivisible point," yet he affirmed that it lies somewhere between justification and death and is "both preceded and followed by a gradual work." Those who were not opposed could scarcely avoid being confused.

Wesley's tendency to use "sanctification" where he meant "entire sanctification" is another instance of his terminological carelessness. This uncritical interchange of terms became especially characteristic of Wesley's later years. It was an unfortunate practice rather generally adopted by many of his followers. The result was that there arose in Methodism two groups using the same term, "sanctification," but with crucially different meanings.

Wesley used the term "holiness" in similar fashion. Sometimes he meant it to be the whole of salvation. Sometimes it was to represent a specific phase. And he had in mind two types of holiness—inward and outward. Often he referred specifically and only to one, though a careful examination of the context is necessary to determine which. Any attempt to systematize Wesley's thought is necessarily complicated by such tendencies. It is quite possible to quote Wesley at length against Wesley.

3. DOCTRINE AND DISCIPLINE

Wesley begins his doctrine with a somber picture of man in his native state. He is a depraved and utterly helpless creature. But the darkness is relieved by Wesley's teaching concerning the possibilities and the operations of grace. Man, thus corrupted, may rise even to sanctity. This hopeful conclusion is prompted by Wesley's concept of God. He sees him not as *Deus absconditus* or wholly other but as compassionate, sanctifying Spirit. As such there is provided for man that community wherein the Holy Spirit is operative for his full redemption. It was Wesley's conviction that the tremendous spiritual enrichment manifested at Pentecost was not for the first-century church alone but was available as an energizing, cleansing, stabilizing force—mediated through the divine community—to all who would prepare themselves for its reception.

His particularization of the steps in this process may be given in Wesley's own description of salvation:

Salvation is carried on by *convincing grace,* usually in Scripture termed *repentance,* which brings a larger measure of self-knowledge. . . . Afterwards we experience the proper Christian salvation, whereby, *through grace, we are saved by faith,* consisting of those two grand branches, justification and sanctification. By justification we are saved from the guilt of sin, and restored to the favour of God; by sanctification we are saved from the power and root of sin, and restored to the image of God. All experience as well as Scripture show this salvation to be both instantaneous and gradual. It begins the moment we are justified, in the holy, humble, gentle, patient love of God and man. It gradually increases from that moment, . . . till, in another instant, the heart is cleansed from all sin, and filled with pure love to God and man. But even that love increases more and more, till we "grow up in all things into him that is our head," till we "attain the measure of the stature of the fulness of Christ." [70]

These last few lines portray the all-important goal. In the heat of controversy over method the place of that goal has been sometimes overlooked.

Here is presented the ideal of maturity. This was the gradual element in Christian perfection, a phase Wesley never surrendered and the preaching of which he felt to be his own "peculiar calling." The relationship of purity to maturity in Wesley's doctrine deserves more than passing notice. The first is held to be a gift of God, consequent upon our complete consecration and our believing faith. It will be noted that this is a perfection not of self-realization but of self-surrender—the unreserved human capitulation to the extended love of God. Eros in consequence is displaced by agape. The second is the result of a discipline of life, energized initially by the grace of God and utilizing the instantaneous enduement in a more expeditious growth toward spiritual maturity.

This concept of maturity appears repeatedly in Wesley's writings. He usually based it upon distinctions in the spiritual life designated as "little children, young men, and fathers," from I John 2:13. It was only the last of these, held Wesley, who was perfected in love in the sense of maturity. This attainment, Wesley taught, was the product of man's earnest and continued cooperation with the constantly extended grace of God. It implied a life unreservedly committed to the requirements of faith and love— a life in which it was "natural, and in a manner necessary . . . to love every child of man." It is a life in which the heart has not merely received an "effusion" of love; it is "established" in that love. Its motives are not only "single" but habitually and spontaneously directed toward obedience to the law of love. Yet it is not a maturity as in fruit, beyond which there is nothing save decay. It is a disciplined and adequate ability, sustained on a moment-by-moment basis, to perform divine requirements which are themselves constantly progressing.

Such maturity implies and usually requires considerable time. But in Wesley's thought the temporal element is not necessarily the regulative factor. Spiritual maturity is more nearly consequent upon perception, faith, and dedication. Thus the process of maturation may be lengthy or brief—all in relationship to the exercise of these factors. It is a psychological rather than a chronological maturity.

However it is acquired, *this* phase of perfection, the gradual work, is the highest and most noble aspect. For necessary as Wesley conceives the instantaneous work to be in bringing "freedom from all sin," he yet declares that it "expresses only the least, the lowest branch of it, only the negative part of the great salvation." [71]

Nor should it be overlooked that all this pursuit of holiness was to take place within and assisted by the Church. Here in the visible community were to be found those means of grace, those counsels, doctrines, and admonitions, which should encourage and guide the seeker after perfection. Only thus could the "beauty of holiness" be given its appropriate and undistorted place. If from time to time those in responsible place in the Church seemed more concerned for the maintenance of "old bottles" than for the infusion of "new wine"—and the inevitable occurred—the result was tragedy for both.

Thus Wesley's system stood, its roots deep in the twin traditions of the Church, a vital synthesis combining a qualified pessimism regarding the nature of man with an unqualified optimism in the possibilities of grace. Such symmetry as it possessed was to be seriously marred in later doctrinal conflict.

CHAPTER III

The Doctrine Transplanted
1766-84

THE PREACHING of Christian perfection as an attainable experience received its great impetus in the British societies around the year 1760. By 1762 the revival of which it was the cardinal feature was at high tide. And for several years thereafter professions to its attainment were numerous and widespread.

In the process of the revival two of Wesley's preachers, Thomas Maxfield and George Bell, became leaders of a group in London who preached and professed perfection in the more extreme fashion. Maxfield had been a stalwart Methodist evangelist for over twenty years. Wesley was extremely fond of him since Maxfield had been the first of his lay preachers, the first "to help me as a son in the Gospel." He hesitated, therefore, to oppose and discipline these "enthusiasts." When he finally did so attempt, he was met with scornful opposition by some, one of whom said, "Sir, we will have no more to do with you; Mr. Maxfield is our teacher." The most extreme features of this party were to be found in the group who followed George Bell. Wesley, having heard charges against them, went to hear Bell preach. "I stood," he said, "where I could hear and see without being seen." Bell prayed for "pretty near an hour." And Wesley, while admiring his zeal, deplored his manner and methods. Finally Bell, certain of his "miraculous discernment of spirits," predicted the end of the world. That event was to take place on February 28, 1763. Wesley took disciplinary action, and Bell left the society on February 4. He lived to an old age, said J. S. Simon, "but he lost his religion." Maxfield indulged in no such rash prophecies, but he did allow certain extreme emphases which brought the doctrine into disrepute and brought him Wesley's open disfavor.

The character of these extremes may be determined from a letter which Wesley wrote to Maxfield and his followers. In it he said:

> I dislike your supposing man . . . can be absolutely perfect; . . . your . . . depreciating justification, . . . appearance of pride, . . . overvaluing feelings . . . ; undervaluing reason, . . . littleness of love . . . ; want of meekness, . . . bigotry and narrowness of spirit, . . . your censoriousness, . . . your affirming people will be justified or sanctified just now: . . . the bidding them say, "I believe": the bitterly condemning any that oppose. . . .[1]

So on April 28, 1763, Maxfield too left Wesley. The fanatics were stopped, but the damage done to the doctrine of Christian perfection was almost irreparable. It now seemed to many a "dangerous delusion."

The next few years found Wesley striving desperately to repair the extensive injury to both doctrine and discipline. In many areas the preaching of Christian perfection had altogether ceased. Thus he wrote to Charles:

> The frightful stories wrote from London had made all our preachers in the North afraid even to mutter about perfection. . . . 'Tis what I foresaw from the beginning—that the devil would strive by T. Maxfield and company to drive perfection out of the kingdom.[2]

In the early part of 1767 Wesley was in London, where he "again began a course of sermons on Christian Perfection; if haply that thirst after it might return which was so general a few years ago." But his efforts were evidently not too rewarding. Three months later he wrote to inquire:

Do they gain ground in London? I am afraid perfection should be forgotten. . . . A general faintness in this respect is fallen upon this whole kingdom. Sometimes I seem almost weary of striving against the stream both of preachers and people.[3]

Apparently he decided to bring the issue to a head; for two days before the Conference of 1767 he wrote to say, "At this Conference it will be determined whether *all* our preachers or none shall continually *insist* upon Christian perfection." [4] But his hopes were too sanguine. The issue was not settled in 1767. Indeed, if it had been settled at this conference, it might well have been with the abandonment of the teaching as a cardinal doctrine. For in May of the following year John wrote to Charles:

I am at my wits' end with regard to two things—the Church and Christian Perfection. Unless both you and I stand in the gap *in good earnest,* the Methodists will drop them both.[5]

A month later and the situation was unimproved. Again he wrote Charles:

But what shall we do? I think it is high time that you and I at least should come to a point. Shall we go on in asserting perfection against all the world? Or shall we quietly let it drop? We really must do one or the other; and, I apprehend, the sooner the better.[6]

Whatever conclusions Charles was to reach, John was not long in choosing what his own position was to be. For two months after the above letter he wrote again:

Blessed be God, though we set an hundred enthusiasts aside, we are still "encompassed with a cloud of witnesses," who have testified, and do testify, in life and in death, that perfection which I have taught these forty years! This perfection cannot be a delusion, unless the Bible be a delusion too.[7]

Nevertheless the declensions continued. And Wesley sadly notes that although many taste of that heavenly gift, deliverance from inbred sin, yet so few, so exceeding few, retain it one year, hardly one in ten, nay one in thirty.[8]

Among the reasons for this he lists "opposition from their brethren" and "want of . . . prudent and tender care." The disaffection was broad and deep.

A few years later, however, Wesley was encouraged to note that

in most parts of this kingdom there is such a thirst after holiness as I scarce ever knew before. . . . Two of our travelling preachers who for some years disbelieved it are now happy witnesses of it.[9]

The pendulum was swinging back from its nadir of reaction.

Nevertheless, whereas the doctrine had before received general, if but tacit, acceptance, there were now areas where it met positive opposition. At Edinburgh, Wesley notes that the society there had gained only five members in five years. Among the reasons advanced by him, he reports the preachers "care not to speak too plain, lest they should give offence" and adds:

When Mr. Brackenbury preached the old Methodist doctrine one of them said, "You must not preach such doctrine here. The doctrine of Perfection is not calculated for the meridian of Edinburgh." [10]

Perhaps the most abiding reaction was not one of open antagonism but a reluctance to insist that perfect love could be attained, as Wesley urged, "now, and by simple faith." His report on the circuit at Launceston could without doubt be accepted as characteristic of a considerable area of Methodism in the closing years of the eighteenth century. The report states:

The preachers had given up the Methodist testimony. Either they did not speak of Perfection at all (the peculiar doctrine committed to our trust), or they spoke of it only in general terms, without urging the believers to "go on to perfection," and to expect it every moment.[11]

70

But while Wesley might reluctantly tolerate such negligence, he would not brook open opposition. In the closing year of his life he wrote to Adam Clarke:

If we can prove that any of our Local Preachers or Leaders, either directly or indirectly, speak against it [Christian perfection], let him be a Local Preacher or Leader no longer. I doubt whether he shall continue in the Society. Because he that can speak thus in our congregations cannot be an honest man.[12]

We can only conclude that the issue which Wesley had intended to place before the Conference of 1767 was still unresolved at the time of his death.

If the testimony of John Hampson may be accepted at face value, we can also assume that the preaching of perfection in the societies was not altogether popular. Since Hampson had broken with Wesley over the Trust Deeds, his testimony may not be completely free of bias. He reports concerning perfection:

For many years it was the Shibboleth of Methodism. . . . Perfectionists and Anti-Perfectionists were the grand divisions. . . . The wags laughed merrily at the witnesses. . . . Even their brethren . . . "eyed them askance," and set a mark upon them; while the Calvinian Methodists, in songs and madrigals and heroics, alternately vented their mirth and their indignation.[13]

More important to the future of the doctrine of Christian perfection in American Methodism than these vicissitudes in the British societies was the exposition of that doctrine by John Fletcher, who had been invited by Wesley to succeed him as superintendent of the Methodist societies. Fletcher had completed his *Checks to Antinomianism* in 1775 and had included as the *Last Check* his *Treatise on Christian Perfection*. His personal prestige, his saintly character, and his literary craftsmanship won him a wide reading on both sides of the Atlantic and throughout the century that followed his death. Since Fletcher's *Treatise* has been called second only to Wesley's *Plain Account* among the "text-books of Methodism on this so little understood question," a brief examination of his views is in order.

Like Wesley he undertook to defend the term "perfection." He cites its accepted usage in secular contexts. He affirms that it is scriptural. Even so, he says, "if we thought that our condescension would answer any good end, we would entirely give up that harmless and significant word."[14] He reveals, however, an unfortunate tendency to regard the term as a convenient password "by which dispirited spies, who bring an evil report upon the good land of holiness, are frequently detected." And so he concludes:

Now the words of my motto, "Be ye perfect," etc., being Christ's own words, we dare no more be ashamed of them, than we dare desire him to be ashamed of us in the great day; Thus much for the word *perfection*.[15]

In proceeding to define Christian perfection, Fletcher readily admits its relative character and quotes an Anglican archbishop to the effect that true Christian obedience has "if I may so say, *imperfect perfection*." It may be called "perfection" because it comprehends a perfect obedience to that law "adapted to our present state and circumstances" which Fletcher calls "the law of Christ." It must be considered relative because "God alone is supremely perfect: all beings are imperfect when they are compared to him." Not only so but "as among rich men, some are richer than others, or among tall men, some are taller than others; so among perfect Christians, some are more perfect than others."[16] Here, as in some other of his analogies, Fletcher is betrayed by a too facile shift from one meaning of perfection to another. If, for instance, he measures perfection by response according to "present state and circumstances," then comparison can be drawn only between a man and his abilities, not between one man and another. On the other hand, if perfection is considered in terms of *ideal* response (or obedience), then one man may be more nearly perfect than another. In no sense can some be more perfect than others. Actually, Fletcher uses perfection in two different senses: (1) the complete realization of an ideal *after its kind,* and (2) the possession of all excellencies. And he does not always maintain his distinctions.

After pointing out the relative nature of Christian perfection, that is, the "possible" as over against the "ideal," Fletcher proceeds to examine "sinless perfection." His solution is so nearly that of Wesley that it does not need reiteration. If one *must* use the term "sinless perfection," then Fletcher insists that it should be always qualified as *"evangelically* sinless perfection," since it means that one is able to render perfect obedience to the "evangelical . . . law of Christ" rather than to the law of "paradisiacal" perfection.[17]

Like Wesley, Fletcher was neither Antinomian nor Pelagian. The major emphases of his polemical *Works* are directed against the first, and the second he specifically repudiates. He maintains, in fact, that "the Scripture-doctrine, which we indicate, stands at an equal distance from these extremes of *Pelagius* and *Augustine.*"[18] Fletcher's teaching concerning original sin was the unrelieved Protestant view of his day. Man is "at variance with his creator," "depraved," "undone," "enslaved," "polluted," "disordered," "helpless and miserable." And in consequence of original sin life could be described as

the almost uninterruped cries of feeble infancy; . . . the tedious confinement of childhood, the blasted schemes of youth, the anxious cares of riper years, and the deep groans of wrinkled, decrepid, tottering old age.[19]

For Fletcher, as with most of his contemporaries, the doctrine of original sin was the foundation of evangelical truth and the principal characteristic which distinguished it from Deism.

But deep-seated and widespread as it is, Fletcher denies the "necessary continuance of indwelling sin and carnal bondage." For him, as for Wesley, original sin is a disease which it is the business of religion to heal. Repeatedly he presents it as "sickness," "corruption," and "helplessness." It is this condition which

73

requires and is answered by the new birth and sanctification, bringing about not merely a change of relationship effected by imputed righteousness but a real healing resulting from infused grace.[20]

To the claim that humility will be lost if the possibility of the destruction of "indwelling sin" be allowed, Fletcher replies, "Who has more sin than Satan? And who is prouder?" [21]

Fletcher was confronted with the argument that his own church opposed his doctrinal views in articles nine and fifteen of its creed: "this infection of nature [original sin] doth reman, yea in them that are regenerated; whereby the lust of the flesh . . . is not subject to the Law of God"; and "if we say we have no sin, we deceive ourselves, and the truth is not in us." He answered by saying: "Our church can never be so inconsistent as to level her articles against what she so ardently prays for in her liturgy." [22] Whereupon he quotes from that liturgy:

Cleanse the thoughts of our hearts by the inspiration of thy Holy Spirit, that we may perfectly love thee, and worthily magnify thy holy Name.
And grant, . . . that we may hereafter live a godly, righteous, and sober life, to the glory of thy Holy name.
Grant to us, Lord, the spirit to think and do always such things as are right.

If it be insisted, he said, that inconsistencies do remain and that the church

sometimes pleads for christian imperfection and a death purgatory: we reply, that, supposing the charge were well grounded, yet we ought rather to follow her, when she soberly follows Scripture, than when she hastily follows inconsistent Augustine.[23]

This was Fletcher's solution to the conflict between the largely Calvinistic nature of the Thirty-nine Articles and the Arminian character of the *Book of Common Prayer*.

Committed then to the possibility of Christian perfection,

Fletcher proceeds to prescribe the method of its attainment. Three quotations will suffice to represent the qualified synergism of his position here:

The way to perfection is by the due combination of prevenient, assisting *Free-grace;* and of submissive, assisted *Free-will.* Antinomian stillness, therefore, which says that free grace must do all, is not the way. Pharisaic activity, which will do most, if not all, is not the way. Join these two partial systems; allowing *Free-grace* the lead and high pre-eminence which it so justly claims; and you have the balance of the two gospel-axioms. . . . To go on steadily to perfection, you must therefore endeavour steadily to *believe,* according to the doctrine of the first gospel-axiom; and (as there is opportunity) diligently to work, according to the doctrine of the second: and the moment your faith is steadily fixed in God as in your centre, and your obedience swiftly moves in the circle of duty [reference to a previous illustration of the two legs of a compass] from the rest and power which you find in that centre, you have attained; you are made perfect in the faith which works by love.[24]

Further he adds:

Ye will so depend upon God's Free-grace as not to fall into Pharisaic running: and ye will so exert your own *Free-will* as not to slide into *Antinomian* sloth. Your course lies exactly between these rocks.[25]

Finally he thus summarizes: "Resolve to be perfect *in yourselves* [and thus avoid Antinomianism], but not *of yourselves* [and thus avoid Pharisaism]."

In Fletcher's thought one of the facets of Wesley's teachings is considerably enlarged. Wesley had stated, though not frequently, that Christian perfection was the portion only of "fathers." Fletcher enlarged on this concept and tended to identify perfection almost wholly with "maturity," accepting, as normal, the temporal connotation. Consequently he could say:

Sanctification is not generally the work of a day nor of a year. For although God can cut short his work in righteousness . . . , it is nevertheless in general a progressive work and of long duration.[26]

He asks if it is wrong to say that *"fruit grown to maturity* is in its perfection" and declares that this is exactly the sense in which he uses the term. It is a term reserved for "that maturity of grace and holiness which established adult believers attain to under the Christian dispensation." [27]

Compatible with this interpretation, then, would be an idea of entire sanctification as only gradually apprehended. And there is much in Fletcher to suggest that this was indeed his view of the matter. He proposes, for instance, a program of "going on to perfection" which includes the following: resolution, reception of the sacraments, proper and appropriate dependence upon faith and works, repentance and heart-searching, the practice of a judicious self-denial, patient resignation in trials, the exercise of faith which "works by love," the practice of "social prayer,"—and two more disciplines which Fletcher considers helpful but not essential: the dynamic use of affliction, and momentary expectation.[28] Wesley would have challenged his program only at the point of its failure to give greater prominence to "momentary expectation."

And yet it must be remembered that Fletcher had set himself here particularly to controvert Antinomianism, and the above program was suggested only after he had first said:

> the most evangelical method of following after the perfection to which we are immediately called, is that of seeking it *now,* by endeavouring *fully* to lay hold on the promise of that perfection through faith, just as if our repeated acts of obedience could never help us forward.[29]

Meanwhile he urges attention to such "acts of obedience" as are available to and obligatory upon ʻthe believer. It was Fletcher's fear that, if this latter phase be disregarded, "we shall fall into solifidian sloth with the Antinomians."

But upon the divisive question of whether Christian perfection is to be regarded as attained instantaneously or gradually, Fletcher denies that a strictly categorical answer can be given. He is perfectly ready to admit the possibility and efficacy of either, and he cites numerous instances from scripture and analogies from nature to support both contentions. The question of method, Fletcher feels, is one which may best be left to the wisdom and providence of God. "If you were sick," he says, "and asked of God the perfect recovery of your health, how would you look for it?" After citing instances from scripture where such healing had been effected by more than one method, Fletcher concludes:

Would ye not earnestly wait for an answer to your prayers *now*; leaving to divine wisdom the particular manner of your recovery? And why should ye not go and do likewise, with respect to the dreadful disorder which we call *indwelling sin?*

He adds that to deny the possibility of instantaneous sanctification

is to deny (contrary to scripture and matter of fact) that we can make an *instantaneous* act of faith in the sanctifying promise of the Father, and in the all-cleansing blood of the Son, and that God can seal that act by the instantaneous operation of his Spirit!

And yet

to deny that imperfect believers may, and do gradually grow in grace, and, of course, that the remains of their sins may, and do gradually decay, is as absurd as to deny that God waters the earth by daily dews, as well as by thunder-showers;—it is as ridiculous, as to assert that nobody is carried off by lingering disorders, but that all men die suddenly, or a few hours after they are taken ill.[30]

Fletcher, then, seems ready to reject as "absurd" and "ridiculous" any effort to say that either one or the other of these methods *must* be the accepted norm. Here is a point, he feels, not clearly enunciated in scripture, witnessed to in both types and therefore liable to more than one interpretation.

The end result, Christian perfection, is expected of the believer and attainable by him in this life. But the means of that attainment are dependent upon so many varying factors that no one formula is universally applicable.

Fletcher's endorsement of the second-blessing schematization would therefore be a qualified one. For with a somewhat inelegant realism he argues:

> Should you ask, how many baptisms, or effusions of the sanctifying Spirit are necessary to cleanse a believer from all sin, and to kindle his soul into perfect love: I reply, . . . I should betray a want of modesty, if I brought the operations of the Holy Ghost, and the energy of faith, under a rule which is not expressly laid down in the Scriptures. If you ask your physician, how many doses of physic you must take, before the crudities of your stomach can be carried off, and our appetite perfectly restored; he would probably answer you, that this depends upon the nature of those crudities, the strength of the medicine, and the manner in which your constitution will allow it to operate; and that, in general, you must repeat the dose, as you can bear, till the remedy has fully answered the desired end. I return a similar answer: If one powerful baptism of the Spirit *seal you unto the day of redemption,* and *cleanse you from all* (moral) *filthiness,* so much the better. If two or more be necessary, the Lord can repeat them.[31]

As to the *nature* of Christian perfection Fletcher is explicit and emphatic. It is a *cleansing*—a cleansing from all sin, "from the guilt and defilement both of actual and original corruption." This idea of cleansing is, of course, suggestive of and compatible with the instantaneous character of entire sanctification. And in spite of his unwillingness to propose any *one* way of attainment, Fletcher not only believed one *could* be so instantaneously "renewed," but his personal testimony to such an experience is a matter of record.

Nevertheless, it is the idea of maturity rather than crisis which dominates Fletcher's exposition of the doctrine. Cleansing, and its concomitant assurance, are but the introductory phases. As for himself he said:

> It seems to me but a small thing to be saved from all sin; I want to be filled with all the fullness of God.[32]

And as he wrote letters of spiritual counsel, he said:

The work of sanctification is hindered . . . by holding out the being *delivered from sin* as the mark to be aimed at, instead of being *rooted in Christ,* and *filled with the fulness of God,* and with *power from on high.*[33]

According to Fletcher, Christian perfection is not only the "cluster" (by which he suggests an "ordering") but the "maturity of the graces which compose the Christian character in the church *militant.*"[34]

Fletcher is particularly denunciatory of the doctrinaire perfectionists. He addresses himself in scatching rebuke to those "perfect Christian Pharisees" who would profess the experience but lack its central characteristic, humble love. He denounces their "narrow, contracted spirit" and their "prejudices," which, he said, they would not sacrifice "to the public good of the whole body of Christ."[35] It is such, he said, who do most to cause men to consider this doctrine a "dangerous delusion." He readily admits that

some gracious persons . . . speak against Christian Perfection with their lips, but cannot help following hard after it with their hearts; and while they do so, they sometimes attain the *thing,* although they continue to quarrel with the *name.* The perfect imperfectionists undoubtedly adorn the gospel of Christ far more than the imperfect, hypocritical, perfectionists, . . . and God, who looks on the simplicity of the heart more than at the consistency of the judgment, pities their mistakes and accepts their work.[36]

Finally, Fletcher joins Wesley in warning against the tendency to make entire sanctification the terminal point in Christian perfection. Wesley had stated:

We have leaned too much toward Calvinism. Wherein? . . . We have received it as a maxim, that "a man is to do nothing in order to justification." Nothing can be more false. Whoever desires to find favour with God should "cease from evil, and learn to do well." Whoever repents should do "works meet for repentance." . . .

Does not talking of a *justified* or a *sanctified* state tend to mislead men? almost naturally leading them to trust in what was done in one moment? Whereas, we are every hour and every moment pleasing or displeasing to God, according to our works; according to the whole of our inward tempers, and our outward behaviour.[37]

Lady Huntington, Fletcher's patroness in his work at Trevecca College, had been particularly offended by what appeared to her to be an attack upon "salvation by faith." She denounced the conference minutes as *"horrible, abominable,* and *subversive"* to the very foundations of the Church. She demanded that her associates similarly disavow Wesley's statement. Fletcher, however, not only further explained but fully defended Wesley's doctrinal stand. In consequence he left Trevecca, "the *servant,"* as he said, "but no more the *President,* of the college." His action cost him not only his position but, what was more painful, a number of friends of long standing.

Fletcher could hardly have done otherwise. With him Christian perfection was—as with Wesley—a "moment by moment" relationship. It could be lost—could, in fact, be retained only by its improvement. His wide use of such terms as "adult," "ripe," and "mature" must not, he warned, be "carried into an exact parallel." For his usage of maturity was never meant to indicate cessation of growth. "Growth in grace" according to Fletcher—and to Wesley—is not canceled but expedited by Christian perfection and is on that very account all the more obligatory. From such a standpoint he wrote his *Checks to Antinomianism.*

The *Checks,* issued seriatim, were especially welcomed by the struggling Methodist societies in the American colonies. These societies had begun with the preaching in New York City of Philip Embury. He was a Methodist local preacher who had come to New York with a group from Ireland in 1760. Piety was not one of the city's outstanding characteristics. The Anglican Church had been established by law, but only a small minority of the populace belonged to that church or were materially affected by it. The Great Awakening, which had shaken New England, Virginia, and Pennsylvania in the 1740's, had scarcely touched the city of New York. There an uncritical tolerance existed by virtue of indifference. And there the new body of immigrants from County Limerick tended to lapse into the careless worldliness of their fellows. It was too much for one of their number, Barbara Heck, who in 1765 urged Embury to start preaching services among his own group. He began with his immediate family and friends, and gradually the circle increased. He was joined a few months later by Captain Thomas Webb, barracks master who had lately come from Albany.

Webb was a fiery and impressive preacher. Charles Wesley in a letter to Joseph Benson when he was trying to persuade Benson not to yield to Webb's appeal to come to America had called Webb an "inexperienced, honest, zealous, loving enthusiast." But John had endorsed him, saying that he was "all life and fire." In America, John Adams was sufficiently impressed to call him the "most eloquent man I ever heard; he reaches the imagination and touches the passions very well, and expresses himself with great propriety." [38] He wore his uniform in the pulpit; and, it is reported, "he reverently laid his sword on the table or desk before him." There can be no doubt that his natural eloquence was strongly reinforced by his martial bearing. It must have taken a certain stiff-necked opposition to authority to resist his calls to repentance.

Not many military men, especially officers, were filling pulpits in New York at this time. And the crowds who came to hear him increased. So great became their number that successively larger quarters for the services had to be found. In 1768 a substantial chapel was constructed on John Street. Methodism was planted in America.

Methodist societies continued to multiply. Robert Strawbridge, another Irish local preacher, had begun in 1769 to preach and organize societies in Maryland, northern Virginia, and Delaware. Shortly thereafter Robert Williams, like Embury and Strawbridge a native of Ireland, began preaching in Virginia. By 1773 he was associated with Devereux Jarratt, rector of Bath Parish in Dinwiddie County, which was then in the midst of a remarkable revival of religion. Williams assured Jarratt that the Methodists were true members of the Anglican Church, aiming only at reviving true religion within its borders. Jarratt thereupon welcomed Williams, and under their combined efforts the revival was extended and intensified. New circuits and societies were soon formed.

From the very first Wesley had been concerned to see that perfection was not neglected by his preachers in America. In 1774 he wrote to Thomas Rankin, who had been sent over the previous year and had just given him a report on the Philadelphia Conference:

I have been lately thinking a good deal on one point, wherein perhaps we have all been wanting. We have not made it a rule, as soon as ever persons were justified, to remind them of going on to perfection. Whereas this is the very time preferable to all others. They have then the simplicity of little children, and they are fervent in spirit, ready to cut off the right hand or to pluck out the right eye. But if we once suffer this fervour to subside, we shall find it hard enough to bring them again to this point.[39]

Here is advice stressing the instantaneous over the gradual that goes beyond Wesley's usual treatment of the doctrine. And this was, in fact, something of a characteristic emphasis in early American preaching of the doctrine.

In New York, for instance, Thomas Webb preached concerning the giving of the Holy Spirit as follows:

The words of the text were written by the apostles after the act of justification had passed on them. But you see, my friends, this was not enough for them. They must receive the Holy Ghost after this. So must you. You must be sanctified. But you are not. You are only Christians in part. You have not received the Holy Ghost. I know it. I can feel your spirits hanging about me like so much dead flesh.[40]

It is not easy to determine just how typical Webb and his message really were. The fact remains, however, that one of the founders of American Methodism emphasized in America, as he had in England, the doctrine of Christian perfection.

Of far greater influence on the development of American Methodism than Webb was Freeborn Garrettson. "Of all the early native preachers," says W. W. Sweet, "Freeborn Garrettson undoubtedly stands at the head of the list in total influence exerted on the development of American Methodism." [41] Garrettson was a native of Maryland who, having heard Strawbridge and Asbury, was converted in 1775 and admitted on trial at the conference of the following year. In the account which he gives of the early years on his circuits in Maryland and Virginia, he reports a routine preaching engagement thus:

The Presbyterian minister was among the crowd and most of his congregation came to hear what the babler [sic] had to say. This man ... I met on the road a few days after. "I was hearing you preach," he said, "and I did not like your doctrine." What was your objection, said I. ... "You preach perfection," said he, "and that I do not believe to be attainable in this life." Then, said I, you do not hold with the doctrine of our Lord and his apostles.[42]

When Garrettson died, his widow was to say, "Blessed be God, he lived and died a witness of that doctrine he delighted to preach, *perfect love.*" [43]

In Virginia the revival which was flourishing under the ministry of Robert Williams and Devereux Jarratt stressed particularly the doctrine of Christian perfection. Jarratt reports phases of this revival during the winter of 1775-76 as follows:

In January, the news of convictions and conversions was common; and the people of God were inspired with new life and vigor by the happiness of others. But in a little time they were made thoroughly sensible that they themselves stood in need of a deeper work in their hearts than they had yet experienced. And while those were panting and groaning for pardon, these were entreating God, with strong cries and tears, to save them from the remains of inbred sin, to *sanctify them throughout, in spirit, soul, and body;* so to *circumcise their hearts,* that they might *love God with all their hearts,* and serve him with all their strength.[44]

Jarratt furthermore defines just what he teaches concerning Christian perfection and what he observed its results to be:

One of the doctrines, as you know, which we particularly insist upon, is that of a present Salvation; a Salvation not only from the Guilt and Power, but also from the Root of Sin; a *cleansing from all filthiness of flesh and spirit . . . ; a going on to perfection. . . .* Several who had believed were deeply sensible of their want of this. I have seen both men and women, who had long been happy in a sense of God's pardoning Love, as much convicted on account of the remains of sin in their hearts, and as much distrest for a total deliverance from them, as ever I saw any for Justification. . . . And I have been present when they believed that God answered this prayer, and bestowed this blessing upon them. I have conversed with them several times since, and have found them thoroughly devoted to God. They all testify, that they have received the Gift instantaneously, and by simple Faith. We have sundry witnesses of this perfect Love, who are above all suspicion. I have known the men and their communication for many years, and have ever found them zealous for the cause of God: Men of Sense and Integrity, Patterns of Piety and Humility; whose testimony therefore may be depended on.[45]

He reports that while in some of the meetings "there have not been that decency and order observed, which I could have wished," it had been on the whole a "great, a deep, a swift, and an extensively glorious work." Months after the peak of the revival he says, "I have the pleasure to inform you, I have not heard of any one Apostate yet." Thomas Rankin's supplement, dated two years later, reports the testimony of a Virginia justice of the peace who said that

before the Methodists came into these parts, when he was called by his office to attend the Court, there was nothing but Drunkenness, Cursing, Swearing, and Fighting, most of the time the Court sat: Whereas now nothing is heard but Prayer and Praise, and conversing about God, and the things of God.[46]

Even if the justice's report was somewhat colored for the edification of his ministerial auditors, it seems apparent that the revival

84

was of genuine value. And Christian perfection as an attainable experience had been one of its distinguishing characteristics.

Such are instances from segments of early Methodist labors in the Colonies. There is no reason to believe them atypical.

Meanwhile, John Wesley, aware of the increasing need and opportunity, was sending missionaries and superintendents to the Colonies. By 1771 he had sent such able men as Richard Boardman, Joseph Pilmoor, and Francis Asbury.

It is impossible to account for American Methodism without giving due consideration to the labors and influence of Francis Asbury. When he arrived in America, he was only twenty-six years of age. He had, however, been preaching an average of three or four times a week since his conversion at fifteen. The physical prowess which he had built up during his six and a half years as a smith's apprentice in England (between the ages of thirteen and a half and twenty) was spent recklessly in his immense itineration as the pioneer architect of Methodism in America.

In 1784 Asbury became a bishop in the newly constituted Methodist Episcopal Church. As such by exhortation and, supremely, by example he shaped the practices and to a considerable degree the doctrinal emphases of early American Methodism. What Asbury thought of the doctrine of Christian perfection is, therefore, relevant. He had early heard the doctrine preached and reports that having been "graciously justified" at the age of fifteen, about a year later he "experienced a marvellous display of the grace of God, which some might think was full sanctification, and was indeed very happy." [47] In the early years of his work in America this is what he reports from time to time in his journal about the preaching of Christian perfection:

January 10, 1773:
> . . . felt much power while preaching on perfect love. The more I speak on this subject, the more my soul is filled and drawn out in love. This doctrine has a great tendency to prevent people from settling on their lees.

85

April 14, 1779:

> My soul was in peace; but I have not sufficiently enforced the doctrine of Christian perfection. This will press believers forward, when everything else is found insufficient. . . . On *Thursday* my mind was deeply exercised on the subject of sanctification; and the result was, a determination to preach it more frequently, and pursue it more diligently.

May 18, 1780 [On which date he has prayed for some who were seeking the experience of entire sanctification. They profess to receive it]:

> I see clearly that to press the people to holiness, is the proper method to take them from contending for ordinances, or any less consequential things.

June 11, 1781:

> Here are a few believers groaning for full redemption, but many more are dying through controversy and for the want of urgent exhortation to purity of heart: it is hard for those to preach this doctrine who have not experimentally attained it, or who are not striving with all their hearts to possess it.

February 7, 1782:

> I find no preaching does good, but that which properly presses the use of the means, and urges holiness of heart; these points I am determined to keep close to in all my sermons.

At this point it appears that Asbury is particularly drawn to the doctrine because he sees it to be the instrument par excellence of keeping the societies from "settling on their lees." An examination of his own intense personal search and his repeated recognition of those who profess perfect love would indicate that it is to him, however, far more than a distant ideal. Two specific aspects of his preaching on the doctrine are revealed: (1) "it must be sought by faith, and expected as a present salvation"; [48] and (2) "it appears to me very difficult to keep professors from placing too much confidence in past experience." [49] He preached it, then, as an instantaneous experience, but he insisted that such an experience was not sufficient for final salvation.

Few men were closer to Asbury in these early years than Richard Whatcoat. Asbury described him as "my faithful friend for forty years . . . a man so uniformly good, I have not known in Europe or America." Whatcoat became a bishop in 1800 and died in 1806. He not only believed in the doctrine of entire sanctification but professed it as a personal experience. In 1781 he wrote of his early religious life:

> I soon found that, though I was justified freely, I was not wholly sanctified . . . after many sharp and painful conflicts and many gracious visitations, on March 28, 1761, my spirit was drawn out and engaged in wrestling with God for about two hours in a manner I never did before. Suddenly I was stripped of all but love. I was all love and prayer and praise.[50]

It was a high point with him when in his itinerary he found others who appeared to have come to a similar point of attainment. His journal reads:

in Thos Odals Class three were justified and Nine Santified
Glory to God

And later:

Met Class at Bror Stewards [. . . .] profest to be Santified
Glory to God [51]

Upon his death his ministerial brethren reported of him:

> He professed the justifying and sanctifying grace of God, and all that knew him well might say, If a man on earth possessed these blessings, surely it was Richard Whatcoat.[52]

With the doctrine of Christian perfection thus highly regarded by the leaders of early American Methodism, it is not surprising that at the Conference of 1781 the traveling preachers present agreed that they would "preach the old Methodist doctrine and inforce the discipline which was contained in the Notes, Sermons and Minutes published by Mr. Wesley." Just what the "old Methodist doctrine" was is made clear by Wesley's earlier remarks. The question had been put: "What can be done to revive the work of God where it is decayed?" And Wesley had replied:

Strongly and explicitly exhort all believers to "go on to perfection."
. . . The Papists say, "This cannot be attained till we have been
refined by the fire of purgatory." The Calvinists say, "Nay, it will be
attained as soon as the soul and body part." The old Methodists say,
"It may be attained before we die." [53]

This passage was incorporated into the *Discipline* of 1784 and
clearly indicates what was included in that which the preachers
of 1781 had agreed to preach.

The doctrinal content of the first *Discipline* of the Methodist
Episcopal Church was fairly well determined before the organiz-
ing conference met in Baltimore at the Christmas season of 1784.
As noted, the traveling preachers had agreed to certain standards
three years earlier. And in October, 1783, Wesley had written from
Bristol:

Let all of you be determined to abide by the Methodist doctrine,
and discipline, published in the four volumes of sermons, and the
notes upon the New Testament, together with the large minutes of
the conference.[54]

There is nothing to indicate that the conference was otherwise
minded. Certainly in this first *Discipline,* Christian perfection was
not neglected. There was the statement already cited which began:
"Strongly and explicitly exhort all believers to 'go on to perfection.'"
And which ended: "Therefore whoever would advance the gradual
change in believers, should strongly insist on the instantaneous."
The usual questions were asked of all candidates for ordination:
"Are you going on to perfection?" "Do you expect to be made
perfect in this life?" Moreover, in order that the candidates might
be informed of what was intended by such questions, the *Plain
Account,* covering almost sixty pages, was incorporated in its
entirety.

The data appear to support the conclusion that American
colonial Methodism in its standards and—more significantly—in
its preaching made the doctrine of Christian perfection one of its
characteristic features. The type of perfection so taught was the

later Wesleyan view which included the concept of an experience attainable "now and by simple faith" and which at the same time made ample provision for corporate Christian nurture. It is reasonable to assume that it was with this connotation that the doctrine was embodied in the first *Discipline* of the Methodist Episcopal Church.

CHAPTER IV

The Development of the Doctrine in American Methodism
1784-1865

WHEN THE METHODIST EPISCOPAL CHURCH came into being at the Christmas Conference of 1784, most of America—everything, in fact, outside the settled areas of the eastern seaboard—was frontier; and the frontier was rapidly expanding. In that same year Congress had taken preliminary steps to open the West to settlement and eventual statehood. Already trappers, fur traders, adventurers, and—above all—the land-hungry agricultural settlers were shaping up a distinctive populace, "childlike, simple, and savage." Into this same frontier the Methodist itinerants poured with a zeal which needed no prompting from an organized missionary society. Instead, "every conference was virtually a home missionary society, every itinerant a missionary." [1] The message and method of these "sons of Wesley" were peculiarly fitted to the task. It is said:

A church with real hopes for success in the West should have been optimistic in its faith, with stress on the importance of the individual. It should have provided social and emotional content. It should have an organization adapted to the widely scattered western population.

Further, it needed a clergy which could speak the language of the crude and hard-working West.[2]

The fact that the Methodist Church met those conditions is indicated by its remarkable growth during these early years. In less than two years after its founding in Baltimore, the church had pushed three circuits west of the Alleghenies and claimed for these circuits a combined membership of 1,210. This was but a beginning.

By 1800 there were at least fourteen circuits west of the Allegheny Mountains: six in Kentucky, two in Tennessee, two in the Ohio Territory, two in southwestern Pennsylvania, and one each in western Virginia and western North Carolina.[3]

When the Louisiana Purchase of 1803 and the opening of the Erie Canal in 1825 enormously accelerated westward expansion, circuits followed the swarming immigration. The Methodists, and their rivals the Baptists, were ideally fitted for their frontier task.

In 1812 the Massachusetts Missionary Society sent out Andover graduates Samuel J. Mills and John F. Schermerhorn "to investigate the religious and moral conditions of the West." They were appalled at the immoral, ignorant, and vicious nature of most of the area they covered. The paucity of Presbyterian or Congregational divines was especially disheartening. The western Baptists, they said, "excite the passions . . . rather than communicate understanding." [4] Nor were they favorably impressed with the Methodist itinerants they encountered, considering them sectarian and generally ignorant. But they did pay high tribute to the Methodist system of circuits, "which," they said, "is by far the best for domestic missions ever adopted." [5]

It was more than this excellent system, however, which made Methodism such a force on the frontier. The message of free will and free grace, the stress on individual responsibility, the emotionally satisfying character of the services—all assisted the circuit rider in the accomplishment of his task. Charles and Mary Beard have described that task as being to restrain the harshness and brutality of the backwoods, to tame the hot passions of men quick with the rifle and the dirk, to introduce sobriety into communities terrified by drunken bullies.[6]

With such an assignment, in such an environment, the preacher must inevitably have felt that the burden of his message should be a warning "to escape the wrath to come" rather than an exhortation "to go on to perfection." Lest this temptation be yielded to, from the highest quarter of Methodism came counsel and advice.

John Wesley, despite the autonomy of the new church and the watery miles that separated him from it, was a dominant influence in American Methodism until his death. At the Christmas Conference one of the first resolutions declared: "During the life of the Rev. Mr. Wesley, we acknowledge ourselves his sons in the gospel."[7] His letters were not, therefore, simply denominational broadsides, half read and wholly neglected. They were respectfully heeded and were in varying degree determinative. During the first year of the history of the American church Wesley wrote as follows to Freeborn Garrettson:

Let none of them rest in being half Christians. Whatever they do, let them do it with their might; and it will be best, as soon as any of them find peace with God, to exhort them to go on to perfection. The more strongly and vigilantly you press all believers to aspire after full sanctification as attainable now by simple faith the more the whole work of God will prosper.[8]

Like his earlier letter to Thomas Rankin, this was a counsel strongly stressing the instantaneous element in perfection. Methodism in America was being urged to revive the "days of Pentecost" which had subsided in Britain.

The bishops of the new church appeared to be entirely in sympathy with such a hope. On September 2, 1784 Wesley ordained Thomas Coke as superintendent of the Methodist societies in America. Later that month he appointed Coke and Asbury as "joint superintendents over our brethren in North America," and at the Christmas Conference of that year both men were unanimously elected to that office. Asbury's interest in sanctification has been noted. Coke's attitude may be discerned in a letter which he wrote from Annapolis in 1789 concerning the revivals then under way in Maryland and Virginia:

Whether there be wildfire in it or not, I do most earnestly wish that there was such a work at this present time in England. In one meeting in this State we have reason to believe that twenty souls received full sanctification; and it is common to have from twenty to fifty souls justified in a day in one place.[9]

Six years later he was counseling Ezekiel Cooper:
"O my brother, labor to stir up our dear American brethren who are children of God to go on to perfection."[10] Coke's interest was sincere and continuous.

Asbury was no less concerned. He reported enthusiastically that in 1789 he "came to Baltimore, and had very lively meetings . . . ; many souls professed to be convicted, converted, sanctified."[11] He commended emphases on the doctrine when he heard of them. He stressed its need and deplored its neglect when he observed such to be the case. During a period of brief illness, which he used for a bit of introspection, he concluded:

I have found by secret search, that I have not preached sanctification as I should have done: if I am restored, this shall be my theme more pointedly than ever.[12]

Reports of such a work came from other quarters. Ezekiel Cooper, one of Asbury's appointees and one of the most able of early Methodist preachers, prepared *A Brief Account of the Work in Baltimore*. In it he said:

About this time [July, 1789] many of the professors of religion felt the need of clean hearts, and were concerned for holiness. There was an encouraging prospect of sanctification taking place in the Church. Some experienced it, but it did not go on to an extensive degree.

A month later, however, at Quarterly Conference he reported a service in which the "mourners and believers were all in full expectation, the professors being on a stretch for purity of heart, and the penitents for pardon." [13]

In order that this deep concern should be regularly sustained, Coke and Asbury in their *Notes to the Discipline* urged the establishment of the Band Societies because, they said, "There is nothing we know of which so much quickens the soul to a desire and expectation of the perfect love of God as this." And they added:

> Wherever also it is practicable, there should be formed *a select society* chosen out of the members of the bands. This should be composed of believers who enjoy the perfect love of God, or who are earnestly seeking that great blessing. . . . *They* also meet once a week for an hour, and the preacher presides among them. Each member is at liberty to speak his or her experience, the preacher giving such advice respecting the grand point their souls are aiming at, as he sees expedient.
>
> Thus does our economy . . . tend to raise the members of our society from one degree of grace to another.

The "first American preacher," William Watters, reports his own attainment of the experience and the consequent spread of that work in his circuits. He says:

> The most glorious work that ever I beheld was in this Circuit amongst believers. Scores professed to be sanctified unto the Lord— I could not be satisfied without pressing on Christians their privilege.[14]

And Benjamin Abbott, a Methodist itinerant from 1789 to 1795 on circuits in New York, Pennsylvania, Delaware, Maryland, and the Jerseys, was reported in the Minutes of the Conference of 1796 to be "an uncommon zealot for the blessed work of sanctification, and preached it on all occasions and in all congregations, and what was best of all, lived it." The doctrine was given stanch proclamation.

But there were problems. The frontier presented one set. New England presented another. There the Wesleyan "invaders" were faced by an entrenched doctrinal system whose extremes were pre-Edwardian Calvinism on the one hand and Universalism on the other. The Great Awakening almost half a century earlier had here and there breached the walls but had by no means opened the gates. Jesse Lee, Methodism's able pioneer to New England, wrote from Boston on January 3, 1791, to Richard Dougless, reporting on a typical difficulty:

My dear Bro.

Since I have been in these parts, I have met with many discouragements, and repeated disappointments. . . . In some places I have been much encouraged, and have cause to bless God for the satisfaction that I have found in preaching to them the everlasting Gospel. But some of my Christian Brethren won't know me, because of my name: the innocent name of Methodist. The m[os]t friendly Society that I have found in Boston is the Universalists. I am permitted to preach in their Meeting House. I see no fruit of my labours here as yet. . . . The Baptist brethren in these parts are not so friendly as they are in your town. They are all close communicants, and mostly rigid Predestinarians. However I believe they have more religion than any other Society of people in Boston. And they continue to improve. . . . I hope you are still determined to follow on to know the Lord. Don't be contented with what religion you have got. Bless God for it, and pray God to give you more. If you rest satisfied with one blessing when God has got another to give you, it will bring leanness into your soul. O my Bro.! live to God. Let him have your whole heart! Keep back no part of the price. . . . I wish you would write to me by some of the Vessils [sic] and direct it to the care of Mr. Taylor Merchant, No. 7 Long Wharf. I am yours in love,

Jesse Lee[15]

The latter portion of this letter tends to substantiate William Fairfield Warren's statement that Lee "set forth the sweet and luminous doctrine of Christian perfection." But New England was stony ground for the Methodist seed.

The distinguishing ensign of the Methodist campaign in this sector was universal (or general) atonement, including the doctrines of regeneration and assurance. What was said of Jesse Lee could have been said also of many another of his fellow itinerants. This was:

> [he] came here, bearing a different gospel from any which had ever been preached in New England: a gospel of free salvation, of universal atonement, of possible conscious conversion and regeneration by the Holy Ghost, and the possibility of having an experience, the subject of which should *know* that he had passed from death unto life, and had become a child of God,—a doctrine unknown and untaught at that time, in all the regions of these New England States.[16]

These doctrines necessarily received prior emphasis. But the doctrine of Christian perfection was not neglected. For this phase of the attack Fletcher's *Checks to Antinomianism* was a rich store of doctrinal ordnance. By 1791 an American edition was published, and by 1820 at least two more editions had come off American presses. The last of these *Checks* was Fletcher's *Treatise on Christian Perfection*.

The preaching of "holiness of heart" was especially prevalent in the Methodist societies during the Second Great Awakening. At this time a number of the preachers sent in accounts of the work on their circuits. The letters were written to their bishops, principally to Asbury; and extracts from them have been preserved. William Mills wrote from New Jersey in 1802 to report that sanctifications were being commonly experienced in the class meetings and that he was "now impressing the necessity of holiness of heart upon those that profess justifying grace." Wilson Lee reported many instances of conversion and sanctification in Baltimore that same year and added:

> I have made it a point to preach perfect love and holiness every Saturday of our quarterly meeting; and the Lord hath blessed this word of his grace, with the witnesses of it.

From Lexington, Kentucky, in 1804 Launer Blackman stated that "the old professors in general are stirred up to seek for perfect love. . . . Numbers have obtained it." Similar reports were given by such well-known early preachers as Daniel Hitt, Richard Graves, Thomas Sargent, Samuel Coate, and James Jenkin. Said Jesse Lee:

> I suppose the Methodist connection hardly ever knew such a time of a general revival of religion through the whole of their circuits, as they had about the latter part of the year 1800.

The Awakening was for Methodism a time of renewed interest in the doctrine of perfect love. The revival continued, and perfection was one of its features. Thomas Coke wrote from Liverpool in 1802 to say:

> The great revival on the [American] Continent rejoices me exceedingly—yea, more, I can truly say, than a revival in any other country in the world. I have read to thousands, and shall read, God willing, to tens of thousands, the account I have already received of the progress of the work. . . .
> I am glad to find by Brother Asbury, that you universally press upon your believing hearers the necessity of sanctification and entire devotedness to God.[17]

In 1805 Francis Asbury declared: "I calculate 1805 to be the greatest year that ever was known in America or the world; only let the preachers of a holy Gospel, be holy and Laborious." Of a camp meeting in Maryland, Asbury reported: "Five hundred and eighty were said to be converted; and one hundred and twenty believers confirmed and sanctified. Lord, let this work be general." [18]

Nevertheless, it should not be assumed that the primary doctrine of the Methodist Episcopal Church during its first two decades was entire sanctification. Christian perfection was a respected but not a dominant feature of the preaching of this period. A review of sermon topics, conference reports, and early biographies clearly indicates that fact. It is entirely possible to read some thoroughly trustworthy and comprehensive accounts of these early years without supposing that perfection was more than an incidental feature. Broader study will indicate, however, that it was definitely more than that. Conversion was the principal theme of early American

97

Methodist preaching, but perfection was a well-remembered corollary. Asbury, for instance, was saying in 1803: "Although I do not consider *sanctification—Christian perfection,* common-place subjects, yet I make them the burden, and labour to make them the savour of every sermon." [19]

But within a few years events conspired to bring about an almost opposite effect. The Conference of 1812, for instance, voted to remove the Doctrinal Tracts from future editions of the *Discipline.*

The removal of the tracts was an action taken purely in the interest of size and convenience. These doctrinal tracts, which included the *Plain Account* and occasionally Wesley's "Of Christian Perfection" had been published in full in the *Discipline.* It was ordered by the conference that the tracts be thereafter bound in a separate volume and so circulated. From 1812, then, the *Discipline* appeared without the tracts. But the separate volumes in which those tracts were to be bound and circulated did not appear until 1832— twenty years after they were removed from the *Discipline.* However necessary and wise the action of the conference, the practical result for the doctrine of Christian perfection was to remove its authorized delineation from widespread circulation and to place it in a less authoritative status. Moreover, during the twenty years in which the tracts were not published, a generation or two of Methodist ministers were rounding out their doctrinal views.

By 1814 there was evidence that those views were already in a process of change. In March of that year Benjamin Lakin entered an account to such an effect in his journal. Lakin had been "admitted on trial to the traveling connection in the Holston Conference of 1795." In 1814 he was on the Limestone Circuit in Kentucky and reflecting on the prevailing spiritual climate as follows:

I have been makeing [sic] some enquirey [sic] into the cause of the gloom that is on the minds of professors and the decline of religion. Lately an old Brother observed that he had observed for some time our preaching to begin with the fall of man, the Redemption by Jesus Christ, repentance and Justification by faith, and here we stoped [sic] and for a long time he had not heard the doctrine of sanctification enforced—I immediately began to make my observation on experiences that I heare [sic], and for a considerable time have observed them go as far as Justification and there stop and no talk of sanctification. I have further observed that professors have loss [lost] (at least too many of them) that bright evidence of their acceptance with God they once had. . . . I concluded the following causes have produced this effect (1) The confused state of affairs and the intrest [sic] every man takes in the event of the war—(2) We have preached the gospel but have been deficient in enforcing the doctrine of sanctification, and (3) the people stoped [sic] In a Justified state without persueing [sic] holiness.[20]

If this doctrinal neglect was due in any way to the war, the ensuing peace was marked by no resumption of interest. In 1819 a commentator on American Methodism could say: "How few and feeble are the efforts of . . . ministers of the gospel in particular, to raise the standard of Christian perfection in the Church." [21]

Among those who did raise that standard was the Rev. Heman Bangs, pastor of John Street Church in 1822. On January 20 of that year he records that he "first—spoke of the doctrine of perfection as the Christian's privilege. Secondly—endeavored to press home the necessity of going on to it." Heman was a brother of the more famous Nathan Bangs, one of the most influential figures in early American Methodism.

Another exponent of Christian perfection was the Rev. Laban Clark. Addressing the New Haven District, of which he was the presiding elder, he spoke of the spirit's influence upon "unawakened sinners" and concluded:

If the gift of the Holy Spirit . . . produces such a moral influence even upon the rebellious, how much more will its renewing and sanctifying influence be exerted in the pardoned believer, to purify him unto God.[22]

That these were illustrations of an infrequent usage is indicated by the Pastoral Address delivered to the General Conference of 1832. It read in part as follows:

Why . . . have we so few living witnesses that "the blood of Jesus Christ cleanseth from all sin?" . . . Among primitive Methodists, the

99

experience of this high attainment in religion may justly be said to have been common; now, a profession of it is rarely to be met with among us.

Is it not time for us, in this matter at least, to return to first principles? Is it not time that we throw off the reproach of inconsistency with which we are charged in regard to this matter? Only let all who have been born of the Spirit, . . . seek, with the same ardor, to be made perfect in love as they sought for the pardon of their sins.

Such exhortation was not, apparently, greatly heeded. Three years later it was charged that "professed Christians" in the church were interested in holiness only to the extent necessary "to escape future perdition." "What a want is there, my brethren," said this plaintiff, "of that deep and uniform piety which should distinguish the Church." [23]

The rising national prosperity which accompanied postwar industrialization was shared in by Methodists. But increasing wealth did not provoke deepening piety. "In common with others of our country," said Nathan Bangs in 1837, "the Methodists are becoming more and more wealthy, and are thereby in equal danger with others of being swallowed up 'with the cares and riches of this world.'" Christian perfection was, in fact, well-nigh swallowed up in a welter of other considerations. Little was said about the doctrine, for instance, in the principal denominational journals between 1832 and 1840. In 1834-35 a spate of articles did appear in the New York *Christian Advocate* pointing out the differences between the Wesleyan doctrine of Christian perfection and certain antinomian teachings then receiving wide publicity. But by and large the "old Methodist doctrine" was becoming a denominational curiosity.

The issues of *The Methodist Magazine and Quarterly Review* from 1830 to 1840 give the impression that this doctrine was of a well-nigh esoteric nature—not seriously questioned nor generally preached. Occasional articles expounded and defended it—usually in strictest Wesleyan terms—but Christian perfection seems not to have been a vital ingredient in general Methodist thought and

life during this period. Between 1836 and 1840 not one article on the subject appeared in the *Quarterly Review.*

Later, Bishop J. T. Peck was to describe these years as a period in which the "subject received less and less attention until, in many places, the publication and earnest enforcement of the old Wesleyan Bible doctrine of Holiness, was in great danger of being regarded as a novelty, and an innovation, even in the Methodist Church!" [24]

Perhaps this is why the bishops felt it necessary to address the General Conference of 1840 as follows:

> We exhort and beseech you, brethren, by the tender mercies of our God, that you strive for the "mind that was in Christ Jesus." Be not content with mere childhood in religion; but, ". . . go on to perfection." The doctrine of *entire sanctification* constitutes a leading feature of original Methodism. But let us not suppose it enough to have this doctrine in our standards: let us labour to have the *experience* and the *power* of it in our *hearts.* Be assured, brethren, that if our influence and usefulness, as a religious community, depend upon one thing more than any other, it is upon our carrying out the great doctrine of sanctification in our life and conversation. When we fail to do this, then shall we lose our pre-eminence; and the halo of glory which surrounded the heads, and lit up the path of our sainted fathers, will have departed from their unworthy sons.

This time the seed fell upon good ground.

The deliberate cultivation of that ground had begun fifteen years earlier. Noting the dearth of preaching on Christian perfection, Timothy Merritt had in 1825 published a small volume entitled *The Christian's Manual, a Treatise on Christian Perfection.* Of Merritt it was said:

> His judgment was remarkably clear and discriminating. . . . He lacked fancy and imagination, but was thereby, perhaps, the better fitted for his favorite courses of thought—the investigation and discussion of the great doctrinal truths of religion. . . . The doctrine of Christian perfection was his favorite theme, and he was a living example of it. . . . No man of his day had more prominence in the Eastern Churches for either the excellence of his life or the importance of his services. [25]

Reported another: "Holiness was the great business he lived to promote." Merritt's discussion of the doctrine is essentially the traditional Wesleyan presentation. He does stress, in a manner that suggests that he considers such stress needed, the distinction between justification and sanctification. He points out that, while there is a partial sanctification (which *begins* in justification), experience and scripture show the need for a more complete work, that is, entire sanctification.

That same year there appeared a series of articles in *Zion's Herald* by Aaron Lummus. Lummus pursues much the same course as did Merritt, but he specifically attacks three errors which were current concerning the doctrine of perfection. Since the articles were published in *Zion's Herald,* it is reasonable to assume that the errors under attack were current in Methodism. They were, said Lummus, (1) a denial of the instantaneous character of complete sanctification, (2) the idea that one can grow toward it but never attain it, and (3) "some err on another ground, viz. they confound regeneration and sanctification, and say we are sanctified when we are converted." His answer is similar to Merritt's—the work of sanctification is begun in regeneration and completed in entire sanctification. Lummus' work suggests that Wesley's synthesis was already under attack.

In 1826 Nathan Bangs, then heading the Methodist Book Concern, completed a series of articles designed to suggest a course of study to younger Methodist ministers. They were published as *Letters to Young Ministers of the Gospel, on the Importance and Method of Study.* In Christian theology Bangs suggested:

On the doctrine of Repentance, Justification, and Sanctification, you can find no authors who have illustrated those subjects with greater clearness and accuracy than Wesley and Fletcher.

He also included Watson (whose first volume of the *Institutes* had just been published) and Baxter with comment on their differing excellencies. As for commentaries he suggested Wesley, Coke, Clarke, Benson, and Henry. Just how much Bangs was heeded, it would be difficult to say; but of the latter writers he mentions, it

was Adam Clarke and Richard Watson whose influence on the doctrine of Christian perfection was most pronounced.

Adam Clarke had few peers in the influence he wielded upon the grass roots of early Methodism. He was an impressive figure, five feet nine inches tall and, though he said he abhorred "men with big bellies," he was given to a "full habit of body." He was able, kind, learned, and unflaggingly industrious. His *Commentary* was his monument—on which he spent forty years (snatched from a busy ministerial and administrative life)—which he completed in 1826.

Clarke's scholarship was acknowledged and questioned. In 1806 the University of Aberdeen conferred on him the degree of Master of Arts and later awarded him the degree of Doctor of Civil and Canon Law. But John Stoughton in his *Religion in England, 1800-1850,* says of him:

> He had an omnivorous literary appetite, but his digestive power was weak. His memory exceeded his judgment. . . . Clarke was more than a commentator, he was a laborious compiler and editor. . . . But he attempted too much to be sufficiently thorough in his undertakings.

His *Commentary on the Old and New Testament* was nevertheless written in a fashion and style that insured for it prestige and popularity. When it was finally ready to submit to the press in complete form, the demand was such that 11,800 copies were printed in the first edition "and successive editions were printed both in England and America." It still enjoys a considerable sale. The following tribute is one estimate of the measure of his influence:

> Adam Clarke was the greatest name in Methodism in the generation which succeeded Wesley. . . . He was not only the greatest scholar in Methodism, . . . but if to all men he was known as a scholar, to his own people he was a father in God and a brother beloved.[26]

And Abel Stevens, one of the outstanding chroniclers of early American Methodism, said that the value of Clarke's *Commentary* to the Methodist ministry was "immeasurably great. . . . It may be said to have initiated critical biblical studies among them." His personal popularity was such that he was invited in the latter part of 1831 to make an extensive tour of the Methodist churches in America. His reply reflects his warmth of spirit and must only have added to his popularity with its recipients. Extracts are worthy of note:

Gentlemen and Rev'd Brethren.

Having been absent in the west of England, for a considerable time, your Letter did not reach my hand till some weeks after its arrival. Your kind Invitation to visit the United States, was gratifying to me and had I been appriz'd of your Intention a few months earlier, I should most certainly have endeavour'd to meet your wishes. . . . But the warning is too short, & I am engaged so far both to England & Ireland in behalf of our missionary cause that I cannot by any Substitute redeem those Pledges. . . .

I respect, & wish well to your *State;* & I love your *Church.* As far as I can discern you are close Imitators of the original Methodists . . . holding the same Doctrines, & acting under the same discipline. . . .

There is no danger so imminent both to *you* & *us,* as departing from our original *Simplicity* in Spirit, in manners, & in our mode of worship. . . . I would say to all, Keep your *Doctrine* & your *Discipline* . . . preach the *former* without refining on them:—observe the *latter* without bending it to circumstances. . . .

As I believe your *Nation* to be destined to be the mightiest and happiest nation on the globe: so I believe, that your *Church* is likely to become the most extensive and pure in the Universe. As a *Church,* abide in the Apostolic Doctrine & Fellowship: As a Nation, be firmly united, entertain no petty differences, totally abolish the Slave Trade (if it be not yet done), abhor all offensive wars; never provoke even the punyest state, & never strike the *first blow.*—Encourage *Agriculture* & friendly *Traffic,* cultivate the *Sciences* & *Arts;* let *Learning* have its proper Place, Space, & adequate share of Esteem & Honour—if possible live in peace with all Nations—Retain your holy Zeal for God's cause & your countrie's weal; & that you may ever maintain your Liberty, avoid as its Bane & Ruin, a National Debt. . . . But whither am I running! will it be a sufficient excuse to allege "The Zeal of *your house,* hath eaten me up!" Truly, truly do I wish you good luck in the name of the Lord. And therefore, With my best Prayers for your civil and religious Prosperity & hearty thanks to each of you individually for the handsome & honorable manner in which you have framed your Invitation, I have the honour to be, Gentlemen & Reverend Brethren, your obliged humble Servant & well wisher.

Adam Clarke[27]

What had one so gallant and influential to say about Christian perfection?

In Clarke the doctrine of Christian perfection as attainable in this life is presented with a dogmatism which now assumed as settled what Wesley was inclined to consider hypothetical. Wesley had said, for instance:

If I were convinced that none in England had attained what has been so clearly and strongly preached . . . I should be clearly convinced that we had all mistaken the meaning of those scriptures.[28]

Clarke, however, some three decades later stoutly affirms, "Suppose not one could be found in all the churches of Christ whose heart was purified from all unrighteousness, . . . yet the doctrine of Christian perfection would still be true." As to the term "perfection" Clarke, like Wesley, admits that there is need for a more appropriate name for the doctrine—this time not because "perfection" connotes too much, but because it connotes too *little*. Said Clarke:

Had I a better name, one more energetic, one with a greater plentitude of meaning, . . . I would gladly adopt and use it. Even the word "perfection" has, in some relations, so many qualifications and abatements that cannot comport with that full and glorious salvation recommended in the gospel . . . that I would gladly lay it by, and employ a word . . . more worthy . . . ; but there is none in our language; which I deplore as an inconvenience and a loss.[29]

Taking the term as it stands, however, Clarke concludes that the perfect is that which fully answers the end for which it was created. And since man was created to love God "with all his heart, soul, mind, and strength, and his neighbour as himself," he who does so is perfect.

The emphasis in Clarke's treatment of the doctrine is upon an experience to be realized instantaneously. In fact, the instantaneous is the only method he recognizes as scriptural. Unlike Wesley and Fletcher he rules out altogether the idea of a gradual attainment. He states:

> In no part of the Scriptures are we directed to seek holiness *gradatim*. We are to come to God as well for an instantaneous and complete purification from all sin, as for an instantaneous pardon.[30]

Purification is the dominant feature of Clarke's view of Christian perfection, though Wesley and Fletcher had held it to be but the lowest phase of perfection. Sometimes he couples with it the idea of readjustment, but perfection as maturity is not an important consideration. For Clarke, to be "saved from all sin" is to be at once "filled with the fullness of God . . . and rooted and grounded in love." The two are concomitant, and the first necessarily implies the other. But like his predecessors Clarke does insist that perfection must be considered as a moment-by-moment relationship, wholly dependent upon the "indwelling Saviour." It can and will be lost except as all the obligations to the proper exercise of faith, love, and good works are observed.

Like Fletcher, Adam Clarke has left a record of a personal testimony to the experience he preached. He was converted in 1778 at the age of eighteen. Six years later when he "had received powerful convictions of the need for entire sanctification of his heart," he received appropriate instruction from a local preacher who "was a partaker of this precious privilege." He began to seek it. He reports:

> Soon after this, while earnestly wrestling with the Lord in prayer, and endeavoring, self-desperately, to believe, I found a change wrought in my soul, which I endeavored through grace to maintain amid grievous temptations. My indulgent Saviour continued to support me, and enabled me with all my power to preach the glad tidings to others.[31]

It should be recognized that with Adam Clarke, Christian perfection was no specialty. His interests were far too broad, his works too extensive. Nor did he minimize the importance of other doctrinal articles. But in his treatment of perfection the almost exclusive emphasis upon its instantaneous phase and his outright repudiation of the gradual pointed the way for the more extreme wings of Wesleyan perfectionism which were to follow.

Richard Watson was Clarke's junior by twenty-one years but died within six months of the latter's demise. The two men offer an interesting study in comparison and contrast. Both were concerned for an adequate presentation of the doctrine of Christian perfection. But their diverse temperaments led to considerably different emphases. Clarke for all his impressive scholarship was basically an evangelist. His presentation of the doctrine of Christian perfection tended, therefore, toward semidogmatic exhortation. When he had completed his exposition, he says: "Arise, then, and be baptized with a greater effusion of the Holy Ghost." Watson, on the other hand, was primarily a scholar. His presentation generally sought the path of noncontroversial elucidation. Therefore, concerning the possibility of attainment he quietly suggests: "There appears no ground to doubt this; since no small violence would be offered to the Scripture . . . by the opposite opinion." Moreover, while Clarke was tending to move to the left of the standard set by Wesley and Fletcher (by his emphasis on the instantaneous), Watson was moving to the right (by his emphasis on the gradual).

The work for which Watson is best known is his *Theological Institutes,* published serially over a five-year period and completed in 1829. As a result of this task he was called the "first systematizer of the theology of Methodism." It is said that "his design in the composition of this work was to assist the junior Preachers of the Wesleyan Connexion in their theological studies." And his work became equally valuable to the preachers in American Methodism. The *Institutes* soon won their place as an exposition of standard Methodist doctrine.

As regards the doctrine of Christian perfection Watson appears particularly concerned to indicate the high place of regeneration in the attainment of such a grace. He says:

107

That the regeneration which accompanies justification is a large approach to this state of perfected holiness; and that all dying to sin, and all growth in grace, advances us nearer to this point of *entire* sanctity, is so obvious, that on these points there can be no reasonable dispute.[32]

In another context he states the work done in initial regeneration in still stronger terms. For concerning the newly regenerate he says:

Believing in his Redeemer and Saviour with the heart unto righteousness, he knows for himself the power of his merit, and the strength of his grace to regenerate. Thus he becomes a holy man . . . and his holiness will increase.[33]

Nevertheless, he holds that these views are

not at all inconsistent with a more instantaneous work, when, the depth of our natural depravity being more painfully felt, we plead in faith the accomplishment of the promises of God.[34]

He points out that to deny the possibility of such an attainment in this life

is to say, that God, under the Gospel, requires us to be what we cannot be, either through want of efficacy in his grace, or from some defect in its administration; neither of which has any countenance from Scripture, nor is at all consistent with the terms in which the promises and exhortations of the Gospel are expressed.[35]

Although Watson grants in the *Institutes* the logical and scriptural grounds for the instantaneous aspect of Christian perfection, he expresses himself with more self-consistency and assurance when in his other works he presents the gradual phase of the doctrine. Here, even more than in Wesley or Fletcher, Christian perfection is viewed as a spiritual maturity to which time and experience must contribute. Life, Watson feels, is the "period in which we are to be trained up for the maturity of holiness, and the perfection and variety of Christian graces." All its vicissitudes and dispensations are intended for the accomplishment of that great end.

Watson, then, does not deny the Wesleyan emphases. In fact, he affirms them in such fashion as has been observed. Perhaps it was this restrained fashion that caused young John M'Clintock, who had been reading treatises on Christian perfection by Mahan, Fletcher, and others, to say of Watson, "How strangely meagre are Mr. Watson's remarks on this subject, both in his 'Institutes' and 'Dictionary'—nay, in his Exposition also." "Meagre" or not, in Watson's exposition there is a discernible shift of emphasis. As Adam Clarke's teachings had in them elements encouraging the tendency to make sanctification a separate and comprehensive article of doctrinal distinction, so Richard Watson's views have in them emphases which tend to merge sanctification with the doctrine of regeneration and thus to lose its significant character. Both such tendencies will later be given specific enunciation.

To supplement such recommended standards, Timothy Merritt had started in 1839 the *Guide to Christian Perfection*—later to be called the *Guide to Holiness*. This was to be a monthly periodical devoted, as the name suggests, to the promotion of the doctrine of Christian perfection. In its treatment of the doctrine stress was laid upon the instantaneous attainability of the experience of entire sanctification. It strove to be nonsectarian though it was by necessary consequence most acceptable to those whose theological background or inclination was Wesleyan. The *Guide* became widely influential and by 1873 had reached a circulation of forty thousand —probably its peak.

Another remarkable promotional agency was the Tuesday Meeting for the Promotion of Holiness. This meeting had begun in 1835 as a joint prayer meeting attended by the women of the Allen Street and Mulberry Street Methodist churches in New York City. Its sponsors were Phoebe (Mrs. W. C.) Palmer and her sister, Mrs. Sarah Lankford—who was to become after Phoebe's death in 1874 the second Mrs. W. C. Palmer. For the first four years it was attended solely by women. But in 1839 Mrs. T. C. Upham, "who had been led to the experience of entire sanctification, . . .

expressed great desire to bring her husband to the next meeting." Not only was this request granted, but other men were invited as well and the meeting was opened to all who were interested. Its specific purpose remained the promotion of the doctrine of entire sanctification. It continued as such for over sixty years, meeting each Tuesday principally in the Palmer home in New York City.

The Palmers were the outstanding exponents of Christian perfection in American Methodism during the third and fourth decades of the nineteenth century. Dr. Palmer was a well-known physician of New York City and a better-known Christian layman. It was his wife, however, who came into greater prominence. Phoebe Palmer was a dynamic and controversial figure. She had married at nineteen. Losing two children in their infancy, she decided that this was God's way of directing her to give more exclusive attention to religious matters. In 1837 she felt herself to be the recipient of entire sanctification. Shortly thereafter "she felt it her duty . . . to strive in every scriptural way to promote this unspeakable blessing among her fellow Christians." The result was her active advocacy of the doctrine and experience. The Tuesday Meeting was her most continuous medium of promotion. There, said Abel Stevens in 1863, "thousands of earnest minds from all parts of the land have sought and found guidance and consolation." But she also stressed holiness in the young women's Bible class of which she was teacher, in the class meetings of which her husband was leader, and later with Dr. Palmer in evangelistic meetings that carried them over the United States, to England, Ireland, and the Continent. Meanwhile she and her husband published hundreds of tracts which were distributed by the thousands (one of the most lively of which was by Harriet Beecher Stowe entitled *Primitive Christian Experience*), edited the *Guide to Holiness* during the period of its greatest influence, and carried on an enormous correspondence with religious leaders around the world. Nevertheless, she found time between 1845 and 1862 to publish seven books on religious themes—most of them dealing with some aspect of Christian perfection.

To many in that prefeminist day such "unwomanly" activity must have appeared slightly monstrous. The record indicates, however, that Phoebe Palmer was able, charming, unquestionably devoted and circumspect, and free from the more distasteful aspects of fanaticism. Bishop Matthew Simpson reported that before his personal acquaintance with her he had feared that she might be a mystic after the order of Madame Guyon. He found, however, that she was instead a thoroughly devoted Methodist, "warmly interested in every form of practical Christianity." He later wrote the introduction to her *Life and Letters,* endorsing her teachings and most of her methods. The introduction to her book, *Pioneer Experiences* was written by Bishop Janes. Bishop and Mrs. Hamline were her warm friends and associates. And Nathan Bangs said of her, "I feel it a duty to record my belief in the deep devotion and the intrinsic usefulness of this Christian woman."

When she died in 1874, T. Dewitt Talmadge of the Brooklyn Tabernacle said of her:

For thirty-seven years . . . every Tuesday, she had a meeting, the sole object of which was the elevation of the standard of Christian holiness; and there were hundreds of Christian ministers, who came in and sat down at her feet, and got her blessing, and went out stronger for Christian combat. It was no rare thing, in her evangelistic meetings in the United States and Europe, to have ministers of the Presbyterian Church and the Baptist Church, and the Methodist Church and the Episcopal Church, and all the churches, coming and kneeling down at the altar, bemoaning their unbelief and their coldness, and then rising up, saying: "I have got it—the blessing." Some caricatured and said there was no such thing as "a higher life" of peace and Christian sanctification; but she lived long enough to see the whole Christian Church waking up to this doctrine, and thousands and tens of thousands coming on the high table-land where once she stood. . . . Twenty-five thousand souls saved under the instrumentality of Phoebe Palmer! What a record for earth and heaven! . . . The Methodist Church cannot monopolize her name. She belonged to that church, she lived in it, she died in it, she loved it; but you cannot build any denominational wall high enough to shut out that light from our souls.[36]

This, then, according to one of her eminent contemporaries was the woman who played so large a part in the revival of holiness in American Methodism. The ensuing holiness movement was a tribute to her influence. Said A. Atwood, one of its early leaders, "All the wide movement of the National Committee is a result of her long and faithful service."

Because Phoebe Palmer was so outstanding and because her efforts were so fruitful, any particular emphasis in her method or message was generally imitated and frequently exaggerated. And some of these emphases tended to deviate from the Wesleyan mean. She taught, for instance, that once the consecration of "body, soul, and spirit" was complete, the believer should then "exercise faith" and, unsupported if need be by any sensible evidence, lay claim to entire sanctification. She was charged, therefore, with teaching, "Believe that you have it and you have it." This she flatly denied, stating that her emphasis was to insist on such a full and complete consecration that faith would be simply the next and necessary step. And yet her messages and instructions seem at least to support the charges made against her. One of her favorite texts was "The *altar* . . . sanctifieth the gift"—that is, that once the gift is on the altar, the consecration made, faith can only affirm sanctification. And she was much concerned that "all who are seeking this blessing were fully aware of the *sinful* inconsistency of unbelief." Some other emphases of her teaching were that the unsanctified go to hell, any failure to "go on to perfection" nullifying previous regeneration. The failure to use specific terms such as "holiness" and "entire sanctification" when referring to Christian perfection bordered, she implied, on the sinful. To fail to give public testimony to the experience was an almost certain way of losing it. Moreover, she chose to say, "Gospel holiness is that *state* of the soul which is attained by the believer . . ."—the type of teaching against which Wesley had warned in his Minutes of 1771. These were not major emphases in Mrs. Palmer's teachings. Most of them were, in fact, purely incidental and in extended exposition so modified as to be virtually nullified. Yet when they appeared even incidentally in tract form under the Palmer aegis, they tended to wide adoption.

112

Many of them became the distinguishing marks of segments of what came later to be called the "holiness movement."

In several of these emphases Mrs. Palmer was opposed by her closest associates. This was especially true with regard to that phase of her teaching which seemed to say, "Believe that you have it and you have it." John S. Inskip, strong advocate of holiness, declared: "In saying we are sanctified through faith, it is not meant that we must believe we *are* sanctified in order *to be* sanctified. This is absurd." Nathan Bangs, ordinarily a stanch defender of Mrs. Palmer, challenged her teaching at this point as "not sound . . . unscriptural, and anti-Wesleyan." Wesley had taught as follows:

> To say every man can believe to justification or sanctification *when* he will is contrary to plain matter of fact. Every one can confute it by his own experience. And yet if you deny that every man can believe *if* he will, you run full into absolute decrees. How will you untie this knot? I apprehend very easily. That every man may believe if he will I earnestly maintain, and yet that he can believe when he will I totally deny. But there will be always something in the matter which we cannot well comprehend or explain.[37]

Bangs endorsed, however, some of Mrs. Palmer's equally disputed teachings. In a series of articles in the *Christian Advocate* he defended the thesis that open testimony was requisite to the maintenance of the fully sanctified life. The controversy which followed agitated the columns of the *Advocate* for some months. Bangs's most ardent opponent and Mrs. Palmer's most relentless critic was the Rev. Hiram Mattison, at that time a teacher at Falley Seminary in Fulton, New York. Mattison especially objected to any implication that testimony to any state of grace was obligatory; and after the columns of the *Advocate* were closed to the controversy, he continued his attack in a brief pamphlet warfare. As with most such arguments this one was not particularly edifying. It apparently convinced no one already possessed of an opinion and succeeded principally in wearying the *Advocate's* readers.

The renewed interest in Christian perfection owed much to the life and labors of Nathan Bangs. His influence can be appreciated only if his place in American Methodism is understood. Said Abel Stevens of him:

Nathan Bangs was not only a public but a representative man, in the Methodist Episcopal Church, for more than half a century. . . . He was the founder of its periodical literature, and of its "Conference course" of ministerial study, and one of the founders of its present system of educational institutions. He was the first missionary secretary appointed by its General Conference, the first clerical editor of its General Conference newspaper press, the first editor of its Quarterly Review, and, for many years, the chief editor of its Monthly Magazine and its book publications. He may be pronounced the principal founder of the American literature of Methodism. . . . Besides his innumerable miscellaneous writings . . . he wrote more volumes in defense or illustration of his denomination than any other man. He became its recognized historian. He was one of the founders of its Missionary Society, he wrote the Constitution . . . of that great cause. . . . During more than twenty years he wrote all its Annual Reports. . . . Few men, if any, have longer or more successfully labored to promote those great interests of the denomination which have given it consolidation and permanence. . . . It has been justly said that he ranks next to Asbury in his historical importance in his Church. Twice did his brethren offer him the Episcopal chair.[38]

Truly his status and influence were formidable. And Bangs both preached and professed entire sanctification. His interest in the theme was early and continuous, and he gave measures for its promotion his wholehearted support. Said Bishop Janes at his funeral:

The Pauline doctrine of sanctification, as defined by Wesley, became his habitual theme of interest and conversation. He delighted to attend social gatherings for prayer on this subject, and during several late years he presided over one of the most frequented assemblies of that kind in our city.

As early as 1840 the work of Bangs, Merritt, and the Palmers began to show results. In 1841 *The Methodist Quarterly Review* observed that the *"work of holiness* is reviving among us" and was thankful for instances of the "clear, sober, and Scriptural professions of that blessed state among our people." The editor was of the opinion that the movement thus started would continue and expand. In May, 1840, the young *Guide to Christian Perfection,* established the previous year by Timothy Merritt, reported: "It is believed that no year of our experience as a Church has been as fruitful in sanctification as the past."

In 1841 Methodist churches in the New York area were listening to lectures on Christian perfection by George Peck, editor of the *Quarterly Review.* These lectures were principally exposition on the doctrine in terms of its presentation by Wesley, Fletcher, and Watson. One of their principal emphases was that entire sanctification would be received by faith and in this life—a point apparently in question. The doctrine was enjoying a resurgent emphasis in American Methodism.

It was also being strongly presented outside the bounds of that particular connection. And its most pronounced and influential exponent outside Methodist ranks was Charles G. Finney. In 1835 he had gone to newly founded Oberlin College to be professor of theology. During the next few years as he held revivals at Oberlin and elsewhere, he became greatly concerned over what he considered the "great state of weakness" in the Christian Church. As a result he said:

I was led earnestly to inquire whether there was not something higher and more enduring than the Christian church was aware of; whether there were not promises, and means provided in the Gospel, for the establishment of Christians in altogether a higher form of Christian life. I had known somewhat of the view of sanctification entertained by our Methodist brethren. But as their idea of sanctification seemed to me to relate almost altogether to states of the sensibility, I could not receive their teaching.

He examined also the teachings of John H. Noyes's antinomian perfection. He could not accept them.

Yet I was satisfied that the doctrine of sanctification in this life, and entire sanctification, in the sense that it was the privilege of Christians

115

to live without known sin, was a doctrine taught in the Bible, and that abundant means were provided for the securing of that attainment.[39]

Not long thereafter as the result of a revival at Oberlin a "very great and important change came over the whole community." President Asa Mahan had been particularly affected, and it was thought that he had come into an "entirely new form of Christian experience." In consequence, said Finney:

In a meeting a few days after this, one of our theological students arose, and put the inquiry, whether . . . sanctification was not attainable in this life; that is, sanctification in such a sense that Christians could have unbroken peace, and not come into condemnation, or have the feeling of condemnation or a consciousness of sin. Brother Mahan immediately answered, "Yes." What occurred at this meeting, brought the question of sanctification prominently before us, as a practical question. . . .

In this form it existed among us, as an experimental truth, which we did not attempt to reduce to a theoretical formula; nor did we attempt to explain its philosophy, until years afterwards.[40]

When they *did* attempt to present the doctrine as such, the emphasis was naturally in keeping with the Reformed idea of divine intervention as against the catholic view of a more gradual nurture.

Finney and Mahan, though opposed at this point by their Presbyterian and Congregational confreres, were outspoken advocates of Christian perfection in a period when it was neglected in many sectors of American Methodism. They came, therefore, to be considered as champions of the doctrine among Methodist groups similarly interested in its promotion. Their Reformed interpretation tended to become the standard view even in these quarters.

Meanwhile, during the early 1840's an unusual revival took place among the Methodists of England and Ireland. James Caughey, an American Methodist minister, was the moving spirit. It is reported, in an unusual estimate which is called "rather under than over the truth," that there were 21,625 justified and 9,222 entirely sanctified. The delegate from the Wesleyan Methodist Conference gave this report a modified substantiation in his address to the General Conference in 1844:

> The great doctrine of *entire sanctification* is exciting increased interest in our church. Many of our ministers and members are rejoicing in that "perfect love" which "casteth out fear," while many others are earnestly groaning for full redemption.

This revival was instrumental in stimulating further American interest, though Caughey's subsequent efforts in this country were not marked with the success which had attended them abroad.

On the American scene the dawning revival of interest in Christian perfection was reflected in the episcopal elections at the General Conference of 1844. Two bishops, E. S. Janes and L. L. Hamline, were elected. They represented to a degree the sectional divisions within the conference. But both were strong exponents of the doctrine of entire sanctification. Bishop Hamline was particularly emphatic in his advocacy. In his address to the Oneida Annual Conference during his first year in the episcopacy he commended that body on the fact that an "unusual number of the members of the Oneida Conference enjoyed the blessing of perfect love." He further exhorted all his ministerial auditors to preach more directly on that subject.

His exhortation was pertinent. In that same year a correspondent to the New York *Christian Advocate* reported that his personal and rather extensive observation was that few among the ministers and laity profess the experience and few preach directly on the doctrine. A young minister, writing to the *Guide to Holiness* in October, 1844, said:

> Among the ministry and membership with which I have become acquainted, but a very small minority have professed to enjoy the blessing of perfect love; and but very few have appeared to be earnestly seeking after it.

George Peck, of Puritan lineage and the editor of the *Methodist Quarterly Review*, had earlier written:

117

Where are the witnesses that the blood of Jesus Christ cleanses from all sin? It is matter of joy, indeed, that many such can be found, but it is to be lamented that their number, in comparison with the great mass of Methodists, is so very small.

Other factors were distracting the church. The Millerite revival, in which William Miller had predicted that the second coming of Christ would take place sometime between 1843 and 1844, had strongly affected the frontier Methodist conferences in the Northeast. Thousands had joined the church in anticipation of the fulfillment of Miller's prophecy. The actual date was finally set, and thousands thronged the hillsides in anticipation. The day passed as had the days before it. Miller then chose a later date; but when that too passed with no fulfillment of the promised event, his great revival collapsed. Methodism's loss from 1845 to 1847 was 56,847. The Mexican War and the slavery controversy were similarly disruptive factors. Nevertheless, the Methodist Episcopal Church is reported to have had a membership gain of around 200,000 during the period from 1842 to 1850.

But Jesse T. Peck, destined to become a bishop twenty-three years later, sadly observed in 1849 that the church was filling up with unconverted who were not even valid seekers after conversion, much less lovers of holiness. Later, in 1851, he states that though he is a stanch believer in the doctrine of entire sanctification, during the first nineteen years of his ministry he saw but few who had professed to find it and had heard practically no distinctive messages on it.

Nathan Bangs, however, had this to say about the doctrinal position of the church as it stood midway in the nineteenth century:

By Methodism I understand those peculiarities of the system by which it is distinguished from all other *isms;* hence it not only includes the doctrines [characteristic of general Protestant theology] enumerated above, by which it proves its orthodoxy, but it brings out more prominently than is done by other denominations . . . that of Christian perfection, or the entire sanctification of the whole man to God, or holiness of heart and life. . . .

118

Now, have the Methodist preachers ceased to preach this doctrine, and to urge it upon their people as an experimental and practical thing? I know that they always, from the beginning of their ministry, held it prominently before their hearers, not only as a privilege, but as a duty, to be "holy in all manner of conversation." But did they all profess to enjoy it? They did not: nor did the members of the church. Some did, both among preachers and people; but I believe a majority did not. Many of the preachers preached it more as a theory, than as something which they knew from their own experience: while all, who were rightly instructed, and were sincere believers in its attainableness, professed to be "groaning after it." This, I believe, has been the general state of the church from the beginning, though there were "times and seasons," when this work of holiness was more prevalent than at others. I may be under a mistake, but I have thought . . . that this subject has very considerably revived within six or seven years past; and that a more than usual number have sought and found the blessing of "perfect love."

I allow that this great and invaluable blessing is not pressed upon the people so generally and so earnestly as its importance demands; but this is not peculiar to the present time. This lack in the ministry and the membership was always a defect painfully manifest.[41]

Bangs's conclusions regarding the revived interest in the doctrine were corroborated by other connectional commentators. In 1848, for instance, the editor of the *Quarterly Review* had reported:

The subject of *Christian perfection* is one which, at the present time, excites as much interest, and receives as large an amount of attention, from the Christian mind of the country, as any other one theological doctrine.

And J. T. Peck in happier vein advanced what he believed to be the causes for this renewed interest. He listed them in this order: (1) increasing publication; (2) increased preaching on the subject— "Presiding Elders' districts may be found where the Presiding Elders themselves, and a large number of the stationed preachers, scarcely omit it in a single sermon. It is so in some western conferences"; (3) the more ready acceptance by the "common Meth-

odist mind" of the doctrine; and (4) the large number of actual recipients of the blessing. The movement, he said, "is of God, and no
finite power can overthrow it." [42] In 1854 it was said that the "witnesses to holiness" were numbered in "hundreds and thousands."

The progress of such a movement was not, however, universally
welcomed. The outspoken advocates of the doctrine came, in fact,
to be regarded as something of a party within the denomination.

At least two factors contributed to this result. First of all, there
had been an extended neglect of the doctrine. On the frontier it
had simply not seemed the appropriate message. As the Methodist
itinerant moved from point to point along his "crude, turbulent,
and godless" frontier circuit, he may have remembered Wesley's
account of his own early evangelical preaching:

At first we preached almost wholly to unbelievers. To those therefore
we spake almost continually of remission of sins through the death
of Christ, and the nature of faith in his blood.[43]

To the great majority of his hearers the "first elements of the gospel"
needed still to be made plain. The pressing and primary task was
conversion. Children must be born before they could come to
maturity. And the average frontier Methodist circuit rider was by
inclination and ability a far better midwife than governess. The
magnitude of the primary task tended to pre-empt the always
limited time, and sometimes limited talents, of even the most
conscientious Wesleyan disciple. In the more metropolitan centers
the desire for community status and institutional growth was a
constant temptation decorously to bypass Methodism's exacting
"peculiarity." Social respectability and financial soundness were
considerably better understood and appreciated virtues than a somewhat intense and suspiciously undemocratic personal piety. Christian perfection seemed somehow too exotic a doctrine. It was preserved but not promoted.

In the second place, the group who came forward shortly before
1840 to espouse a revival of the doctrine had evolved a growing
particularization concerning the manner of its presentation. It was

emphasized, for instance, that the attainment of entire sanctification here and now was absolutely necessary for salvation here and hereafter. The necessity of giving public testimony to such an experience, once it had been received, was no less compelling.

Principally for these reasons there tended now to be stirrings of opposition not only to what were considered extreme emphases but to those features of the doctrine which seemed to give excuse for such extremes. Consequently there arose those, apparently few in number and small in influence, who were charged with teaching that Christian perfection was to be attained "in the order in which vegetation reaches its consummation." "Efforts have not been wanting," wrote George Peck, "to modify the true Scriptural and Wesleyan theory." And those efforts, it seemed, were in the direction of identifying justification and sanctification with the result that "no distinct blessing, under that name, is to be sought or expected subsequently." These were straws in the wind, significant intimations of flourishing dissent. But as yet they were local and fragmentary—minor annoyances rather than major threats. And so they received only passing notice.

In brief recapitulation the 1820's and early 1830's may be characterized as a period when the doctrine of Christian perfection with an emphasis on entire sanctification was generally acknowledged to be one of the standards of American Methodism. There was little or no opposition at that point. If it was not actively opposed, however, it was definitely neglected. The issue was practical rather than theological. It was not a general acknowledgment of the doctrine that was lacking; it was the absence of any considerable effort to make personal appropriation of the experience that doctrine implied. In the late 1830's and early 1840's sectors of the church were agitated by a resurgence of holiness teaching. This resurgence was self-conscious and well implemented. And for various reasons it was not unanimously welcomed.

In 1848 opposition to this new emphasis was brought clearly into the open. Merritt Caldwell, a professor at the Maine Wesleyan Seminary, published in that year *The Philosophy of Christian Perfection*, "embracing," he said, "a Psychological Statement of the Principles of Christianity on which this Doctrine rests: together with a Practical Examination of the Peculiar Views of several Recent Writers on this Subject." Caldwell was apparently motivated by a desire to express in philosophical and psychological terms those aspects of the doctrine for which he felt biblical and orthodox terms to be inadequate. He was not ostensibly in revolt against the Wesleyan concept. However, his work was generally so interpreted. W. C. Hosmer in an extended article in the *Quarterly Review* approved such revolt and further argued that salvation must be considered as a whole, all of which is demanded—and given—instantly. Therefore whatever distinctions theologians may have imposed have no *real* meaning. If there seem to be stages, it is only seeming; for "they must all be passed through in the same moment, or they are not all necessary to salvation."[44] It is of no particular concern here to evaluate the character of this argument. Its conclusions alone are significant in that they reveal theological tendencies. Hosmer argues as follows: All that is necessary to salvation is given in regeneration. If sanctification is necessary to salvation, as its proponents claim, then sanctification is given in regeneration. If sanctification is given in regeneration, then there is no essential difference between the two. Therefore sanctification and regeneration are for all *real* purposes identical. Hosmer is merely proving what Wesley had long ago admitted. But in the now specialized language of the holiness advocates sanctification had come to mean entire sanctification. Therefore what Hosmer proposes of the first is intended to be popularly interpreted as true of the second. Hosmer's major premise is, moreover, a deliberate challenge to the contention that entire sanctification is (in every case) necessary to salvation. The importance here is not the validity of the argument but the significance of the theological affirmation. The relevant fact is that in 1849 a prominent contributor to the *Methodist Quarterly Review* and a professor in a Methodist seminary have to all appearances argued strongly against the Wesleyan teaching of the necessary distinction between regeneration and sanctification.

The challenge was responded to. George Peck, now retired from the editorship of the *Quarterly Review,* issued in 1849 a new edition of his book on Christian perfection. The feature of the re-issue and its *raison d'être* was a lecture on the difference between regeneration and sanctification—a restatement of distinctions Wesley had previously made. John M'Clintock, now editor of the *Quarterly Review,* called Peck's work the "only extended and scientific discussion of this great theme extant among us." Two years later, in 1851, R. S. Foster published his views on this sub-ject in a book entitled *The Nature and Blessedness of Christian Purity,* an able and noncontroversial exposition of Wesley's views with a special emphasis on the distinctiveness of sanctification as a doctrine and entire sanctification as a phase of that doctrine. Shortly thereafter J. T. Peck, by this time president of Dickinson College, further elaborated this position, concluding with:

> We humbly submit, therefore, that they [regeneration and sanctifi-cation] ought not to be used interchangeably, and that attempts so to use them have caused nearly all the confusion which has embarrassed these great points in theology.[45]

The question as to the distinctiveness of the doctrine of sanctifi-cation was now in the open. In the first round of polemical inter-change the traditional answer secured the greater measure of sup-port.

This position was strengthened by the wording of the Pastoral Address to the General Conference of 1852. The address dealt not only with the statement of the doctrine but also with its ex-perimental application. It urged:

> We would . . . exhort you, dear brethren, that the doctrine of *entire sanctification,* or *entire holiness,* be not confined to our standards; but that it may be a matter of experience in our hearts, and may be con-stantly practised in our lives. We advise you, however, in speaking or writing of holiness, to follow the well-sustained views, and even the phraseology employed in the writings of Wesley and Fletcher, which are not superseded by the more recent writers on this subject. Avoid

both new theories, new expressions, and new measures on this subject, and adhere closely to the ancient landmarks.

In the years immediately following this conference doctrinal controversy tended to subside, overshadowed by the impending struggle between North and South. Not one article directly on the subject of Christian perfection appeared in the columns of the *Methodist Quarterly Review* from 1853 to 1861.

By this time the Methodist Episcopal Church had undergone several noteworthy schisms. Most of these had nothing to do with the doctrine of Christian perfection. The O'Kelly schism of 1792 and the organization of the Reformed Methodists in 1814 resulted principally from differences over matters of representation and administration. The doctrine of Christian perfection was heartily endorsed by the mother church and by her schismatic daughters alike. It was not an issue. No more was it concerned with the organization of the Methodist Protestant Church in 1828-30. The division here arose out of the long-continued, and finally unsuccessful, effort to effect a more democratic system of securing ecclesiastical officials. While perfection did not enter into the controversy, the doctrine did find a generally favorable reception in the younger church. In 1877 a specific doctrinal statement on sanctification was added to its Articles of Religion.

The far greater separation which brought into being the Methodist Episcopal Church, South, was likewise without reference to Christian perfection. The principal issue, as with so many denominational divisions at this time, was slaveholding. The General Conference of 1836 had condemned abolitionism, and in the annual and district conferences every effort was made to eliminate discussion of the slavery issue, but it was brought to a head at the General Conference of 1844. There it was voted that Bishop James O. Andrew, who had by marriage become an owner of several slaves, should not exercise his episcopal prerogatives until such time as he had ceased to be a slaveholder. This action brought into the open the whole disputed issue of the respective authorities of the General Conference and the episcopal office. For the

124

most part the southern conferences felt the action taken against Bishop Andrew was extrajudicial. The northern conferences, on the other hand, felt that a failure to carry such action through was a surrender of Methodist discipline. The views were irreconcilable. Efforts for compromise and pacification failed. The Board of Bishops recommended that action on the case of Bishop Andrew be postponed until the next General Conference. The recommendation was tabled by a vote of 95 to 84. In the closing hours of the conference a Plan of Separation was adopted which provided ways and means for a division of property and for the peaceful withdrawal of such churches as chose to do so. On May 1, 1845, the southern conferences were represented in a convention held at Louisville, Kentucky. There, using the Plan of Separation as a guide, they established the Methodist Episcopal Church, South. The Methodist Episcopal Church repudiated the Plan of Separation at the General Conference of 1848, and extended litigation ensued. At no time was perfect love the point at issue.

Nor can it be said that the doctrine of Christian perfection was the disruptive factor which led to the organization of the Wesleyan Methodist Church in 1843-44. That organization was primarily a reaction against the Methodist Episcopal Church at the following points:

(1) The Methodist Episcopal Church having no rule forbidding slaveholding by private members; and by declaring that slaveholding is in harmony with the Golden Rule, and by allowing Annual Conferences to say that it is not a moral wrong, makes itself responsible for slavery; (2) the government of the church is aristocratic; and (3) its attitude toward dissenting brethren is uncharitable.[46]

The moving spirit in this schism was the Rev. Orange Scott, self-educated, energetic, courageous, and impatient. Scott was Vermont born, a member of the New England Conference, and a "thorough going abolitionist." In 1835 he had written to the Rev. J. A. Merrill:

Dear Brother Merrill:

I forgot to say to you that we have a meeting of *true abolitionists* at

125

the meeting house at Lynn Wood End Monday evening at ½ past 7 o'clock. . . . We want to agree among ourselves on the best, and most *prudent measures* to pursue in conference on the subject of Slavery. Invite any of your district whom you know to be *thorough going abolitionists*—say nothing to others—*Let us beware of "spies"*— . . . *Be firm my brother.* Everything depends now on *firmness.* . . . If we are firm and independent at this *particular crisis* much good will result. . . . I know the state of feeling so well through the conference, that I have no doubt but three forths [*sic*] of the conference will be with us. . . .

Yours

O. Scott [47]

But Scott misjudged the strength of his support. The General Conferences of 1836 and 1840, determined to maintain peace between northern and southern sectors, invoked increasingly severe measures against agitators. Finally, in 1843 a call was issued by Scott and others for a convention to meet that year in Utica, New York,

to form a Wesleyan Methodist Church . . . free from episcopacy and slavery, and embracing a system of itinerancy under proper limitations and restrictions, with such disciplinary regulations as are necessary to preserve and promote experimental and practical godliness.[48]

Clearly, perfection was not a recognized point of disagreement.

A *Discipline* which was published that same year does not, in fact, contain any reference to sanctification in its Articles of Religion. This early omission is explained by the fact that "this doctrine was so fully taught in the other part of the doctrinal standards, Wesley's Sermons and his notes, that no one thought it necessary to make any more specific statement of this doctrine." [49] Whatever the reason, Christian perfection, though not given immediate and specific affirmation, was a basic tenet with the great majority of those who were responsible for the organization of the new church. At the 1843 convention in Utica, New York, the Pastoral Address closed with these words:

126

But above all, brethren, we exhort you to make *holiness* your motto. It is holiness of heart and life that will arm you against every assault.[50]

And when the first General Conference was held in 1844, an article on sanctification was prepared for submission to the yearly conferences. As presented, the article read:

Sanctification is the renewal of our fallen nature by the Holy Spirit, whereby we are delivered from the pollution, inbeing, and reigning power of sin, and are enabled to love God with all our hearts and walk in his holy commandments blameless through the grace of our Lord Jesus Christ.[51]

After being submitted to the annual conferences during the quadrennium 1844-48, it was ordered inserted in the *Discipline*. But it appeared in that *Discipline* in a statement more specifically perfectionist than the one originally submitted:

Sanctification is that renewal of our fallen nature by the Holy Ghost, received through faith in Jesus Christ, whose blood of atonement cleanseth from all sin; whereby we are not only delivered from the guilt of sin, but are washed from its pollution, saved from its power, and are enabled, through grace, to love God with all our hearts, and to walk in His holy commandments blameless.

Later the doctrinal formula was again changed to include these words: "It is a distinct, instantaneous, and subsequent work to regeneration, and is wrought when the believer presents himself a living sacrifice, holy, acceptable unto God." The Wesleyan Methodist Church was thus early identified as a holiness church, and its subsequent history increasingly confirms that identification.

In the Methodist Episcopal Church this separation was primarily considered as an unfortunate abolitionist answer to the mounting tension between North and South. It had the effect of increasing antislavery sentiment in the northern conferences since many came to feel that the measures protested against were, in fact, ill-conceived.

Nine years later a more specifically perfectionist schism began. The year 1857 was a memorable one on several counts. A depression gripped the nation. The "Prayer Meeting Revival" was getting under way—a religious phenomenon, carried on principally by businessmen, which was to sweep from coast to coast within the next two years. And in the Genesee Conference of the Methodist Episcopal Church factional differences were approaching a climax. In this conference there were two groups, which could be designated as the "conservatives" and the "liberals." They chose to refer to each other as the "Nazarites" and the "Buffalo Regency"—or "Preachers-come-back-to-the-Discipline Society" and "New School Methodism." The issues were both practical and doctrinal.

In the first category such matters as secret societies, amusements, dress, and abolition were matters of contention. In the second the doctrine and preaching of second-blessing holiness was the disputed point. The liberals were allegedly opposed both to the doctrine and to the camp-meeting methods by which it was promoted. The incident which provoked decisive action was the publication of an article entitled "New School Methodism" by B. T. Roberts, one of the leaders of the conservative group. In that article Roberts deplored what he felt was a departure from the standards of original Methodism. He denounced the general worldliness which, it appeared, was becoming a characteristic of the church. He decried the failure to enforce discipline and the reluctance to urge revivals. He especially attacked the growing tendency of Methodist ministers to affiliate with secret orders and the influence which he considered such orders to wield in church appointments. At the annual conference of the following year Roberts was reproved for the tone and character of his article. When that article was republished, though he denied all responsibility for its second appearance in print, Roberts was expelled from the conference as guilty of "unchristian and immoral conduct." He appealed to the General Conference of 1860. The committee which considered his case voted 19 to 19 on the question of affirming the condemnation and 18 to 20 on the question of reversing the decision of the annual conference. The decision of that conference thus stood; Roberts was out. Other ministers of similar points of view and practice withdrew or were in some instances expelled.

Consequently in 1860 a call was sent out which read:

A convention will be held in Pekin (New York) for the purpose of adopting a Discipline for the Free Methodist Church, to commence August 23. All societies and bands that find it necessary, in order to promote the prosperity and permanency of the work of holiness, to organize a Free Church on the following basis are invited to send delegates:

1. Doctrines and usages of primitive Methodism, such as the witness of the Spirit, entire sanctification as a state of grace distinct from justification, attainable instantaneously by faith; free seats and congregational singing, without instrumental music in all cases; plainness of dress.

2. An equal representation of ministers and laymen in all the councils of the church.

3. No slave-holding, and no connection with oath-bound societies.[52]

Thus a group of about eighty laymen and fifteen ministers voted to organize a new church to be called the Free Methodist Church. This church would stress in particular the entire-sanctification phase of Christian perfection. As that doctrinal statement was incorporated in their early *Disciplines,* it read:

Merely justified persons, while they do not outwardly commit sin, are nevertheless conscious of sin still remaining in the heart. They feel a natural tendency to evil, a proneness to depart from God, and cleave to the things of earth. Those that are sanctified wholly are saved from all inbred sin—from evil thoughts and evil tempers. No wrong temper, none contrary to love remains in the soul. All the thoughts, words and actions are governed by pure love.

Entire sanctification takes place subsequently to justification and is the work of God wrought instantaneously upon the consecrated believing soul. After a soul is cleansed from all sin, it is then fully prepared to grow in grace.

Such a statement was said to be "exactly according to the teachings of John Wesley" [53]—but it was an emaciated and partial Wesley, lacking his careful qualifications and devoid of the insights of his "catholic spirit." Moreover, this and similar remarks about "merely justified persons" (although the "merely" was later dropped) appeared to confirm the contention that, when sanctification was stressed, justification was disparaged.

Thus mid-nineteenth-century American Methodism was marked by two schisms in which the doctrine of Christian perfection played a significant part. And two American churches of some consequence and continuing history emerged.

The history of these two churches illustrates the growing tendency of the holiness emphasis of this period to identify sanctification with an individualistic puritanism. As time passed, the proof of orthodoxy tended to become strict adherence to a set of stringent and sacrosanct regulations. Thus the Wesleyan Methodist Church, organized in the earliest flush of the revival of the 1840's, reflects in its history, a system relatively liberal at the outset but which grew increasingly insistent upon the observance of rules as it became a more distinctively holiness church. The Free Methodist Church, on the other hand, coming out of a later phase and self-consciously identified as a holiness church, began with a fully enunciated set of stringent regulations.

Meanwhile in the Methodist Episcopal Church the sweep of the holiness revival continued. Its progress was especially notable in the West. In Illinois by 1860 regular weekly prayer meetings emphasizing holiness were being established. President Dempster of Garrett Biblical Institute had contributed an article to the press the purpose of which was "to explain the nature, show the attainability, and hint at the importance of Christian Perfection." From Kansas a correspondent to the *Beauty of Holiness* reported: "The President of Baker University, located at this place, is a man 'full of faith and the Holy Ghost,' and preaches a full and present salvation." Bishops Hamline and Simpson gave the movement their active support.

Reaction to the continuing holiness revival was mixed. In some sectors it was ignored; in others it was "viewed with alarm." The secession of the Free Methodists gave a schismatic stigma to the whole revival. Thus in 1860 the bishops had this to say to the General Conference of the Methodist Episcopal Church:

The Methodist Episcopal Church has always been remarkably harmonious in doctrinal views. By the divine favor, this doctrinal unity still prevails among us. For several years, however, there have been a few persons in the Church whose presentation of the doctrine of Christian perfection has been supposed to vary somewhat, in the terms and forms of expression used, from those employed by our standard authors.

These individuals claim to be strictly Wesleyan in their views of the doctrine, and probably are so substantially. Nor do we impugn their motives. But, in our judgment, in denouncing those in the ministry and laity who do not sympathize with them and adopt their measures, and in some instances, by employing and encouraging erratic and irresponsible persons to conduct religious services, they have erred, and unhappily agitated some of our societies, and in a few instances caused secessions. It is our opinion that there was no occasion for these specialties.

But the prayer meetings and associations continued to multiply.

In the southern church the doctrine of Christian perfection had not received the same attention as in the North. The principal reason for this neglect was the preoccupation of the new church with the practical issues which had arisen from separation. Doctrinally, however, the church accepted the views of Wesley and Fletcher without question. At the first General Conference the Pastoral Address reminded that body that its "true original vocation" was to "spread Scriptural holiness" over "every land in which we may be found." The Course of Study carried an item on "Sanctification, in the sense of Christian Perfection: what it is, and how to be attained." And the *Discipline* included everything relevant to the subject to be found in its northern counterpart. The evidence is scant, however, that in these early years there was any considerable preoccupation with or intensive presentation of the

131

doctrine of Christian perfection. *The Quarterly Review* carried nothing on the subject from 1847 when it began publication until 1861 when for a time publication was suspended.

The publishing house of the Methodist Episcopal Church, South, did issue in 1857 William Arthur's remarkably successful *Tongue of Fire*. This was an American imprint of a work which shortly before had been published in England. It is a well-written study of the work of the Holy Spirit. In it Arthur pungently describes the dearth of vital religion in the typical institutional church and ministry. He speaks with the incisive candor of a prophet, yet there is much more of Hosea than of Amos in his message. He asks for all that the most pronounced holiness advocate demands, and his views on the possibilities of divine grace are exaltedly Wesleyan. Yet he avoids the controversial, and often threadbare, terminology of traditional theology. He makes no plea for some unvarying method. He is apparently ready to trust that the honestly seeking heart and the always searching Spirit will in ways best devised by themselves find each other. In such fashion he escapes both compromise and controversy. His was a pattern of holiness preaching too seldom followed.

Aside from this publication little else is apparent during these pre-war years to indicate a lively interest in the doctrine of Christian perfection.

During the period of the Civil War the preaching of Christian perfection was considerably diminished. Between the two branches of Methodism "patriotism in both North and South too often became the only consideration, and as a result Christian forgiveness and the Golden Rule gave way to bitter vindictiveness." [54] This was not the milieu for the development of Christian perfection. There were, it is true, reports of religious interest in both the Union and Confederate Armies that approached at times the status of revival. But perfection, as might be expected, was not the dominant note. In fact, said a report, there was a general decline of interest in holiness and in religion generally.

CHAPTER V

The Doctrine Modified
1865-1900

THE RELIGIOUS INERTIA and moral depression which followed the Civil War were of concern to leaders in all segments of American church life. They were a special challenge to those in the Methodist Episcopal Church who considered that the mission of that body was to "spread scriptural holiness over these lands." To effect that end against the general irreligion called for a response beyond and above the ordinary. They were, however, encouraged to believe that such a response was possible, for their ranks had been greatly increased.

In 1866, since abolitionism was no longer an issue and the church had at last taken a clear antislavery stand, a large number who had previously withdrawn and joined the Wesleyan Methodist Connection decided to return. Around 125 ministers, including a number of the original founders of the Wesleyan Connection, returned to the Methodist Episcopal Church. With them came large numbers of the laity. As a result the ranks of outspoken holiness advocates in the church were considerably augmented.

At the same time it was felt by many that the church itself was in a slough of spiritual despond. Discipline, it was asserted, was sorely neglected, the class meetings were going or gone, there was too much conformity to secular practices and goals, and re-

133

vivals were in disfavor.[1] In 1866 it was said of Christian perfection, "This doctrine is the great want of the world today . . . not needed simply as a doctrine believed and preached, but *inwardly experienced.*"[2] A few months later the New York *Christian Advocate* reported that Randolph S. Foster—soon to become professor of systematic theology at Drew—

felt that a crisis is upon us. He thought that the secret of our loss of power as Methodists lies in the fact that many Church members in an unconverted or backslidden state are retained among us.

Moved by such considerations, a group of Methodist preachers met weekly in New York City to consider ways and means of responding to this crisis. Among the proposals offered was one by John A. Wood. He suggested that the ideal medium for the restoration of vital spiritual life would be a camp meeting organized, advertised, and administered specifically for the promotion of holiness.

The camp-meeting idea was certainly not new to Methodism. Asbury had given it unqualified praise. But with changing social conditions it was tending toward desuetude. Wood's suggestion, however, appeared to be the "sun-burst of a new revelation" to John S. Inskip, English-born evangelist who was already coming into leadership among holiness advocates. The idea was given encouragement. Consequently in June of 1867 a meeting was held in Philadelphia, and "arrangements were made for holding the first camp meeting *ever held* for the specific and special purpose of promoting the work of entire sanctification."

One month later the National Association for the Promotion of Holiness was formally organized at Vineland, New Jersey. The efforts of the first two years were primarily directed toward the promotion of the New Jersey camp meeting. But at the close of the second year a permanent organization was established with John S. Inskip as its first president. It was interdenominational in character though its greatest support came, naturally, from Methodists. The association had as its sponsors such men as Bishop Hamline, James Caughey, John A. Wood, and Alfred Cookman.

The national association emphatically denied any schismatic intention. The call for its first camp meeting was issued by the presiding elder of the New Jersey Conference.

Before long it was national in scope as well as in name. The Palmers were its representatives in meetings in Michigan, Illinois, Ohio, Missouri, and Kansas. Numerous auxiliary associations were organized, working usually in close harmony with their national counterpart. By 1871 mass meetings were being held throughout the West in such centers as Salt Lake City, Sacramento, Santa Clara, and San Francisco. As a result it was reported that year that "near a thousand souls were sanctified including the leading members of the churches."

Its grand objective, if not its program and methods, seemed exactly what was being asked for in episcopal pronouncement. In 1870, for instance, the bishops of the Methodist Episcopal Church, South, addressed the General Conference of the body as follows:

We fear that the doctrine of perfect love . . . as taught in the Bible, and explained and enforced in our standards, as a distinct and practicable attainment, is too much overlooked and neglected. This was a prominent theme in the discourses of our fathers; and . . . they urged religious people to "go on to this perfection" of sanctifying love. . . . If we would be like them in power and usefulness, we must resemble them in holy consecration. Nothing is so much needed at the present time, throughout all these lands, as a general and powerful revival of scriptural holiness.

And as though in response, there followed reports of revivals marked by the "conversion of sinners and . . . the sanctification of believers." [3]

In the Methodist Episcopal Church also the doctrine of Christian perfection was receiving active advocacy. Wrote L. R. Dunn of the Newark Conference in 1873:

Never before was this privilege so clearly and extensively proclaimed. Never were there so many living witnesses of its experience. Never were there so many of our ministers and people really "groaning after perfect love." [4]

Nevertheless, when the General Conference of the Methodist Episcopal Church, South, convened in 1878, the bishops again said:

We cannot omit from this [admonitory] category the insufficient stress, in our day, laid upon the doctrine of "entire sanctification." . . . The infrequency of its proclamation from the pulpit and the irregularity of its experimental power in the Church have proved a serious detriment to the robustness of our piety, and to the specialty of our mission, "to spread scriptural holiness over these lands." Let us more than ever reassert this great doctrine.

The admonitions were evidently heeded. A few months later the Nashville *Christian Advocate* was reporting that the entire church was being pervaded by an interest in holiness: "Venerable and holy men are calling attention to it. Multitudes of awakened believers are seeking it." In this southern area the revival was stimulated by but not yet a part of the organized holiness movement.

In the North and West the movement continued to expand. By 1878 holiness camp meetings were regularly held in Missouri, and a weekly newspaper for the specific promotion of the doctrine was started. A year later the Southwestern Holiness Association was organized in Kansas. In 1880 the Western Union Holiness Convention came into being at Jacksonville, Illinois. Delegates to this convention were principally members of the Methodist Episcopal Church. The Free Methodists were the next largest group; and listed in the order of their numerical strength, there were also members whose denominational affiliations were Baptist, Missionary Baptist, Free Will Baptist, Evangelical, Presbyterian, Christian, Congregational, Methodist Protestant, Swedish Methodist, Wesleyan Connection, Methodist Episcopal Church, South, Church of God, and the Salvation Army. Seven states were represented.

By this time the magnitude of literature published on this theme was said to be enough to "astonish even the friends of holiness." Tracts, journals, and songbooks poured from the presses. Much of this literature was criticized for its limited range—"nearly everything except doctrine, experience and news from the forces in the field being excluded." Nevertheless, or perhaps therefore, the movement steadily grew in size and influence.

The First General Holiness Assembly convened in Park Avenue Methodist Episcopal Church in Chicago in May of 1885. With this meeting the organizational framework was completed—from the local association to the national general assembly. The formation of a new church would have been relatively easy. But strong sentiment against such a move prevailed.

The assembly was predominantly Methodist, though delegates connected with at least ten different denominations were present. Amid such diversity the need for a statement of "things commonly believed" seemed advisable. Therefore a Declaration of Principles was adopted which included the following Doctrinal Statement:

1. The State of Justification . . . including these particulars:
   (1) The pardon of sin, so full and free that all the transgressions of the past life are blotted from the Book of Divine remembrance, and by this act of Divine mercy, the individual is accounted righteous before God, notwithstanding his actual past unrighteousness. (2) The new birth, or moral regeneration, quickening him into spiritual life, and renewing him in the spirit of his mind. (3) Adoption into the Divine family and consequent heirship, witnessed distinctly to the personal consciousness by the Holy Ghost. This great act of justification is received alone upon the ground of the infinite merit of Christ's atoning sacrifice, in the exercise of faith in that atonement, preceded by true repentance, which consists of deep sorrow for the sins committed, restitution, and a full renunciation of sinful habits and associations.
2. Entire sanctification . . . that great work wrought subsequent to regeneration, by the Holy Ghost, upon the sole condition of faith, such faith being preceded by an act of solemn and complete consecration;—including three particulars:
   (1) The entire extinction of the carnal mind, the total eradication of the birth principle of sin. (2) The communication of perfect love to the soul. . . . (3) The abiding indwelling of the Holy Ghost. . . .
   There is such a close connection between the gifts of justifica-

137

tiᴗn and entire sanctification, and such a readiness on the part of our Heavenly Father to bestow the second as well as the first, that young converts should be encouraged to go up at once to the Canaan of perfect love.

3. Testimony. It is the duty of all who are made partakers of entire sanctification . . . to testify thereof to the praise of the Giver. Such testimony should be very definite, as much as possible in the use of Bible terms, and in . . . a spirit of humility. . . . If such testimony be withheld the light of the soul will soon become darkness.

4. Holy Character. The portraiture of . . . The Sermon on the Mount, and the thirteenth Chapter of first Corinthians. . . .

5. The attractive Graces. The quieter graces of the Spirit. . . .

6. Growth in Grace . . . should be rapid, constant, and palpable.[5]

On these points there was unanimity. Justification and entire sanctification were two "gifts." Sanctification as a "gradual work before" does not appear to have been considered. Young converts are to "go up at once to the Canaan of perfect love." It is experience minus process.

The revival continued. By 1887 the national association could report that it had held "sixty-seven national camp meetings and eleven Tabernacle meetings . . . distributed through sixteen states of the Union, extending to both shores of the Continent, and to the far-off East." Its representatives had carried its message and methods to Canada, England, Germany, India, and Australia. In the United States holiness associations were active in the South and Southwest. By 1888 the list of holiness associations included twenty-six of state or local character, two in Canada, three national in scope, and one claiming to be international. There was a Young People's Methodist Alliance which had Christian perfection as its stated emphasis. Each week there were 201 "stated meetings for the promotion of holiness" scheduled and advertised. The names and addresses of 206 holiness evangelists were listed. Four years later the list of evangelists had grown to 304 and the "stated meetings" to 354. The movement was strongly organized, implemented, and publicized.

Publishing interests were, in fact, a major concern. In 1888 it was reported that not less than four publishing houses were engaged in the exclusive publication of holiness materials. Twenty-seven holiness journals were being periodically issued, most of them on a monthly basis. By 1892 there were forty-one such periodicals. Holiness literature was abundant in scope if limited in content.

Adverse reaction to a program of this sort was inevitable. As early as 1878 D. D. Whedon, editor of *Methodist Quarterly Review,* had spoken out vigorously against both the theology and the program of the movement. He flatly declared:

The holiness association, the holiness periodical, the holiness prayer-meeting, the holiness preacher, are all modern novelties. They are not Wesleyan. We believe that a living Wesley would never admit them into the Methodist system.

A few years later W. D. Kirkland, editor of the *Southern Christian Advocate,* in an article which was both criticism of the holiness associations and challenge to the church said similarly:

No self-constituted and irresponsible "association," with its many objectionable features, must be allowed to stand forth before the world as the only, or even as the chief, exponent of holiness. . . . The remedy then is in the Church herself. She must vindicate the claim that her highest aim is to spread Scriptural holiness over the land.[6]

But there were also defenders of the movement. In the South, Leonidas Rosser, a presiding elder and editor of the *Southern Methodist Review,* warned that there were two extremes which the church must avoid—"liberty without law, and law without liberty." In the mounting criticism of the holiness associations he felt that the latter extreme was being approached. He further stated:

We have no law prohibiting voluntary associations for the promotion of holiness, provided such associations are not in conflict with our prescribed order, nor in conflict with our doctrines. . . . Methodism, itself a great holiness association, was organized in the Church of England. . . . Let all opposers of these associations . . . show their errors, excesses, and evils, or withdraw their opposition; for in opposing them they oppose Methodism.

And Bishop Foster somewhat earlier had said of these associations, "They have been driven to separate and class effort from the indifference and coldness of their brethren and in many instances of the pastors." His analysis had been corroborated by Daniel Curry, editor of the *Methodist Quarterly Review,* who presented an extensive study of the movement, especially in the Northeast, and concluded that it had been both needed and beneficial.

Charges and countercharges were hurled, especially at the point where schism was threatened or actually in process. The holiness associations were charged with being the seedbed and sponsors of what was coming to be called "come-outism." T. J. Wheat, a presiding elder in one of the western conferences of the Methodist Episcopal Church, characterized the holiness associations in Illinois, Iowa, Missouri, Nebraska, Kansas, and California as follows:

The leaders in the holiness movement are all, or nearly so, zealous advocates of come-outism. For the last ten years in some of these States the Holiness Associations have been a standing menace to the spirit of the Gospel of Jesus Christ. As associations they have been, and are to-day, religious anarchists.

Undoubtedly there were those within the associations and on its fringes who by overt act or inferential statement justified these charges. But the associations as such strove earnestly to discourage such a temper and to disengage themselves from those who persisted in it. At one of the earliest meetings of a major association a paper was presented on *Current Errors Among Teachers of Holiness.* The first two errors listed were: (1) "the silly dogma of no-churchism" and (2) advocacy of the "organization of a distinctively Holiness Church." Apparently neither the Free

Methodist Church nor the Wesleyan Methodist Church were regarded at this time as distinctly holiness churches.

Tendencies to "come-outism" were recognized as active in the holiness movement but were opposed and denounced as errors. The North West Texas Holiness Association stated, in fact, that it had been organized "for the special purpose of reviving scriptural holiness in the Methodist Episcopal Church, South, and to protect our people from the inroads of fanatical 'come-outers' and others of that sect." The Iowa Holiness Association went on record in similar fashion, writing its opposition to "come-outism" into its constitution. The most influential holiness publications echoed this sentiment. "We revere our chief ministers—we have a profound respect for church authority," said the *Guide to Holiness*. "Loyalty to church relations," said the editor of the *Holiness Year Book,* "should characterize all the friends of holiness." Perhaps the most revealing statement of attitude appears in the Declaration of Principles adopted by the General Holiness Assembly of 1885. On "Church Fellowship" that body declared:

The Church is the body of Christ . . . . The privilege of membership therein is very precious and to be highly esteemed. Every saved individual should be connected with the organic Church. . . . Professors of holiness should not voluntarily surrender their Church privileges for trivial causes. But, if an oppressive hand be laid upon them in any case by Church authority, *solely* for professing holiness, or for being identified with the cause of Holiness, depriving them of the privileges of Christian communion, they should then adjust themselves to circumstances, as may be required in order to have the continued enjoyment of the ordinances of our holy religion.

In that declaration the holiness associations presented their countercharge. The principal issue, they said, is "crush-outism" of which "come-outism" is but the result. This was not a new charge. The Free Methodists had earlier felt that they had been "forced out of the ranks of the regular ministry in their churches." In 1859 the *Guide to Holiness* had charged that the action in the Genesee Conference (the expulsion of B. T. Roberts and others)

141

was but an example of what was going on in the entire church. And in 1869 Phoebe Palmer had written to Mrs. L. L. Hamline that

a Presiding Elder . . . had actually taken pains to crush out all definite testimony on the subject of holiness, as far as his influence extended, and [said] to the ministers on the district that it must be crushed out, as he regarded it as synonymous with free Methodism.

Finally a subscriber to the New York *Christian Advocate* asked a somewhat rhetorical question of the editor:

A minister of the Methodist Episcopal Church was so enraged against holiness that he sent for a policeman to take out of his church a member who would testify that the blood of Jesus Christ cleanses from all sin. . . . Deserves such a minister a place in any church?

Thus when a holiness-association report speaks of "those who seem to be driven out of the Methodist Episcopal Church by its opposition to the definite work of holiness," there are grounds for the statement.

It may be assumed that such extreme measures were unusual. The very fact of their publicity seems to support this conclusion. But the attitude suggested may have been fairly general. The following account seems to indicate that it was. The aging L. R. Dunn, builder of almost seventy churches, describes the situation as he sees it in an "address to the Bishops" of the Methodist Episcopal Church. He speaks of his long-proved loyalty to the church. He states that he has enjoyed the personal friendship of "Hedding, Morris, Janes, Simpson, Ames, Foster, Newman, Bowman, Foss, Warren, Goodsell, Harris, and others, and most of your number have been welcomed at my humble board." He then points out that the bishops "can not fail to have observed" that the man who becomes known as an advocate of holiness finds himself discriminated against, if not set aside. He attributes this to the "worldliness" which he feels is "well-nigh regnant in the Church." Reflecting a similar outlook, the *Guide to Holiness* exhorts its readers to "stand the test" during these "storms of slander and ridicule."

Spokesmen for the associations maintained that false positions were assigned to them and that they were then attacked on the basis of those improper charges. And, wrote H. R. Withers in the southern *Quarterly Review,* "if we defend, we are 'mad, show temper, very unsanctified.' If we submit in silence we are 'whipped, can't answer, overcome.'" Concerning the holiness advocates, he further maintained:

> Methodists of this theory . . . are today the most loyal of all Methodists. Their harmless but useful holiness associations, that have no machinery except to provide times and places to hold revival meetings, are clothed by the heated imagination of a godless prejudice with the most formidable harness of reckless knighthood, intent on revolution and treason. Truly they are in peril among false brethren.

It appeared exceedingly difficult for either side to detect virtue in the objectives of the other.

The Methodist Church was coming into a period when diverging estimates of the nature of the Christian faith were giving rise to separate camps whose theological positions would be mutually incomprehensible. This was, for instance, an era of remarkable growth for Methodist educational institutions. There was needed, and at once, a corps of adequately trained professors. Increasingly, Methodism's more promising students took their graduate training in the universities of Germany, returning to occupy seats of philosophy and theology in Methodist schools and seminaries. And with them came the views of Hegel and Schleiermacher, Feuerbach and Comte, Lotze and Ritschl, first to question and then openly to attack a startled traditionalism. It is true that some, such as Ritschl and Schleiermacher, had doctrines of perfection clearly enunciated in their theological systems. They were, however, of no support to the traditional Wesleyan formulation. In the first place, their perfectionism was generally ignored by those who otherwise acclaimed their doctrinal offerings. Secondly, their views at this point were set in a framework generally antagonistic to the orthodoxy of that period. They appeared as aliens, if not indeed as enemies. Darwinism and the new claims of a confident science rudely disturbed a once-complacent faith. Philosophy, which had been for so long the docile handmaid of theology, now seemed about to destroy or unseat her.

Quite naturally traditional theology sought to protect itself from this invasion. Sometimes, uncertain of its bearings, it took refuge in obscurantism and appalling dogmatism. And when it did, it inevitably drove from it those who recognized in these competing ideologies values ignored or denounced by the defenders of tradition. To them the new liberalism offered a haven. It was a haven in which humanism, however, came to be considerably more at home than theocentric piety.

The social reformers, moreover, dismayed at the indifference to human misery on the part of the average churchman and discouraged at the paltry results of the social program of orthodox Christianity, turned elsewhere for the dynamic of their gospel. They found it in the positivism of Auguste Comte and in the neo-rationalist "sociology" of such men as Henry George and Lester Frank Ward.

From pulpits in Columbus, Ohio, and Burlington, Iowa, Washington Gladden and George D. Herron delivered some of the earliest manifestos of the social gospel. In Topeka, Kansas, Charles M. Sheldon was writing *In His Steps*, destined to be one of the all-time best sellers. The burden of these messages was that society could be redeemed only through individual sacrifice. To many the specific proposals of these men seemed little short of socialistic. They did have a passion and a social concern which would not be denied expression.

In a Methodism conditioned from its earliest days to an awareness of social need, such an approach found sympathetic consideration. It called for sacrifice, and it accomplished results. Alongside the dynamic message of the new social gospel Methodism's "doctrines of experience" appeared to an impatient many as a theological façade for egotistic reaction. The message of the holiness advocates sounded strangely, and irritatingly, irrelevant.

144

This was the increasingly wide theoretical background of opposition to the promotion of the doctrine of Christian perfection.

Objections arose to certain practical issues also. There was, for example, the insistence by holiness advocates that testimony to entire sanctification was a duty. This soon led to the teaching that one was derelict if he failed to testify whenever occasion afforded, regardless of how that testimony might be received. Wesley, it is true, did teach that it was a violation of conscience for one who had received perfect love to be always silent concerning it.[7] He did not, however, teach that such a one was violating conscience unless he was always professing it. Moreover, he discouraged stereotyped phraseology. He encouraged such profession as could be made "with the deepest humility and self-abasement before God" to such as would hear it profitably. Faced frequently now, however, by a certain antagonistic skepticism, these testimonies were apt to be more belligerent than winsome. There were inevitably those within the movement who relied more upon dogmatic assertion than upon transparent sanctity to substantiate their high claims. Bishop J. T. Peck, a most active holiness protagonist, mildly observes: "When . . . a man did not live well . . . loud professions . . . do great harm."

There was also the tendency to clannishness—to be warmly alive to those within and antagonistic to or oblivious of those without the fellowship. Bishop R. S. Foster, another holiness advocate, warned against this tendency to separateness and "class-religion." But the issue which most aggravated ecclesiastical dispositions was the unregulated activity of holiness evangelists, many of whom were not ordained and stood in no regular relationship to the church.

The evangelist problem was of long standing and had been steadily growing more acute. In 1879 the Illinois Annual Conference attempted to meet the issue by passing resolutions which urged: (1) that its ministers preach *all* the doctrines "including that of perfect love—plainly, clearly, and in the spirit of Christ"— and (2) that its people "be true to their covenant vows" and allow no services, and invite no evangelists without the consent and supervision of the pastor. The resolution was plainly directed toward the regulation or prohibition of holiness evangelists. But the action by the Lay Electoral Conference at that same session included the statement that the "spread of Scriptural holiness . . . is now, as formerly, of importance paramount to all other considerations." And the next year in that same city the Western Union Holiness Convention was organized. The Missouri Annual Conference of 1880 reported that leading the list of its problems were: "self-constituted specialists, who, in some instances, are members of our own Church and yet pay little or no regard to our rules of discipline." Other conferences faced a similar situation. In 1886 and 1890, consequently, the General Conference of the Methodist Episcopal Church, South, was memorialized to make provision for the appointment and regulation of evangelists. The memorials were not favorably acted upon. The General Conference of 1894 commented on this situation:

We are confronted with a new condition. Evangelists are numbered by scores and hundreds, and multiply fast. They belong to various denominations; some of them are ordained, others unordained, and even unlicensed to preach or exhort; all act without appointment or supervision in this special work.

Whereupon the action of the previous conferences was concurred in. There was to be no "office of evangelist." But the problem was recognized, and the bishops recommended that the *Discipline* be changed to guard against "such interference, whether by local or itinerant preachers." Consequently, in addition to and given priority over all other duties previously listed, the *Discipline* of 1894 specified that the first duty of the preacher in charge was "to preach the Gospel and, in the absence of the Presiding Elder or Bishop, to control the appointment of all services to be held in the Churches in his charge."

With these repairs to the disciplinary fences the local pastor was given authority and responsibility to see that all unauthorized preachers were kept out of his church and later out of the bounds of his charge. In some areas it was made crystal-clear that the activities of the holiness associations were now considered extralegal and were therefore no longer to be condoned. The crisis of decision was inescapable, and for many that decision, which had heretofore been *both/and,* had now become *either/or.* The rise of numerous holiness sects within the next few years was the inevitable result.

These were climactic years. The church protested vigorously that it was promoting entire sanctification as much, and in the same sense, as were the associations, "It has not abandoned the truth of entire sanctification taught by its founder," said the 1890 General Conference of the Methodist Episcopal Church, South, "nor turned away from his expressed aim to 'spread scriptural holiness through these lands.'" E. T. Clark, commenting on this period, refers to such declarations as "verbal gestures to the doctrine of entire sanctification but showing no sign of returning to it as a vital experience." [8] The associations were unimpressed. They noted instead what they considered to be a rising tide of formalism and modernism. Thus in 1893 the editor of one of their widely circulated publications states what he feels to be the sentiment of the associations:

The question is being definitely presented: Shall God's great ideal of a New Testament Church be realized, viz.: a spiritual and holy church; or shall it be inundated with formality and worldliness? This is the great question and must be squarely settled. To this end a living ministry and membership are set to work out the New Testament design, a holy church, "without spot or blemish, or any such thing." Their faces are set like a flint, and they will not yield an inch of ground, nor compromise in any degree.[9]

The gauntlet was thrown down.

The answer came a year later in the bishops' address to the General Conference. It had a fairly long preamble:

The privilege of believers to attain unto the state of entire sanctification or perfect love, and to abide therein, is a well-known teaching of Methodism. Witnesses to this experience have never been wanting in our Church, though few in comparison with the whole membership.

147

Among them have been men and women of beautiful consistency and seraphic ardor, jewels of the Church. Let the doctrine still be proclaimed, and the experience still be testified.

And now the gauntlet is picked up:

> But there has sprung up among us a party with holiness as a watchword; they have holiness associations, holiness meetings, holiness preachers, holiness evangelists, and holiness property. Religious experience is represented as if it consists of only two steps, the first step out of condemnation into peace, and the next step into Christian perfection. . . . We do not question the sincerity and zeal of these brethren; we desire the Church to profit by their earnest preaching and godly example; but we deplore their teaching and methods in so far as they claim a monopoly of the experience, practice, and advocacy of holiness, and separate themselves from the body of ministers and disciples.

The truce had expired.

Within the next six years not less than ten separate religious bodies were organized with entire sanctification as their cardinal doctrine. All ten of these were dominantly Methodist in former church affiliation. All of them came out of the Holiness Movement. Most of their members were recruited from advocates of that movement who no longer felt at home in their own communion. These bodies were:

1. The New Testament Church of Christ, which was organized at Milan, Tennessee, in 1894 and which "soon spread throughout western Texas and Arkansas."

2. The Burning Bush movement, which in 1894 grew out of a protracted revival in the Metropolitan Methodist Church of Chicago. It subsequently "spread through several states" and took the name the Metropolitan Church Association.

3. The First Church of the Nazarene, organized at Los Angeles, California, in October, 1895. Its founder, Phineas F. Bresee, had been a presiding elder in the Methodist Episcopal Church and was later to become the first general superintendent of the Church of the Nazarene.

4. The Association of Pentecostal Churches of America, a union in December, 1895, of several Holiness churches in and around New York City.
5. The Apostolic Holiness Union, organized at Cincinnati, Ohio, in 1897 by a Methodist minister to work as an interdenominational agency in the promotion of holiness in the major denominations.
6. The Missionary Church Association, organized at Berne, Indiana, in 1898 on an emphatically definite platform of regeneration, sanctification, healing, and premillennialism.
7. The group of Holiness churches organized in Texas in 1898 by holiness evangelists from California.
8. The Pentecostal Alliance (later Pentecostal Mission), organized as a missionary holiness association in 1898 at Nashville, Tennessee.
9. The Pentecost Bands of the World (later the Missionary Bands of the World, Inc.), organized in 1898 in Indianapolis principally as an arm of the Free Methodist Church but soon an autonomous group with a major emphasis on missions.
10. The Independent Holiness Church, organized in 1900 at Van Alstyne, Texas, and soon expanding to include "twenty church organizations."

Some of these groups, the Burning Bush Movement and the Missionary Church Association, have a continuing history as independent organizations. But most of them sooner or later merged with other groups of similar emphases. Over half of those listed above united with related groups in 1907 and 1908 to form the Church of the Nazarene.

With regard to the doctrine of Christian perfection these groups were united in presenting it with a strong, if not exclusive, emphasis upon its instantaneous feature—entire sanctification, almost always defined as a "second definite work of grace, subsequent to regeneration." It was early recognized as, and has remained, the distinctive doctrinal emphasis in these organizations. Their ministers and in large part their lay leadership are expected not only

149

to endorse but to have come into the actual experience of entire sanctification.

Among these groups the term "Pentecostal" meant primarily that the organization stressed entire sanctification, of which Pentecost was conceived to be the prototype. The name did not indicate any addiction to charismata. These organizations tended to be, in fact, vigorously opposed to any speaking in tongues. As the term "Pentecostal" came to be increasingly associated with glossolalia, most of these groups dropped it from their name.

Thus by 1900 the greater part of the outspoken advocates of holiness—by which was meant principally Christian perfection in its entire-sanctification aspect—had withdrawn from or been encouraged to leave American Episcopal Methodism. The holiness movement had fully entered the period of separation and sect formation.

While these disciplinary issues were being thus brought to a decision, the doctrine which had given rise to them was being strenuously assailed. In 1866 Samuel Franklin, a member of the Illinois Annual Conference, had written *A Critical Review of Wesleyan Perfection,* denying that sanctification accomplished anything not previously done in regeneration. His book opens with a quotation which indicates its general temper:

These are systems of theology yet rearing their venerable heads, defying the assaults of reason, because shielded by the aegis of authority.

Franklin's argument is unduly elaborate but rests rather largely on the thesis that if man were "generated" perfect, he is "regenerated" perfect. Therefore regeneration brings spiritual perfection. Of this work Phoebe Palmer wrote:

I think this is a very unprofitable book. . . . I would not pronounce it tame but dangerous. . . . It is due the cause of truth to say, that the man who prepared this book for publication . . . has been blending his efforts largely in selling this book, in which (thank God) he has been very unsuccessful.

Not long thereafter A. J. Endsley in a sermon printed in the Pittsburgh *Christian Advocate* maintains as did Franklin, that regeneration does all that entire sanctification is purported to do. He particularly objects to the usage which makes sanctification a second work. "Who says so?" he asks. ". . . No reader of the Bible of ordinary intelligence says so." Endsley's article suffers from the heated partisanship characteristic of this period of doctrinal warfare.

Supporting this same general denial of any doctrinal distinctiveness to sanctification is the position taken by D. D. Whedon. Whedon—a former professor of logic, rhetoric, history, and literature—was a formidable adversary. His teaching strongly reflects the views of Zinzendorf, who had taught that man's holiness was completely "in Christ," never "of himself." The believing Christian was therefore as holy at justification as he could ever be thereafter. Whedon argues that in justification "God beholds the soul as being in Christ perfectly innocent, perfectly pure from the guilt of sin. In *that sense* he is at that moment *perfectly holy*." The believer is also in possession of sufficient power to keep him "with more or less continuity" in that realm where he was at justification "pronounced . . . , through Christ, perfectly innocent of sin." It is this power which Whedon designates sanctification. He says:

We think one of the best definitions of sanctification is: The power, through divine grace, more or less complete, and more or less permanent, so to resist temptation and avoid sin as to live in the fullness of Divine favor.[10]

For an illustration of sanctification Whedon chose a certain spring iron feature of railroad tracks known as "snakes' heads." These must be kept fastened down or are otherwise able, said Whedon, to wreck a train. From spiritual "snakes' heads" we are never delivered, he said; but sanctification is that force which keeps them "more or less completely" suppressed. Quite naturally his view became known as the "snakes' head" theory.

Whedon's views gained unusually wide circulation since he was for many years editor of the *Methodist Quarterly Review*. As such he attacked with ardor and ability the second-blessing teaching concerning sanctification. Articulate as he was, there are certain areas of his view which allow various interpretations. He even granted, for instance, that there may be situations where one might profess entire sanctification, a privilege which he specifically declined. The net result of his exposition, however, was to add the weight of his influence to the tendency to identify regeneration and sanctification. And editor J. M. Buckley of the New York *Christian Advocate* declared that Whedon's view was a concise statement of acceptable Methodist theology on Christian perfection.

A view which Whedon heartily endorsed was one which was presented by J. O. A. Clark of Macon, Georgia. Said Clark: "Every believer whose sins are truly forgiven, and who is begotten of God, is pure in heart, free from sin, and *sanctified*." So far Clark is Wesleyan. But he further denies the place of or need for entire sanctification. Is it, he asks, "some special and extraordinary grace, some second blessing . . . ?" And his obvious answer is No. Instead he says that Christian perfection may be entirely "summed up in a single word, and that word is, *growth*." He and Whedon are agreed in their rejection of entire sanctification. They differ in that Whedon considers holiness something given and to be *maintained* while Clark considers it something promised and to be *moved toward*.

But in Methodism during the last decades of the century, the traditional view still had its able and willing defenders. L. R. Dunn was in the vanguard with an extended article on "Entire Sanctification." He argued with extensive reference to Wesley's *Plain Account* and *Sermons* and to Watson's *Institutes* that regeneration and sanctification are and have been always regarded in Methodist theology as distinct doctrinal concepts.

Another who regularly maintained this emphasis was Bishop J. T. Peck, who thus addressed the ministerial candidates of the Southern Illinois Conference:

I desire, my brethren, to assure you that in the doctrines of The Methodist Episcopal Church on this subject there is nothing hidden or doubtful. The Church has no question about this doctrine. For it does seem to us that the idea that there is no definite blessing which ought to be sought, called entire sanctification or perfect love . . . is not true.

The tendency to alter traditional interpretations of doctrine was as always disquieting. Where lies the difference between liberality and infidelity? The bishops of the Methodist Episcopal Church sought to provide some line of demarcation. To the General Conference of 1880 they said:

We regret to say that in some quarters a spirit of latitudinarian speculation has been introduced into the Church. . . . We are in full sympathy with freedom of thought and freedom of speech. . . . But when a minister has been admitted into official position in the Church, professing to believe its doctrines, and pledging himself to maintain and defend them, . . . he is under sacred obligations to be faithful to his vows.

In other areas similar views were being expressed.

At the Centennial Methodist Conference of 1884 the traditional view, maintaining the distinctiveness of sanctification, was most clearly affirmed. Representatives from American Methodism were there in force. And from the Methodist Episcopal Church, South, J. B. McFerrin had this to say:

Mr. Chairman, . . . they tell us it is time for the creeds of the Church to be remodeled. Well, that may do for some people's creed, but not ours. . . . Justification by Faith, the Witness of the Spirit, Sanctification of Heart and Life, these are the grand peculiarities of Methodism, and let them be preserved forever.

Speaking for the Methodist Episcopal Church, J. E. Evans quoted extensively from the Scriptures and from Methodism's standard authors, continuing with:

These evidences from the standards of Methodism might be multiplied almost indefinitely that sanctification is distinct from and a

153

higher state of grace than regeneration and the new birth. Whosoever, therefore, teaches contrary to this is not a Methodist in doctrine, and if a Methodist, he violates the first Restrictive Rule of the Discipline.

Finally in the Pastoral Address official members from the churches represented besought the conference as follows:

> These . . . doctrines have been the rallying cry of Methodism in the past, and must be in the future—they are repentance, faith, justification, adoption, the witness of the Spirit, sanctification, and Christian perfection. Out of these come all . . . our connectional institutions. . . . Take from Methodism these doctrines of experience, or even the emphasis given them, . . . or confuse them by any conceivable departure from their simplicity so that they shall become only doctrines of the creed, unverified in the soul as the very essence of salvation, and then our glory is departed forever. . . .
>
> We remind you, brethren, that the mission of Methodism is to promote holiness. . . . In all the borders of Methodism the doctrine is preached, and the experience of sanctification is urged. We beseech you, brethren, stand by your standards on this subject. Our founders rightly interpreted the mind of the Spirit. . . . Let us not turn from them to follow strange lights.

It would seem that officially the great burden of the church's concern was to maintain both in doctrine and in experience the traditional Wesleyan emphasis. The degree of its concern is indicative of the strength of the tendency to depart from that emphasis. Four years later, in 1888, the General Conference of the Methodist Episcopal Church was again reminded of the "urgent need for line upon line, and precept upon precept, to keep the experience and practice of our people in line with our doctrinal teachings."

In that same year, however, appeared a work about which it was said, "No book, by a Southern author, and published by a Southern house, has been discussed so extensively." This was J. M. Boland's *The Problem of Methodism*. That problem, thought the author, was the doctrine of sanctification. Boland maintains that it is impossible to determine from Wesley's own writings

THE DOCTRINE MODIFIED, 1865-1900

what he *did* believe in regard to the distinctive place of sanctification—especially as it was distinguished from regeneration. But Boland *is* certain that Wesley came to repudiate his earlier belief concerning "sin in believers" and consequently abandoned the concept of entire sanctification as a second blessing. This sweeping conclusion he reaches by assuming that, when Wesley revised the ninth article (Church of England), in preparing the Twenty-five Articles of Religion for the American church, he "publicly rejected the residue theory of regeneration by expunging the clause in which it was baptized into the creed of the Church."

This was building a weighty assumption on a flimsy deduction. It is true that in revising Article IX, which refers to "Original or Birth-Sin," Wesley omitted the statement "and this infection of nature doth remain, yea in them that are regenerated. . . ." Boland has assumed that *this* particular statement was Wesley's reason for excising over half the article, the complete portion omitted reading:

The flesh lusteth always contrary to the spirit; and therefore in every person born into this world, it deserveth God's wrath and damnation. And this infection of nature doth remain, yea in them that are regenerated; whereby the lust of the flesh, called in the Greek, *phronema sarkos,* which some do expound the wisdom, some sensuality, some the affection, some the desire, of the flesh, is not subject to the Law of God. And although there is no condemnation for them that believe and are baptized, yet the Apostle doth confess, that concupiscence and lust hath of itself the nature of sin.

If Boland is right, then Wesley was remarkably inconsistent; for his letters and sermons after 1784 are replete with references, direct and implied, which testify to his continuing belief in "sin in believers."

A more defensible explanation is offered by Henry Wheeler, who says:

Why the latter part of the article was omitted is easily seen. Wesley could not indorse its teaching. The flesh does indeed lust against the Spirit, but it does not follow that "therefore in every person born into

155

this world, it deserveth God's wrath and damnation." The English divines who subscribe to the Articles are not agreed on this subject, some following the views of Augustine and others rejecting them. The interpretation of the Article is modified and accommodated to the views of each party. . . . It is better to omit than to retain what needs such an equivocal exposition.[11]

Wesley's objection to the teaching of inherited *guilt* was, said Wheeler, the real reason why he set aside the latter half of the ninth article.

Despite the inaccuracy of its principal thesis Boland's book received wide circulation and considerable acclaim. Its conclusions were cited by John E. Edwards, a prominent member of the Virginia Conference, as sufficient grounds for radical doctrinal revision. He proposed:

It is time for the expurgation, not of scriptural holiness, Christian purity, and "perfect love," but of all that recognizes a "second change," involving a second cleansing as the condition of the attainment of Christian purity and maturity, not only from our hymns, but also from our standards of doctrine, as they are called. It could be done . . . without the surrender of more than a half-dozen stanzas from our hymns, together with a few of Mr. Wesley's earlier sermons.[12]

His objection reflects the heat of controversy; his solution, the blight of inaccuracy. But it was obvious that despite the appeal of the bishops the standards were being increasingly challenged.

By now, as a matter of fact, a new set of Methodist standards were in process of establishment. H. C. Sheldon in the 1890's could say:

Among formal systems of theology, Watson's Institutes have long been regarded as a compendium of Methodist teaching. Recently a new era of productiveness in Methodist theological literature has been inaugurated. The works of W. B. Pope, M. Raymond, and D. D. Whedon have been introduced to the public; also, more recently, those of John Miley, T. O. Summers, [and] R. S. Foster.

The earliest of these is the *Systematic Theology* of Miner Raymond, published in 1877. Raymond, professor of systematic theology at Garrett Biblical Institute, accepts in Wesleyan fashion the possibility of and necessity for entire sanctification. He flatly declares that "not all of original sin or natural depravity is removed in regeneration." But as a theologian he admits a difficulty, for

sanctification, being a matter of experience, and therefore known only by experience, and being variable, different in different persons and in the same person at different times, is incapable of logical definition; that is the precise idea can not be revealed to one otherwise ignorant of it by any formula in language.[13]

But the Scriptures "recognize," Raymond maintained, "a state of grace which they speak of as a state of maturity," and they "call that grace perfect love." Christian perfection, therefore, despite the difficulty of definition includes at least these two ideas: maturity and perfect love. Explore those concepts and the breadth of the doctrine is evident.

As to the *manner* in which Christian perfection is wrought, we again face that variable datum personal experience. Recognizing the differences in the "mental constitutions, habits, and conditions of the persons sanctified," the difficulty of arriving at any one pattern is obvious. Raymond is inclined to say that such perfection is accomplished

generally by a gradual process, perhaps sometimes instantaneously, as the subject improves his privileges, grows in grace and knowledge, and comes to the exercise of an intelligent, evangelical, saving faith for this special attainment, this higher Christian life.[14]

In this statement Raymond is referring, it seems, to the length or brevity of the period preparatory to the "exercise of . . . saving faith." In another context he insists that the testimony of thousands must be accepted to a "sudden instantaneous transition from a low state of religious enjoyment to a consciousness of completed salvation." Moreover, even when the work be considered as gradual, "there is an instant when it is done, completed, and finished." And as a process of maturation "there is, somewhere, a point that is in Scripture designated as a point of maturity."

But the variations are well-nigh infinite. On the one hand, there is the child who is so reared in Christian nurture "as that he will never knowingly and voluntarily transgress the law of God —in which case he will certainly grow up into regeneration and final salvation." On the other hand, there are those in whom the habits of sin are deeply established and who "in most cases . . . are not wholly emancipated till after many a struggle and many a baptism of holy cleansing." In view of these obvious differences Raymond warns that "no man's experience should be the basis of another's man's faith."

It is his conclusion that what one may not be able adequately to define, one may yet come fully to experience. For there is, he says, a "state of grace which may be sought, obtained, and enjoyed."

The work which came to be most influential during this period was the three-volume *Compendium of Christian Theology* by British theologian William Burt Pope. Differing in some respects from the typical American exposition of the doctrine, it is an able theological and historical summation of the Wesleyan position. In Pope's discussion of Christian perfection the Methodist position is almost entirely indicated by rather full quotations from the *Plain Account*. Pope's choice of quotations and supplementary comment is marked by caution. Whereas his exposition allows the propriety of the instantaneous interpretation of entire sanctification, it further reveals his belief in the necessity for an extended period of gradual growth toward that event. The *Compendium* grants that assurance is a concomitant of the completed work. And Wesley is quoted to show that he gave a restricted and guarded endorsement to public profession of the attainment of perfect love.

But it is in his *Higher Catechism of Theology*, where quotation is largely dispensed with, that Pope indicates his own views. And here in one or two particulars he differs from the statement given in his *Compendium*. For instance, under "tendencies to error" he says:

A distinct assurance, connected with the moment of final deliverance from sin, and as it were apart from the silent seal of the indwelling Spirit, is sometimes looked for without any express warrant of Scripture.

And with regard to testimony, as would follow from such a view of assurance, he remarks: "As employed by the individual Christian concerning himself, it is a term more appropriate to his aspiration than his professed attainment." What Pope is most concerned to emphasize about the doctrine, he gathers under the heading "cardinal teaching." And this is

that perfection is solely the Spirit's work in the believer; but implies his most strenuous co-operation: as to the former, it is received merely by faith, and hence may be given instantaneously, "in a moment"; as to the latter, "there is a gradual work, both preceding and following that instant."

Here was Wesley in undistorted miniature.

Pope was characterized by D. D. Whedon as a "Wesleyan of the strictest type, and especially of the school of Watson." But R. W. Moss with greater discernment sees him as one who "though . . . his intellectual sympathies were mainly with the past, . . . stood as a theologian at the parting of the ways." [15] He was a transition character, intent on conserving the values of the past even as he opened the door to further departures from tradition.

One who entered upon such a departure was John Miley, benign and methodical professor of systematic theology at Drew Theological Seminary. In his *Systematic Theology*, published in 1894, he makes his views clear at two focal points. First, he inclines to question the doctrinal necessity of such a work as entire sanctification as it was customarily presented. He sees no reason to assume that what is postulated for this "complete" work cannot be and is not accomplished in regeneration. Moreover, he states that there is no explicit scriptural support for the idea of an "incompleteness of regeneration." As a consequence, he says, "there is perplexity in the notion of entire sanctification," and "it should not be thought strange that some question the truth of this doctrine, or even oppose it." Second, and more emphatically, he opposes the view that entire sanctification must always be considered a second blessing. He holds that such may be a *possible* mode, but he objects to the insistence that it is the *only* mode. Here, he feels, is the crux of the controversy. He observes:

> Right here is the occasion of unfortunate differences among us. However, much of the evil consequence . . . would be avoided through a spirit of mutual forbearance. Let those who hold rigidly the second-blessing view preach sanctification in their own way, but let them be tolerant of such as preach it in a manner somewhat different; and let such as hesitate respecting that special view be tolerant of those for whom it possesses great interest.[16]

It was a fourteenth-chapter-of-Romans appeal for peace, though it was rather obvious as to whom Miley considered the "weaker brother."

In the theological position which he had taken, Miley acknowledges that he is in divergence from the teachings of John Wesley; and this is due to the fact, he says, that Wesley's views on regeneration, as reflected in his "On Sin in Believers," are defective. Wesley was more nearly correct, he holds, in the views which he expressed in "The Marks of the New Birth." It is of interest to note that Wesley preached "The Marks of the New Birth" in 1743 and "On Sin in Believers" twenty years later. Of these two sermons E. H. Sugden (editor of Wesley's *Standard Sermons*) says, "The first sets out the ideal of the Christian life; the second makes the qualifications which practical experience shows to be necessary." Miley would reverse that judgment. Moreover, he felt that Wesley's adherence to the second-blessing theory was principally because "he gave too much doctrinal weight to individual professions of experience." In fact Miley is ready to say the true view of the doctrine may be quite near Zinzendorf's idea of entire sanctification in regeneration—provided that doctrine is guarded against its "tincture of Antinomianism."

Having cleared the ground by stating the areas where he is in disagreement with the traditional doctrine, Miley proceeds to give his positive views. He believes, for instance, that entire sanctification is a privilege "at once so thoroughly Scriptural and Wesleyan that from it there is among us only the rarest dissent." But this doctrine has two aspects which need to be, but often are not, kept clearly distinguished. The first might be called a subjective purification and is "operative within the moral nature." The second may be designated "maturity" and has specific reference to the actual Christian life. The first is the necessary ground of the second, but the second should not be considered the *immediate* product of the first.

With regard to this subjective purification Miley is ready to admit that it is generally, but not necessarily always, instantaneous in character. But with regard to maturity he affirms that there must be an allowance made for time—time for growth, time for the perfection of "Christian graces." This time element will, of course, vary with the capacities and temperament of the individuals concerned.

Miley's views were variously received. Within the church his reviews were favorable, those of differing points of view finding qualified haven within his theological system. Thus the editor of the *Methodist Quarterly Review* finds that Miley "wisely discredits the 'second blessing' theory." While the editor of the *Quarterly Review* observes that Miley gives circumspect, though unequivocal, endorsement to the theory. Actually, Miley had allowed the views of both groups to be acceptable but had denied the claim of either to be exclusively so.

Miley's views are in part the expression of a revolt against what he considers extreme and factional presentation of the doctrine. In his positive emphases he concedes most, if not all, of that for which Wesley, Fletcher, and the more thoughtful of the holiness advocates were contending. They, too, distinguish between inward and outward holiness, between purity and maturity. In addition,

however, he strengthens considerably the trend to identify regeneration and sanctification. Watson's qualified suggestions have
become Miley's outright emphasis.

This trend was to be strongly challenged. The holiness advocates
in and out of the church stoutly maintained the traditional emphasis. Regeneration and sanctification were clearly distinct and
especially so at the point of entire sanctification. They held with
undeviating loyalty to the doctrinal statement adopted at the
General Holiness Assembly of 1885. One of their spokesmen
could say with confidence:

> We are now prepared to give a formal definition of sanctification or
> Scriptural holiness, which would probably be accepted by the three
> hundred teachers and preachers in the National Holiness Association
> of America . . . : Entire Sanctification is a second definite work of
> grace wrought by the Baptism with the Holy Spirit in the heart of the
> believer subsequent to regeneration, received instantaneously by
> faith, by which the heart is cleansed from all corruption and filled with
> the perfect love of God.[17]

This definition had something of the force of an "apostles' creed"
within the holiness movement. It was limited as was that first
great formulary to the specific issues in controversy and was
effective to expose the uncertain and to rout the disaffected. This
was the phraseology in which the doctrine was presented, and its
strength lay in its intensity.

The heavy attacks were directed at any distinction in the process
of salvation. Defensive exposition and exhortation were focused
therefore on entire sanctification.

It was inevitable that this should be so. Entire sanctification as
a second definite work of grace was felt to be the *sine qua non*
of Christian perfection. Its omission or neglect was to render further
discussion of the theme purely academic. So reasoned those active
in the associations and in the holiness movement generally. Asbury
Lowrey, editor for some time of *The Christian Standard,* a periodical speaking for the National Association for the Promotion of Holi-

ness, stated that entire sanctification was a neglected theme in the leading pulpits of Methodism, and

if discoursed upon at all, it is rather represented as a . . . ripening process. Such is the general treatment of the theme now by the Methodist pulpit, excepting those who are accused of making holiness a hobby. And on account of this unkind accusation, many who feel a deep interest in the matter are deterred from giving it prominence. . . . The great subject, by neglect on the part of the regular ministries in the Church, has been relegated to outside and, in some sense, irregular agencies.[18]

Disregard had led to disproportion.

The defenders of the traditional view were not all in "outside and, in some sense, irregular" relationships. Among the new standards mentioned had been the works of T. O. Summers and R. S. Foster. These men held high place in the southern and northern churches respectively. And both were outspoken defenders of the distinctiveness of sanctification and the requisite place of entire sanctification.

T. O. Summers had been from 1847 until his death in 1882 secretary of all the sessions of the General Conference of his church. From 1858 until 1882 he was, besides, the editor of the *Quarterly Review*. And in 1875 he became dean of the biblical department and professor of systematic theology at Vanderbilt University. It was said of him, in the fulsome tribute to which church historians incline, that during this latter period he was "universally recognized as the foremost theologian of the Church." [19] But Bishop McTyeire at Summers' funeral described him as, a "vat into which all learning had been poured, as incapable of originality as he was of sin."

Summers was, however, influential and articulate, and he directed his remarks primarily against the growing tendency to identify sanctification and regeneration. "Who would have thought," he wrote, "that Osiandrianism and Zinzendorfianism would be revived in the close of the nineteenth century? Yet such is the case." Over against this growing tendency he cites

Wesley's extensive arguments for sin in believers. He maintains that the essential need is for the church to find a medium between the "rationalists" who deny innate depravity and the "fanatics" who distort the doctrine of entire sanctification.[20]

His most explicit statement of the doctrine, *Holiness, a Treatise on Sanctification,* was so Wesleyan as to be almost a transcript of various statements from Wesley. For Summers, tradition was its own authority. In his *Treatise,* therefore, he rested his case on appeals to the traditional view and gave a thorough analysis of what that view was. Perhaps his most distinctive emphasis was his teaching that all advances in the Christian life

are made under the influence of faith; and when that faith covers over the broad extent of our necessities, and the promise of sanctifying grace, then we are cleansed from all sin, and our hearts are filled with perfect love.

Sanctification for Summers was both a distinctive doctrine and an enriching experience.

Randolph S. Foster, whose works were mentioned among the newer standards, had strongly encouraged the holiness revival throughout his career as pastor, professor of systematic theology, president of Drew Theological Seminary, and bishop in the Methodist Episcopal Church. He has been called "one of the greatest and most magnetic thinkers of American Methodism," a man of "gigantic intellect." In his later years his *Studies in Theology* gained for him a certain eminence as a theologian. But his views on Christian perfection are most clearly reflected in his earlier *Nature and Blessedness of Christian Purity.* This is a practical and earnest treatise in which Foster stresses the distinctiveness and attainability of entire sanctification, at the same time insisting that there shall be no deprecation of any of the other doctrines of the church. He gave a more careful and philosophical presentation of his views, still essentially unchanged, in his later Merrick Lectures delivered before the Ohio Wesleyan University. His works reflects both the spirit and content of Wesley's teachings on Christian perfection.

There were many others who defended, ably and otherwise, the traditional Wesleyan position. Some of them were more influential than those listed above. Thomas N. Ralston of the Methodist Episcopal Church, South, whose *Elements of Divinity* were "long a standard in the Church and a textbook in the Conference course for ministers," consistently upheld that view. At Boston University, Daniel Steele gave it impassioned exposition—in classroom, the *Christian Advocate,* and in his own published works. And John R. Brooks of the southern church, with an impressive marshaling of testimony and quotation, presented by his *Scriptural Sanctification,* an able defense of the doctrine. He had in preparation polled the bishops of his church on the question "Do you teach that regeneration and entire sanctification are separate and distinct, one from the other, and therefore received at different times?" Not all the bishops replied. Some were away, said Brooks. But from those who did he selected this answer as typical:

No doubt a person who should experience the right kind and measure of faith might and would be wholly sanctified at the same instant he should be regenerated. But such instances, if they ever occur, are extremely rare. *Usually the two works are quite distinct, both in nature and in time,* as our standards teach.

The other replies, Brooks reported, did not differ significantly from this view.

Besides these who had published more or less influential works, there were other defenders of the same view in consequential periodicals. John J. Tigert of the *Quarterly Review* maintained a consistent and circumspect advocacy. Leonidas Rosser of the Richmond *Christian Advocate* was outspoken in defense of the doctrine and its advocates. And such strictly holiness periodicals as the *Christian Standard, Christian Witness, Pentecostal Herald,* and *Guide to Holiness* enjoyed a relatively wide circulation and reflected a consistency of emphasis.

But traditional theology, and tradition in general, were even then under heavy attack on many fronts. At Yale, William Graham Sumner despite his clerical background was "turning his back upon theological economics" and teaching a course in political economy interlarded with broad assignments from the writings of Herbert Spencer. He had accepted his post at New Haven out of a conviction that the role of the clergy was to be increasingly irrelevant. Said Wilbur L. Cross of him, "No other teacher of those days exerted so profound an influence upon his students as did Professor Sumner. It was tremendous." [21] And when Sumner discussed religion, he was apt to say:

When two religions appeared in the primitive community the one favoured by respectable cattle thieves was practiced as religion and the other was called illicit medicine or black magic.

Sumner's attitude and outlook may be considered in a sense representative of the general intellectual climate. Certainly it was also evident in areas outside New Haven.

At Boston University, one of Methodism's oldest, this growing spirit of revolt against tradition was perceptible. Daniel Steele, stanch defender of tradition, retired in 1894 from his teaching responsibilities. The next year Olin A. Curtis, finding the increasingly liberal atmosphere uncongenial, withdrew to spend a year abroad and then to accept a post at Drew Theological Seminary. And the most influential man on the faculty was Borden Parker Bowne.

Bowne had come to Boston University as professor of ethics in 1876, after having studied abroad at Paris, Halle, and Göttingen. In 1888, already well known as an able and independent metaphysician, he was made professor of philosophy. As teacher and author he became a notable, and often disturbing, agent in the yeasty ferment of American theology. In the 1890's he was in the process of establishing a new theological approach in which traditional evangelicalism had little, if any, place.

It was a period for clearing the ground, and Bowne was unsparing in his application to the task. So with incisive brilliance he blasts the "traditionalist who confuses theology with experience." The testimony of experience, Bowne held, was always suspect and often absurd. Actually Bowne was part of a general revolt against that

166

type of religion which had been satisfied to express itself in shibboleth and self-adulation, often oblivious both to personal inadequacy and to social need.

But the revolt which followed had gone too far. The roots of genuine piety had been injured in the attack upon the parasitic growths which fed upon it. William James described the result as follows:

> When I read in a religious paper words like these: "Perhaps the best thing we can say of God is that he is *the Inevitable Inference*," I recognize the tendency to let religion evaporate in intellectual terms. Would martyrs have sung in the flames for a mere inference, however inevitable it might be? Original religious men, like Saint Francis, Luther, Behmen, have usually been enemies of the intellect's pretension to meddle with religious things. Yet the intellect, everywhere invasive, shows everywhere its shallowing effect. See how the ancient spirit of Methodism evaporates under those wonderfully able rationalistic booklets (which every one should read) of a philosopher like Professor Bowne.[22]

Traditional theology at Boston University was definitely in process of decisive alteration.

Such a processs was not merely regional. It was similarly under way at Vanderbilt University, still distinctively Methodistic. In 1891, it is said, the son of a Georgia clergyman, his theological views considerably disturbed by his readings in Renan and Haeckel, sought counsel in the office of Chancellor Garland. That counsel was reported as follows: "Men never amount to much until they outgrow their fathers' notions, sir." Nine years earlier Wilbur F. Tillett had become professor of systematic theology at Vanderbilt. If he did not completely subscribe to Chancellor Garland's views, he nevertheless did not share the profound respect for tradition which had characterized his predecessor, T. O. Summers. With regard to the doctrine of Christian perfection, for instance, Tillett, while paying it high tribute, saw no necessary difference between regeneration and sanctification and no good reason why the results traditionally ascribed to the latter might not be realized in the

167

former. The instantaneous element in what was considered the Wesleyan view was, said Tillett, largely the result of the teachings of the fanatical Thomas Maxfield and George Bell, "who had had, as we have seen, so much to do with starting the 'instantaneous sanctification' or 'second blessing' movement." [23]

Tillett further taught that concerning Christian perfection Wesley in his later years

quietly "let it drop." This does not mean that he abandoned his doctrine, for he did not; it means that he let all insistence upon *instantaneous* sanctification quietly drop. Hence his writings immediately before and ever after 1784 contain very few allusions to inbred or indwelling sin, but he seems from this time on to regard a "voluntary transgression of a known law of God" as the only definition of sin consistent with Scripture. [24]

Tillett was evidently influenced in these conclusions by Boland's *Problem of Methodism,* which had made much the same claim. The answers to Boland at this point would be, therefore, answers to Tillett. Actually Wesley never did diminish his exhortations to seek perfection "now" and "by simple faith"—though he continually coupled with such exhortation the teaching of a "gradual work."

Students of Tillett must, however, have received the impression that any instantaneous sanctification had been essentially repudiated by Wesley and was, in fact, unsupported by sound scriptural exegesis or representative Christian experience. It was, they were told, doctrinally weak and experimentally misread. Those who insisted otherwise were apt to be considered mentally retarded. Bishop E. R. Hendrix, in fact, referred to such as "good brethren with sad indications of 'arrested development.'"

But while traditional theology was under attack, religion in America was not moribund. When the World's Fair was held in Chicago in 1893, Dwight L. Moody hired the big tent of Forepaugh's Circus for Sunday services and preached to overflow crowds. Under his direction the city was zoned, and certain churches were designated as evangelistic centers. Sermons were preached in

Polish, Hebrew, French, German, and Swedish. Theaters were hired as preaching centers, and on some Sundays the aggregate attendance "exceeded a hundred thousand." At that same World's Fair the Evangelical Alliance was holding one of its General Conferences to consider the function of the church in the increasingly complex social and industrial order. While the delegates in attendance would not have filled Forepaugh's Circus, the problems with which they dealt were deep and relevant. It was a serious and sincere recognition by churchmen of the responsibility of religion for the alleviation of social ills. Amid these expressions of religion, evangelistic and sociological, theology, however, held a relatively low priority. Its traditional expressions were apt to be avoided, were, in fact, openly suspect as invitations to controversy rather than as aids to the accomplishment of desired goals.

In American Methodism it was the doctrine of Christian perfection which suffered most from this widely shared attitude. The vexing issue had come to be generally referred to as the "second blessing question." Wesleyan or not, it was under attack.

In the South, A. G. Haygood while president of Emory College had gone on record as saying, "Entire sanctification is not instantaneous." And the editor of the Nashville *Christian Advocate*, E. E. Hoss, when asked to state his opinion on the second blessing, had replied that it was an "ill-assorted compound of impossible psychology, absurd exegesis, and misread experience." There is nothing to suggest that the opinion of these two men changed when later they were both elected to the bishopric. Bishop J. C. Granbery, whose pamphlet *Entire Sanctification: The Second Blessing* received wide circulation, stated that his personal view was "that God completes the purification not 'a little before death,' as Wesley held, but at the instant of death." And in the columns of the Nashville *Christian Advocate* it was argued that

the truth is, sanctification in its primary sense and on the human side is prerequisite to, and on the divine side is a necessary part of justification. In neither case, nor sense, can it be a blessing subsequent to and distinct from regeneration, or justification.[25]

To accept a theory merely because Wesley espoused it, Morris Evans declared, was slavish. Other articles were in similar vein.

In the North there were outspoken dissenters also, though not usually in such influential connectional posts. From Illinois in 1898 came a booklet by I. Villars entitled *The Theory of the Second Blessing—Is It Either Wesleyan or Scriptural?* Villars contended that Wesley's doctrine of sanctification "was nothing more or less than our doctrine and experience of Justification by Faith." The next year a rather elaborate study entitled *Sin and Holiness* was published by D. W. C. Huntington, chancellor of Nebraska Wesleyan University. The thesis of this work is that Wesley's concept of "inbred sin" was faulty in essence and confused in presentation. Huntington concludes that regeneration and sanctification are essentially synonymous. This book received wide circulation and a favorable review in the *Methodist Quarterly Review* which included the significant remark that "watchful observers of tendencies say that Dr. Huntington's book is in the direction of the general present drift of thought in our Church." The traditional formulation of the doctrine was being engulfed by new streams of interpretation.

Meanwhile there were three expositors of the doctrine whose works defy easy classification. These men were J. T. Crane, C. W. Rishell, and James Mudge.

Crane, prominent and influential member of the Newark Conference, had written on the subject considerably earlier than the other two. But in many significant respects his work *Holiness the Birthright of All God's Children* is similar to theirs. He opposes, for instance, the idea that entire sanctification is *necessary* as a second work of grace in order to cleanse the soul from such sin as will keep it from the presence of God. Therefore he argues that Wesley's sermon "On Sin in Believers" overstates the case—due to the fact that Wesley was concerned to controvert the "high perfectionists." Therefore what Wesley called "inbred sin" continuing in the believer should more accurately have been called a congruency to temptation, something which Crane insists is not sin. Nevertheless, says Crane:

170

There are times in the life of the most faithful follower of Christ when new light seems to beam upon him. He sees opening before his spiritual vision new possibilities of faith, and hope, and love. . . . He does not feel that the wrath of God is upon him, because of the smallness of his spiritual stature, but he realizes that with all this new light he cannot rest content with his present attainments. . . . He seeks [God] in humble, importunate, believing prayer. And then comes the baptism of the Holy Ghost, rich, full, abundant, filling his soul with peace, and blessing, and salvation.

And thus the Christian rises from a lower to a higher plane of experience.

Crane's book was written, as most of these works were, in the midst of controversy. And he frequently says more than he seems to mean. He is in specific protest against what he feels is a disparagement of regeneration which, he holds, brings one into the complete favor of God. Entire sanctification is not, therefore and strictly speaking, a requisite for a barely safe hereafter but a necessity for an abundantly satisfactory here and now.

In an extended article written for the *Methodist Quarterly Review* in 1892, C. W. Rishell, who was soon to accept the post of professor of historical theology at Boston University, points out that an undue stress upon intention had resulted in an inadequate concept of sin. It must be recognized, he says, that the "weight of a moral fact to any individual is determined by the delicacy of his conscience." He holds further that we do not detect *all* areas of sinfulness at one time. We do detect *some* and in bringing those to the fore are delivered from them. Just how this affects the doctrine of sanctification, Rishell points out:

So far as the intention is concerned sincere consecration is always entire, but as far as reality is concerned it is only entire when the full compass of that act is comprehended by the mind. The penitent sinner makes an entire consecration so far as he knows. . . . But his idea of consecration, as his idea of the significance of the Christian life, may be and generally is very imperfect.

To the charge that God would not do an imperfect work of cleansing, Rishell replies that this overlooks God's method with souls. "Better, as man is constituted, is an imperfect work of grace with our concurrence than a perfect one without it." If these premises be allowed, it is inevitable, states Rishell, "that sooner or later a second blessing will become a necessity to the earnest soul." But since salvation from sin progresses with the development of comprehension and aspiration, the second blessing may be on a much higher level for one than for another. An absolute standard at this point is, therefore, not possible. Moreover, says Rishell, "there is room for a new consecration and a still higher salvation." Concerning this he states:

It is entirely possible that a third crisis . . . and a third blessing of a nature similar to the second be received. But it is more likely that the state of enlightenment in a person who has reached this stage of experience will lead to a gradual discovery of the defects, and separation from them. . . . But for growth in grace subsequent to this experience [perfect love] the recognition of its limitation is a necessity. One who feels that the work is all accomplished can make no progress. . . . To fail of a lively sense of our need of more light is to exhibit a state of contentment with ourselves indicative not of spiritual life but of death.

Here was a view all the more Wesleyan because not apparently concerned to defend the literal Wesleyan formula.

Completing this group is the work of James Mudge, former missionary to India where he edited the *Lucknow Witness,* and for several years secretary of the New England Conference. In many ways his exposition parallels that of Rishell's, though his language and general approach reflect more strongly the controversy of which he was a part. The very title of his book was provocative—*Growth in Holiness Toward Perfection or Progressive Sanctification.* And he begins by asserting that with regard to Christian perfection Wesley "groped eagerly for the light; but the fog was thick about him, and he never quite emerged"—a fairly brash analysis sufficiently *lèse majesté* to call for immediate retaliation by offended sensibilities. He follows Rishell in close particular, concluding that "God is obliged to proceed in this gradual way . . . , step by step, as we are able to bear it and to give the intelligent cooperation of our own will to the work of grace." As for regeneration and sanctification Mudge makes the following rather rough distinction:

> While every regeneration is a sanctification, all sanctifications are not regenerations. A man is born again only once; he is sanctified or purified a great many times, just as many as may be needful for the completion of the work which . . . is never completed at the beginning, because of the weakness of the human factor [but] is repeated again and again. . . . Regeneration is a completed work; sanctification is a progressive one.

With Crane, Mudge insists that the new convert is made sinless in regeneration—but he needs to walk in new accessions of light if he is to retain this holiness. And Mudge states that he is in full agreement with those who feel that

> the great mass of the members of our Churches are in a very unsatisfactory condition and need a further work of purification wrought upon their hearts. . . . We further agree that, in order for them to reach this most desirable state, a crisis must in most cases be brought on, very similar to what they went through at conversion.

But he maintains that no sense of *finality* is to be given to this subsequent work. There must always be kept in mind the need for further blessings, though the initial purification may seem indeed like a second blessing. It is easier to discern Mudge's intention than it is to comprehend his attempted doctrinal distinctions.

His apparent belligerency, his somewhat cavalier treatment of Wesley and the standard writers, and his readiness to scrap traditional terminology—all these brought Mudge inevitable criticism. But the book was also hailed as "one of the most remarkable books on this topic ever published within the bounds of Methodism," a "hallowed and sacred volume." It was widely influential. In the controversy which followed, Mudge stoutly maintained that he was completely Methodistic and orthodox. Later, after the heat of this period had subsided, Mudge rewrote his views. And then, looking back, he said:

> Nearly all the controversy has been over words, and because there has been woeful lack of clear definitions. Whole octavos have been wasted in refuting what nobody holds, and proving what nobody doubts.[26]

In the light of this later volume it appears that Mudge was not so much opposed to the traditional doctrine as he was in disagreement with some of its stereotyped emphases. Certainly he was concerned for the encouragement of the quality of life that doctrine was intended to promote.

These three—Crane, Rishell, and Mudge—do not fit easily into the pattern of those who advocated the second-blessing concept or of those who opposed it. They did not fit because they were not sufficiently pro or con. They allowed too much for one group, too little for another. And yet they were nearer Wesley's concept of the doctrine than were the extremists in either opposing party. They were strongly opposed to any disparagement of regeneration, as Wesley had been; so they lifted it above his own interpretation. But he too had a very high view of regeneration and might have preached a supplement to his "On Sin in Believers" had he faced the tensions of their period. They were strongly fearful that a sense of Pharisaic satisfaction would follow upon one interpretation of entire sanctification, so they argued against a finality in that experience. Wesley had been similarly fearful, though he sought a solution in his doctrine of "growth in grace." And even in their doctrine of additional blessings they mirrored Wesley's doctrine of degrees. Certainly they may have claimed Fletcher as a doctrinal forebear. But the general synthesis embodied in their teachings was not heeded by an age absorbed wholly with thesis and antithesis. It is true that many holiness advocates would have agreed with the broad concerns of these men, though they would have disagreed with the terms used to express them. But for the most part these defenders of the traditional doctrine were engaged at just one point of it—entire sanctification. And one of their own spokesmen revealed the result when he said:

> We have pre-eminently erred in the want of clearer, fuller teaching as to the after experiences of the sanctified state. We succeed in leading many into the incipient experience, but largely fail to lead them beyond it. . . . We need to be taught that there are experiences innumerable in the after widening and deepening of the holiness stream.[27]

During the last three decades of the nineteenth century, then, those who advanced doctrinal views on sanctification fall for the most part into two major groups: (1) those who contended that man's holiness, as effected by the grace of God, is accomplished in regeneration; and (2) those who held that man's holiness, as effected by the grace of God, is accomplished by further infusion of grace subsequent to regeneration. Many who declared themselves on this subject, however, had overlapping and sometimes contradictory elements in the systems they advocated. It is therefore possible to order such views into separate categories only on the basis of *emphasis,* not on specific and guarded utterance. The names given are from the discussion above. The list is by no means exhaustive.

Sanctification indistinct from regeneration	Sanctification distinct from regeneration
Man's holiness, *as effected by the grace of God,* is accomplished in regeneration.	Man's holiness, *as effected by the grace of God,* is accomplished by further infusion of grace subsequent to regeneration.
And sharing this conclusion are those who differently teach that	And sharing this conclusion are those who differently teach that
1. Complete deliverance from all sin is accomplished in re-	1. A complete purification is instantaneously accomplished

Sanctification indistinct from regeneration	Sanctification distinct from regeneration
generation, the "residue theory" being denied (Boland, Clark, Edwards, Endsley, Franklin, Hayes, Huntington).	in the crisis of entire sanctification (Brooks, Foster, Lowrey, Peck, Ralston, Rosser, Steele, Summers, Tigert).
2. Complete deliverance from inbred sin is never accomplished in this life; and, therefore, regeneration does all that may ever be done in this sense (Whedon, Granbery).	2. A completed purification may be gradually wrought in the process of continuing sanctification (Haygood[?] Hoss, Kelley, Miley, Pope).
	3. A progressive purification is wrought through a sanctification combining crises and process (Crane, Rishell, Mudge).

But however well phrased, doctrinal polemic was finding a diminishing welcome. When in early 1896 James Mudge requested a review of his controversial work, Bishop J. F. Berry replied:

I read your book with very great interest and thoroughly admired its clear, strong chapters. The fact is, however, I do not believe in controversies over the "Holiness" question. To me it looks like rather an unholy business. We have had in the Methodist Episcopal Church within the last twenty-five years so much debate on the subject that a good many people have in that way grown tired of and prejudiced against the doctrine. Don't you think we ought to stop debating about it now and begin to be holy? [28]

There was a genuine weariness of controversy. Pleas were made for moderation and conciliation. It was suggested that a moratorium be called on traditional doctrinal terms, especially since such terms were so often used with differing meanings by those who represented opposing points of view. It was felt, moreover, that appeals to Wesley offered no solution, "each one selecting his 'Wesley says' according to the particular sentiment he wishes to sustain or the doctrine he desires to prove." Said J. W. Mendenhall:

Let us have done with theorizing, moralizing, philosophizing, and Wesleyizing on a teaching that shines in the New Testament with the clearness of the sun in the heavens.[29]

Theology was in bad odor. The head was asked to make way for the heart. With the rather careless expansiveness that marks much of his writing, Daniel Curry declared, "Theories of religion . . . are less valuable than the faith that accepts, without a theory, the grace that brings salvation."

In the South there was a determined effort to effect a cessation of doctrinal hostilities. Addresses from two of the bishops, E. R. Hendrix and J. C. Granbery, were printed in pamphlet form and widely circulated. The temper was irenic and the intention conciliatory. In these pamphlets the instantaneous element was allowed and the gradual was favored. John J. Tigert hailed this effort and believed that it

should do much to put an end to the controversies that have so long and painfully distracted our Zion. . . . If the spirit of come-outism anywhere exists, let it be put away at once and forever. If the spirit of crush-outism has anywhere found expression, let it not be so as mentioned among brethren . . . —"let us have peace."[30]

And peace of a sort was had. From 1896 to 1900 no article on this subject appeared in *The Methodist Review*.

In this area, therefore, the ending of doctrinal controversy was effected on relatively high terms. Those terms were stated as follows: that while the church maintained the distinctiveness of the doctrine of sanctification, it also held that "it is not vital that we hold the work done instantaneously" and "it is not essential that a man make a specific profession of the experience."[31] To the outright holiness advocates this must have seemed a surrender of the vital issue. Some kept up the battle from such beleaguered areas of resistance as Asbury College. But more withdrew to join the burgeoning sects.

In the North solutions were sought for on terms calculated to avoid disruption. The doctrine and experience of perfect love were given explicit endorsement. The General Conference of 1896 was told by the bishops:

We have insisted on the glorious privilege and duty of all men becoming saints, of immediately being made perfect in love, and of gradually ripening into Christian maturity in all faculties. This doctrine was never more definitely stated, clearly perceived, nor consistently lived by greater numbers than now.

The New York *Christian Advocate* continued to give prominence to articles on perfection by Daniel Steele and to print extended biographies of such holiness champions as Nathan Bangs and Bishop Hamline. The editor hoped for the day when "holiness [would] dominate the church" and reported in August, 1898, the spread of a "holiness revival in China." The cause seemed flourishing.

From other quarters, however, came reports not so encouraging. For some time it had been noted that the leaders who championed the holiness cause were passing away and their places were being left vacant. Such bishops as Janes, Simpson, Peck, Foster, and Haven had been quite active in the holiness movement. Their replacements seemed less likely to be. Ocean Grove Camp Meeting was still conducted and apparently well attended. But it, too, was changing. In 1872 the report from Ocean Grove to the *Guide to Holiness* had been, "Multitudes were sanctified wholly and many sinners were born into the Kingdom;" and in 1878, "Nearly six hundred . . . in converting, sanctifying and reclaiming grace." In 1894, however, the report said, "Several persons were at the altar and some were converted." The difference cannot be wholly a matter of reportorial accuracy. The active promotion of perfect love as an experience was in evident decline.

The doctrine was not preached because in the colleges and seminaries it was no longer taught. The abuse of the doctrine by its

178

more intolerant advocates had led to a reaction against any sort of encouragement. It was not, moreover, in keeping with the most recent, and apparently more relevant, trends in theology. In consequence it was either ignored or virtually explained away in courses of systematic theology. As the century drew to its close, Bishop Stephen Merrill reported this fact and noted its result:

Large numbers have come into the pulpits of Methodism with little knowledge of the early struggles of our founders, or of the doctrinal contests through which they passed in reaching the conclusions which have become our inheritance. These young men come with theological opinions molded in schools where Methodist standards are not the text-books, and where there is large desire to keep abreast of the times in modern exegesis and criticism. With commendable zeal they enter the pastorate as Methodist preachers, with slight appreciation of the symbols of our faith and of the peculiarities which distinguish us from the Churches around us.[32]

It was the bishop's opinion that the promotion of such a doctrine as Christian perfection ought not to be left to specialists but that the leaders and pastors of the church should seek to re-establish the doctrine in its rightful place. "The preachers must lead," he said. "Much can be done in our theological schools, and much in our Conferences."

But the re-establishment of the doctrine of Christian perfection was far down the agenda. The trend was in another direction altogether. Theology was in the process of denying its relevance. Scientific humanism was just beginning to assert its omnipotence. A rather naïve liberalism was in vogue, and its limitations were not yet discerned. The traditionalist, who must perforce voice opposition, would for some time seem merely and hopelessly reactionary.

In Methodism the determined advocates of a particular point of view had for the most part departed to more congenial associations. A muted tolerance was the order of the day. And as the members of the General Conference of 1900 looked back upon the century just passed, they were solemnly reminded:

179

That many changes have occurred in the outward forms of Methodism is obvious. Which do they indicate, growth or decay? . . . The strenuous contention for this or that particular doctrine or usage of Methodism, once common, is now rarely heard: is this indifferentism, or is it, in part, a better discernment of that which is vital to the Christian faith, and, in part, the result of an acceptance by others of the once disputed opinion?

Whoever in the presence of such conditions hastens to pronounce judgment on the general question of growth or decay is evidently unequal to the task.[33]

CHAPTER VI

Summary

A. Concerning the Doctrine

THE DOCTRINE of Christian perfection has too ancient and continuing a history to be classified merely as Wesleyan. And John Wesley would be among the first to point this out. He emphatically repudiated any suggestion that it was *his* doctrine. He recognized it as implicit in the promises of the Gospels, the assumptions of the Pauline letters, and the exhortations of the Johannine writings. In such recognition he but reflected an insight common to much of the devotional literature—though not to the representative preaching —of his day. Long before Wesley, Law, or Taylor, however, the Greek Fathers, especially Irenaeus and Clement of Alexandria, had presented the doctrine in extended exposition. Even before them the Christian Church bore witness that this teaching was within its recognized tradition. Said R. N. Flew:

> The doctrine of Christian perfection—understood not as an assertion that a final attainment of the goal of the Christian life is possible in this world, but as a declaration that a supernatural destiny, a relative attainment of the goal which does not exclude growth, is the will of God for us in this world and is attainable—lies not merely upon the by-paths of Christian theology, but upon the high road.[1]

181

It is true that at times the doctrine found what seemed only a precarious place among issues more pressing or clamant. But always, somehow, the church was never without its witness to the possibility through grace of the attainment of an elevated and dynamic piety. Even in its hours of near apostasy this ideal would not down. It rose up to reprove and inspire. It was part of the church's charter and commission—rebuking moral lassitude and tormenting its prodigal sons with a high homesickness. The doctrine of Christian perfection has been the church's "holy grail" from its earliest days.

Wesley's distinctive contribution issued from the fact that he considered the doctrine as a practical way of life available to and necessary for every regenerate Christian. The idea of perfection as an esoteric privilege available only to an endowed few was repugnant to him. Moreover, there was little of the speculative in his presentation of the doctrine. Recognizing its claims, he began an intensive search, seeking to recover in his own soul the "image of God," never quite able—or willing—to profess its attainment. Meanwhile he undertook to provide a medium by which others might be assisted in a similar search and through which holiness might find methodical and social expression. His societies arose as a consequence of this purpose.

Wesley's formulation of the doctrine did not leap, Minervalike, full grown from the mind of its builder. Instead it grew slowly, like a cathedral whose architect tries many materials before he finally brings his structure to completion. Wesley had early seen his goal— "simplicity of intention and purity of affection"—and that he never changed. But for a number of years the approaches he pursued proved in whole or in part unsatisfactory. In his heart-warming experience at Aldersgate he felt he had found the key. Sanctification, like justification, was to be won "by faith." This he taught, at first uncertainly, finally with assurance.

The element that provided this assurance was the testimony of "living witnesses" who, beginning around 1744, reported that they had attained what he had been tentatively preaching. In the revival of 1759-63 Wesley saw a confirmation of that work which he had glimpsed in individual Moravians twenty years before. From that time on his doctrine was a completed system, somewhat mellowed with the passing of time but never changed in basic structure. The "old Methodist doctrine," the "proper Methodist testimony," became the declaration that Christian perfection might be entered into by a work of divine grace called "entire sanctification" and available "now and by simple faith." Wesley held that to fail to emphasize this possibility of the immediate reception of such an experience was effectively to cut the nerve of any real expectation of it. To delete the instantaneous was to cancel the gradual as well.

Though Wesley never afterward changed the form of his doctrine, there were times when he seemed ready to abandon it. Such a reaction followed a period of its fanatical promotion. Like a medical researcher who sees his carefully compounded formula used by awkward and careless practitioners with disastrous results, Wesley observed the debacle wrought by perfection in the hands of Thomas Maxfield and George Bell. Sick at heart, he momentarily considered letting it quietly drop. But he found he could not. Even when he writes out of the depths of an unfathomable depression to his brother Charles, he ends his letter by saying:

O insist everywhere on *full* redemption, receivable by *faith alone!* Consequently to be looked for *now.* You are *made,* as it were, for this very thing. . . . Press the *instantaneous* blessing: then I shall have more time for my peculiar calling, enforcing the *gradual* work.[2]

This gradual element was one of the very basic stones in the doctrinal structure he was erecting. Here the high morality of the Greek Fathers and the practical discipline of the English mystics were incorporated. The key that opened the door was faith, and heights otherwise remote were gained by its power. The upreaching, day-by-day path, however, was marked by discipline—works of faith and acts of love, attendance on the means of grace, attendance to the needs of men. Wesley's idea of holiness was a concept deeply rooted and widely spread. Personal salvation was focal, but in the last analysis he knew no holiness but "social holiness."

Actually to understand Wesley's doctrine, it is necessary to see the individual recipient of the grace of God in his inescapable relationship to the spiritual community through which that grace was mediated. For Wesley was a churchman. The sacramental nurture of the Church of England was as normal and necessary to him as were food and drink. It was as a churchman that he turned back from following after the Moravians, appalled by what he considered their quietism. Aldersgate had not affected that basic attitude. With growing certainty he felt that to follow any guide who slighted any of the means of grace was to court religious disaster. His lifetime opposition to any tendency within his own societies toward separation from the church is, of course, well-known. On his deathbed his words were few, but they included these:

We must be justified by faith, and then go on to sanctification. . . . We thank thee, O Lord, for these and all thy mercies: bless the Church and King; and grant us truth and peace, through Jesus Christ our Lord, for ever and ever!

Here was an insistence on justification, an exhortation to sanctification, and an Anglican "prayer for the Church." For to the end this evangelical preacher of holiness was also a priest of the church. This was the environment in which the doctrine was formulated. That was the milieu in which it was to be lived out.

Thus the doctrine must be seen, not as a self-sufficient entity, but as an integral part of the whole system of faith and nurture which characterizes the church at its best. It was a part, and a valued part, of that doctrinal cluster by which the church nourishes the widely varying needs of its communicants. When it was neglected, the result was atrophy; when it was lifted out of its regulative setting, the result was distortion.

It is true that Wesley does not stress this particular aspect of the doctrine in such an exposition as the *Plain Account*. He saw no reason to. He was addressing his remarks to those who, if they did not entirely share his views, were amply familiar with them. His societies were not intended to be substitutes for, nor even supplements to, but vital cells *of* the church. They were to be active and organic agents in helping to answer its petition when it prayed:

"O gracious Father, we humbly beseech thee for thy holy Catholic Church. . . . Where in any thing it is amiss, reform it."

Not all of his followers, as a matter of fact, *did* share such views. In 1762 Thomas Maxfield's ties were thin; for when he left Wesley, he also left the church. And George Bell had reached the point where, he said, he needed no further attendance on any means of grace beyond his own ecstatic unit. It was in the hands of these two that Christian perfection became "dangerous delusion."

But within the sacramentarian framework Wesley cherished intense personal devotion and ardent application to the pursuit of holiness. There was a tremendous immediacy about his doctrine, the search for and assurance of an exalted personal relationship. There was the never-blunted concept of crisis—the enforcement of the idea that the crucifixion of self is no casual affair, that mortification is more than a term, and that purification is at last not without its inner testimony. There is a substantial measure of mystical theology in Wesley; and though it brought him ridicule and misunderstanding, he never played it down.

Finally, Wesley's doctrine was a doctrine of grace. It recognized that depravity, however dark, and evil circumstance, however real, do not necessarily consign man to hopeless defeat. Realistic as Wesley was in his estimate of the nature of man, he nevertheless refused the arbitrary dictum that the grace of God can go only so far and no further in its redemptive efficacy. With Wesley the vision of God was not an invitation to despair but a "call unto holiness," and "God does not command the impossible." His doctrinal goal, therefore, was something other than the seventh chapter of Romans.

It was in the area of practical methodology that Wesley's doctrine met its most serious difficulty. He had proposed that Christian perfection could be realized through the process of sanctification. This process was usually marked by a crisis called entire sanctification which was, at least logically, instantaneous in its apperception and to be received by faith. Generally, if not always, such an experience was to be both preceded and followed by a gradual work of nurture and guidance. The long-term nurture of the

185

church and the constant regulative oversight of devotional cells were presupposed. However, such safeguards came to be freely ignored during the period when holiness received its most intense promotion. During the revival years of 1759-63 ecstatic experience was often considered even by Wesley the all-sufficient and self-validating testimony to the attainment of perfection. Emotional states came to be more valued criteria than ethical behavior. And though Wesley belatedly attempted to clarify and strengthen the regulative discipline of his bands, he found the task well beyond him. His select societies were rife with Pharisaism. Throughout his spiritual domain the wheat fields were thick-sown with tares. Discipline surrendered to delusion. The reaction which followed was well-nigh sufficient to "drive perfection out of the kingdom."

Nevertheless, though tempted, Wesley abandoned neither the doctrine nor its typical method of promotion. He did qualify his methodology, freely granting the efficacy of variations from it. But he did not give it up. There were, he was certain, too many who had by it found a new resource, a new level of sanctity and power. He would not abandon the method by which that host had come into an "established habit of goodness." Wesley therefore continued to urge that entire sanctification be sought for "now and by simple faith," hesitant to stress qualifications in the face of belligerent reaction. He was convinced that the "work of God does not prosper where perfection is not preached."

The really critical feature in Wesley's formulation of the doctrine is his teaching that holiness or perfection may be actually and consciously attained. In considering this feature, two possible alternatives have to be faced. If the answer is Yes, immediately Pharisaism threatens. Can it be escaped? If, on the other hand, the answer is No, moral complacency tends to take over. Can aspiration after a never-to-be-realized goal be long sustained? In other words, what can save the teaching from spiritual pride on the one hand or from acquiescence in spiritual mediocrity on the other? These are the Scylla and Charybdis of the doctrine of Christian perfection.

Spiritual shipwreck has occurred at both these points. There have been those whose profession of attainment was so redolent with self-righteousness as to be insufferable. They have manifested a pseudo sanctity, harsh and censorious, bearing little if any resemblance to that true piety which is always gentle and winsome. On the other hand, where attainability has been categorically denied, the tendency has been to accept some compromised ideal as the goal itself. For the denial of the attainability of an enjoined moral ideal leads inevitably to the practical repudiation of that ideal. If realism determines that only compromise is possible, then compromise becomes the goal. It is sought for, acceded to, enshrined. Acquiescence displaces aspiration.

There were in Wesley's doctrine, however, provisions for escape from the horns of this dilemma, provisions that have been generally ignored. Wesley insisted, for instance, that any attainment must recognize its wholly relative character. There was no "perfection of degrees." Even the attainment of perfect love left broad areas of personal excellence still unrealized. There was an infinite distance between any possible attainment here and now and that "full conformity to the perfect law" which stands as the absolute ideal of the child of God. As over against what remained to be won, present attainment was calculated to prompt penitence rather than pride. Any present perfection was always imperfect; and none there were who did not need to say, "Forgive us our trespasses."

Attainment, moreover, was never to be considered a personal achievement. Perfect love came not by accomplishment but by reception. Even when considered as maturity—the ripening of Christian character, the full ordering of Christian virtues—it was wrought by a God-given faith, made effectual by God-tendered grace. There was nowhere place for pride of personal achievement. The whole process from first to last was the work of the Holy Spirit. It was the Spirit who convicted, who pointed out areas of deeper need, and who—in response to consecration and faith— provided the dynamic to meet those needs. Moreover, this life of the Spirit was maintained on a moment-by-moment basis. Wesley had insisted: "We feel the power of Christ every moment resting upon us, whereby alone we are what we are . . . , and without which, notwithstanding all our present holiness, we should be devils the next moment." [3] In such a relationship spiritual pride was as unseemly as any "voluntary transgression of a known law of God." It was, in fact, more deeply sinful.

As attainment was not to be considered personally achieved, neither was the judgment concerning it to be personally determined. In Wesley's teaching there was "no holiness but social holiness." Only the devotional cell, the church society, was qualified to evaluate the sanctity of any of its members. In these class meetings and select societies there were to be operative those spiritual influences which should both encourage and regulate the aspirations and attainments of the individual members. Personal assurance was to be thus fortified against mere eccentricity. The witness of the Spirit was clarified as it was mediated through the regulative community. Wesley was also deeply concerned to restore the "neglected disciplines" and the full sacramental nurture of the church. This was the climate in which Christian perfection might come to undistorted fruition. This was the climate which he hoped might pervade his newly planted societies in America.

B. Concerning the Development of the Doctrine in American Methodism

During the early years of the establishment of American Methodism, especially in the New England sector, the doctrinal emphasis was almost entirely on universal redemption, Methodism's aggressive contradistinction to the long-defended particular redemption. Consequently Christian perfection followed somewhat afar off. But in the Virginias under the congenial Anglicanism of such a rector as Devereux Jarratt perfect love flourished in healthy fashion. And when the new Methodist Episcopal Church went its way in 1784, Christian perfection was not only an officially accepted doctrine but a recurrent theme in the messages of its major representatives.

As circuits pushed into the unchurched and generally irreligious frontier, the doctrine went into an abeyance that soon amounted to neglect. For Christian perfection, as Wesley had presented it, called for a sacramental setting unknown and alien to the American frontier—a fact to which Wesley seemed completely oblivious. The teaching of perfection in love had been in general nurtured by select societies—specialized groups operative within the general Methodist organization, itself a society within the Anglican Church. The promotion of perfection was a task which called for sensitivity, devotion, and spiritual insight. On the American frontier such traits fought a losing battle. Primitive demands had to be met with primitive methods. Life inevitably tended to coarsen. Restraint and sensitivity were early casualties in the battle against a stubborn wilderness environment. Danger and toil sharpened basic instincts but provided little opportunity for the cultivation of quiet saintliness. The promulgation of Christian perfection faced very real and often insurmountable difficulties. Its neglect followed.

In the 1840's, however, the doctrine was revived. Active among its protagonists were Charles G. Finney and Asa Mahan, whose affiliations and theology were in general Presbyterian-Congregational. In their presentation of Christian perfection the concept of divine intervention tended to predominate. The instantaneous virtually eclipsed the gradual. The prominence of Finney and Mahan and their outspoken advocacy tended to stamp the doctrine with their particular interpretation even in Methodistic circles. In those circles the revival of Christian perfection was undertaken by special groups who met to do what the church was apparently failing to do—encourage aspiration after the "higher life." In many ways their purposes were identical with those undertaken by Wesley. But as the movement developed, certain charactertistics became apparent which distinguished their treatment of the doctrine of Christian perfection from Wesley's more mature views.

That doctrine, as it was promoted in most of the special meetings and associations from 1850 until the end of the century, was essentially the unqualified Wesleyanism of 1760-62. Under the sponsorship of Phoebe Palmer, who felt that most of her views concerning its special promotion had been given her directly from God, this particular presentation of the doctrine tended to become the orthodox view. In its emphasis upon entire sanctification as attainable "now and by simple faith," it was unmistakably Wesleyan. But there were omissions and variations which set it apart.

Wesley, for instance, had come to a fairly general tolerance of method. The holiness movement, on the other hand, maintained a strict and unvarying methodology. And opponents of the method were apt to be considered opponents of the doctrine. Wesley had encouraged testimony only when the time, place, and motive were propitious. In the later emphasis testimony was pronounced a duty, to be given however adverse the reaction. And where Wesley had conceived the doctrine as part of the broad, general nurture of the church with a gradual work always preceding and following entire sanctification, it was now being presented as almost wholly comprehended in the specific experience, any prior or subsequent nurture being merely incidental—sometimes irrelevant. There were other differences, but these were most significant.

What brought about such a movement, and why were some of the emphases so extreme? The movement as an organized effort arose as a result of the low spiritual tone generally characteristic of organized religion following the Civil War. It is sometimes assumed that the movement was primarily an expression of an economically and culturally submerged group finding in the high promises of religion compensation for their poverty in other areas. It may be possible to illustrate this thesis by examples from later periods. But the post–Civil War revival of holiness cannot be so explained. Economic and sociological factors undoubtedly played a part. But the more basic motivation for those who were active in the holiness movement within the Methodist Church must be sought for in the realm of theological and psychological predisposition.

In this latter area it has been evident that outstanding holiness advocates have tended to be persons who were impatient of restraint, who considered the unhampered pursuit of the "glorious vision" not simply a right but a duty. They were "men of the warm heart," and they frequently found themselves at odds with their brethren who placed greater importance upon order, discipline, and institution. Even John Wesley, methodical and authoritarian, had enough of his mother's fiery dissent sorely to disturb the episcopal

190

matrix which he cherished but against which he from time to time rebelled.

The holiness advocates of the nineteenth and twentieth centuries were not, however, irresponsible schismatics. Until schism actually threatened, the movement numbered among its leaders and supporters some of Methodism's most prominent figures. Bishops, representative ministers, educators, and prominent professional people were active in its ranks. They were united in their high regard for tradition and in their feeling that Methodist piety was being threatened by new and dangerous tendencies. In working together they sought two things: first, to revive a neglected doctrine; and second, to check a threatening "modernism."

They tended to give greatest stress to that doctrinal area which, they felt, had received greatest neglect. Hence entire sanctification came to receive almost exclusive attention. The result was their own neglect of the equally important features of Christian nurture and growth in grace. Many factors contributed to this one-sided presentation: precedents from Wesley's own developing thought, frontier attitudes, revivalistic promotion, Calvinistic advocacy, sectarian emphases—all united to interpret sanctification in terms of the instantaneous as over against the gradual.

To determine the basic responsibility for these extremes, it is necessary to decide whether it was the general neglect of the doctrine by the church or the exclusive preoccupation with it by the specialists. And the facts sustain the conclusion that the first was to the second as cause is to effect. The church's failure to give witness to this high aspect of its gospel, to encourage this unlimited aspiration in its worship, was the primary reason for the one-sided advocacy of the doctrine by the associations. If that advocacy was partial, it was because it was out of its rightful sacramental context. And in far too many instances that context was closed to its expression.

On the other hand, many of the advocates of holiness were its poorest recommendation. Amid the host of sincere and committed seekers after perfect love there were that blatant number who mistook censoriousness for sanctity, denunciation for devotion, and high profession for holy practice. Too often, goaded by their detractors, they proceeded to prove the validity of the charges made against them.

While one sector of the church was intent upon a revival of the traditional emphasis, another sector was restive under that tradition. It welcomed instead the sweep of nineteenth-century theological optimism. Between a confident humanitarian morality and a traditional piety which appeared unconcerned with the society of which it was a part, the sympathies of this sector of the church were with the former. Thus two groups with antithetical points of view were mutually repelled by the extremes each saw in the other. The result in some instances was the rise of "come-outism" and "crush-outism." Reaction provoked reaction, and extreme begot extreme.

In the doctrinal controversy that arose out of these varying stresses and emphases, the really determinative opposition to the traditional doctrine was not actually manifest. Its representatives were engaged in establishing new bases of interpretation and were not interested in debating conclusions whose very premises they questioned. Borden P. Bowne, for instance, tended to ignore the whole issue. Wesley's doctrine could scarcely interest one who declared: "Sin itself, as we find it among men, is largely the willfulness of freedom which has not learned self-control." [4]

Those who did take up the cudgels generally argued for the doctrinal identity of regeneration and sanctification. Their views received wide acceptance. It must be admitted, however, that a great part of the war of words was fought between individuals whose views, calmly considered, were not basically incompatible.

Sensing this, a demand arose for peace. Such peace was possible only if each side was willing to make certain concessions. Such concessions were proposed. On the one hand, entire sanctification should be accepted as a distinctive doctrine and as a possible experience. On the other hand, stress on the instantaneous should be muted. For one group the concession, being primarily theoretical, was not too difficult. For the other group the concession, being basically experiential, was well-nigh impossible. The result was a withdrawal from the church and the organization of various sects. [5]

Thus as the century drew to its close, the doctrine of Christian perfection was presented in differing fashion by two Methodistic groups, both claiming Wesleyan authority for their positions. In the sects it was an abbreviated Wesleyanism—in many respects characteristic of his unmodified 1760 views, stressing his instantaneous teaching and neglecting in large part his emphasis on the gradual. In the church it was an uncertain Wesleyanism—in many respects characteristic of his 1745 views, mildly hopeful of the efficacy of a gradual approach but ignoring for the most part his emphasis on the instantaneous.

CHAPTER VII

Conclusions

DURING THE FIRST HALF of the twentieth century the fortunes of the doctrine of Christian perfection in Methodism have not changed greatly from the pattern established in the closing decade of the previous century. It has continued to be a waning emphasis. But among certain of the smaller religious bodies, most of them Methodist in derivation, it has remained a crowning doctrine. During the first three decades of the century revival meetings stressing "holiness of heart and life" swept recurrently across the nation. For the most part they were attended with a substantial measure of success, and the churches under whose auspices they were conducted became for a time some of the fastest growing religious communities on the American scene.

As these bodies developed their institutions and strengthened their order and polity, however, this emphasis became less prominent. The *sect* with its particular concern became the *church* with its general responsibilities. Even so, holiness conventions are still held, and entire sanctification is still preached as a doctrine and sought as an experience. It is nevertheless true that even in those churches dedicated to its promulgation this once-distinctive characteristic has become diffused if not in fact subdued.

Currently, perhaps, this deliberate cultivation of the "life of the Spirit" is most apparent in groups which are generally related to but not always part of the organized church. In prayer groups, research groups, "Camps Farthest Out," Ashrams, and various other fellowships the disciplined search for a "higher level of spiritual life" is being carried on. Results vary widely, but the very existence and multiplicity of these groups testify to the spiritual hunger of the modern heart for something more than traditional pulpit fare.

The most startling ecclesiastical phenomenon in this century thus far has been the remarkable growth of Pentecostal, Assemblies of God, and "Latter Rain" churches. With a vitality and insouciance difficult for their older brethren to comprehend, these groups have moved across the continent, appealing primarily to the humble but manifesting an increasing attraction also to his more sophisticated neighbor. Their growth has been repeatedly analyzed and their popularity usually ascribed to sociological factors. It may be possible, however, that their emphasis on some of the neglected doctrines of holiness, even with overtones of speaking in tongues, has gained for them the extraordinary reception they have received.

In the Methodist Church candidates for ordination are still asked the Wesleyan question "Are you going on to perfection?" and occasionally a Bishop John Hamilton will add, "If not, where *are* you going?" The question is usually answered in the affirmative. Moreover, at the General Conference of 1952 the bishops pointed out to the delegates of the now-united church:

We believe in Christian perfection. God's grace is manifested not only in the forgiveness of our sins but is also creatively redemptive, the power that works in us to make us perfect in love. Nothing short of perfection, Christlikeness in thought, word, and deed, can measure God's loving purpose for us. It is our faith that the fundamental change wrought in the individual by regeneration is a dynamic process which by growth in grace moves toward "mature manhood, to the measure of the stature of the fullness of Christ." We may quench the Spirit and fall from grace but our divine destiny is perfect love and holiness in this life.

In all candor, however, it can scarcely be maintained that in the teaching and preaching of the Church the doctrine holds today, anything like the significant place given it by Wesley or by the delegates to the Christmas Conference of 1784.

Yet Christian perfection can scarcely be discussed without relating it to Methodism. John Wesley described it as the "grand depositum which God has lodged with the people called Methodist." Abel Stevens reports it as the "great potential idea of Methodism." Philip Schaff calls it Methodism's "last and crowning doctrine." And Frederic Platt identifies it as "pre-eminently the distinctive doctrine" of Methodism.[1] Among the most representative and saintly leaders of that church are those who have not hesitated to affirm their attainment of its promises.

As Nolan B. Harmon in his *Understanding the Methodist Church* has said:

The doctrine of Christian perfection has been the one specific doctrinal contribution which Methodism has made to the Church universal. John Wesley called it, the "peculiar doctrine committed to our trust." In all else we have been, as we should be, glad and energetic followers in the main stream of Christian belief. But in this one doctrine we stand by ourselves and utter a teaching that reaches up fearlessly and touches the very Scepter of God.

If, therefore, in the history of Methodism abuses have marked periods of its promotion, if neglect has spawned mutation, if the doctrine has been forced into narrow and unvarying methodology, if unwise preoccupation with experience has brought about neglect of nurture—it would appear that the answer should be not abandonment but re-examination and wise restoration. For Wesley considered that this doctrine was Methodism's principal *raison d'être*—"and for the sake of propagating this chiefly He appeared to have raised us up." [2] To that end Wesley had labored to establish a workable synthesis of faith and nurture. That synthesis, not always strongly ordered, has been often distorted as its separate elements have received undue stress or unwarranted neglect. It nevertheless remains a heritage from which the Church may deeply profit. So reasons also Bishop Paul B. Kern, who says:

196

Modern Methodism has sense enough, has spiritual insight sufficient to rescue this New Testament doctrine of holiness from the hands of its cynical despoilers and set it forth once more as the precious experience of humble saints who love the Lord with all their minds and hearts. We need a new and modern interpretation and proclamation of the redeemability of these human natures of ours from all sin, and the possibility of attainment, through His grace and sustaining strength, of Christian perfection. The cynicism that scorns the doctrine tragically reveals the desperate need of the truth it so casually rejects.[3]

Doubtless there are many who would argue contrariwise. Why, they might well ask, should we again concern ourselves with a doctrine whose history has been so marked with controversy? The fact is, however, that the controversy itself is but one evidence that there is something in the doctrine that will not leave the Church undisturbed. There is an ideal embodied in the teaching by which spiritual complacency is constantly discomposed. By it the Church is reminded of that quality of righteousness, the hunger for which is her badge of identity. "If we have no hunger and thirst after that righteousness which is Christ," says W. R. Inge, "we are not Christians . . . at all." To quiet Wesley is not to hush the call to perfection. Thus Bishop Kern can say:

> In ridding ourselves of this Methodistic emphasis we are embarrassed by the New Testament. . . . The fact is the world needs a more absolute type of Christianity. The lukewarm mediumness that characterizes much of our church life simply does not possess the power of spiritual transformation which characterized New Testament Christianity.[4]

This is an indictment not to be ignored. It points to a serious weakness in a critical hour.

The truth is that in no period of its history have greater demands been laid upon the Church. And its adequacy to meet those demands is seriously and generally questioned. Anglican Bishop S. C. Neill, discussing "The Church's Failure to Be Christian" before the Amsterdam Assembly of the World Council of Churches, declared:

Most educated men in the world to-day have some knowledge of the Gospels, and some mental picture of the character of Jesus. They realize, perhaps better than many professing Christians, that the only true criterion of Christianity is likeness to Christ. The heart of their complaint, though perhaps they would be hard put to it to frame it in words, is that they do not see in Christianity and in the Church that likeness to Christ which they have a right to expect. Real holiness is impressive and attractive; if the Church has failed to hold the respect of the ordinary man, may the cause not be, in part at least, that the children of the Church have failed to set before the world the challenge of unmistakable holiness after the manner of Christ? [5]

It is currently demanded of the Church that it give living expression to its professed ideals. Its critics are not impressed by numbers, nor satisfied with an indifferent morality. They ask to see in its life as well as in its creeds the "beauty of holiness." They look for that "city of God" whose members are sensitive both to the high resources of religion and to the deep needs of men.

The Church must seek therefore to recover, or discover, the spiritual dynamic which may arm it for its task. It has truly lived only when the transforming power of the Spirit has been manifest in its ongoing order. One of its major tasks, therefore, is to be certain that such power is operative. It is better to be challenged with the problems of vitality than to be complacent with uncomplicated impotence. To turn from an exalted search because that search has been beset with problems is to buy peace at too high a price. It must be, then, a serious charge against any system of religious discipline wherein a spiritual dynamic is refused encouragement merely because its regulation may be difficult.

Protestantism, particularly, needs to reconsider its treatment of a doctrine long recognized and presently alive in Catholic tradition. The encyclical of Pope Pius XI written for the third centenary of Francis of Sales had this to say:

Christ constituted the Church holy and the source of holiness, and all those who take her for guide and teacher must, according to the divine will, aim at holiness of life: "This is the will of God," says St.

Paul, "your sanctification." What type of sanctity is meant? Our Lord himself explains it in the following manner: "Be ye perfect as your heavenly Father is perfect." Let no one think that this invitation is addressed to a small, very select number and that all others are permitted to remain in a lower degree of virtue. As is evident, this law obliges absolutely everybody without exception. Moreover, all who reach the summit of Christian perfection, and their name is legion, of every age and class, according to the testimony of history, have experienced the same weaknesses of nature and have known the same dangers. St. Augustine puts the matter clearly when he says: "God does not command the impossible, but in giving the commandment, He admonishes us to accomplish what we can according to our strength, and to ask aid to accomplish whatever exceeds our strength." [6]

In keeping with this interpretation Réginald Garrigou-Lagrange writes, "Perfection is an end toward which all must tend, each according to his condition," and "assuredly actual graces are progressively offered to us proportionate to the end to be attained, for God does not command the impossible. He loves us more than we think." [7] "Who," asks H. R. Buckler, "can set a limit to the work of sanctification which the Holy Ghost has begun in us?" [8]

Yet Protestant thought has frequently tended to deny such a work altogether. Any congruity of human nature with divine grace is often and arbitrarily denied. The two are held to be not only different but wholly different. Granted such a premise, any real doctrine of perfection must of course be rejected. But the result is a theology whose emphases lie somewhere between moral indifferentism and heroic despair.

The Wesleyan formulation of the doctrine of Christian perfection has something to say at such a juncture. It is the answer, or rather the saving supplement, to the Barthian disparagement of man. With Barth it affirms man's radical evil; against Barth it denies man's utter discontinuity with the Spirit of God. The truth in the modern criticism of humanism, which Wesley preserves, is that man is but the *instrument* of the divine grace—a consciously voluntary instrument. He finds his fulfillment not in self-abasement, nor in self-exaltation, but in self-surrender. His piety is not and cannot be egocentric; it is and can only be theocentric. Thus any attempt to impose arbitrary limits approaches impiety. For if it is presumptuous to profess the attainment of perfect love as one's own achievement, it is no less presumptuous to deny that the grace of God can bring the surrendered soul into perfect integration. Who can say what the grace of God can do? Who dares say what it cannot do?

It may be discovered that at this exalted level Protestant and Catholic enjoy a highest common denominator. If so, let it be explored and shared gladly. It may also be discovered that in this search for perfection there is a shared aspiration with the deeply pious of other faiths.

Perhaps in this difficult but inescapable doctrine of the Spirit lies an approach to unity more significant than those frequently proposed. In the face of a spreading and militant atheism surely some common meeting ground for believers must be sought. Why should we not then seek the highest? Perhaps we may find, after all, that as men sincerely draw nigh to God, they draw nigh also to each other.

Appendixes

A
John Wesley: The Problem of His Testimony to Entire Sanctification

IN DISCUSSING CHRISTIAN PERFECTION, W. B. Pope says, "It is the privilege of the covenant, and not the avowal of it, with which we are here concerned." In any doctrinal study this is, of course, a proper discrimination. And yet there are those who are interested, not unreasonably, to know whether or not John Wesley ever gave explicit testimony to the experience he so earnestly preached. To determine the answer has already been called an insoluble problem, But if the data are indeterminative, they are not irrelevant.

By his own testimony Wesley was in active search of this goal of Christian perfection as early as 1725. He says that it was as he read à Kempis' *Christian Pattern* that he saw

that "simplicity of intention and purity of affection," . . . are indeed "the wings of the soul," without which she can never ascend the mount of God.

And said Wesley, "I sought after it from that hour." His unsuccessful search has been described. He really did expect, however, that at Aldersgate he had won by faith the goal he sought. For Peter Böhler, Wesley had said shortly before, "amazed me more and more by the account he gave of the fruits of living faith— the holiness and happiness which he affirmed to attend it." And a heart-warming experience such as his is usually interpreted in the terms according to which it is expected.

Was Aldersgate *really* Wesley's second blessing? Augustin Léger had called his decision of 1725 *"la première* conversion." Did he mean Aldersgate to be considered the *"second* conversion," as such an experience was and is called? Others have referred to the Aldersgate experience as Wesley's "Pentecost," though it is not clear in just what sense it was meant.

The point at issue, however, is what Wesley himself considered it to be. He did avow five months later that sin no longer had dominion over him as a result of the May 24th, 1738, experience. But he was at the same time seeking for something more, which he described in Moravian terms as the "witness of the Spirit" and which brought "deliverance . . . from every outward and inward sin." His period of depression in 1739-40 has been briefly examined—a period which Wesley came to designate as "desertion," God's testing of the soul by apparent withdrawal. And when in 1742 he wrote his "Character of a Methodist," he placed upon the title page the words "Not as though I had already attained." This action is often cited as though it closed the issue on this entire question. Actually, as Wesley pointed out, this tract was intended to be an "ideal" picture to which he hoped some day the Methodists might attain. It was patterned upon Clement of Alexandria's ideal description and contained claims as extreme as some Wesley later was to repudiate. At any rate it comes from a far too early period to be *ipso facto* proof of Wesley's finished testimony. The general tenor of Wesley's remarks during the period following Aldersgate indicates, however, that as far as his own judgment was concerned, he had not attained the "great salvation."

An interesting account to the contrary appeared in the May 19, 1938, issue of the New York *Christian Advocate.* There Wesley is (presumably) quoted as having said that after his conversion he saw that salvation was not complete without holiness, whereupon he (allegedly) said:

I mourned day and night in agony to be thoroughly sanctified. On "the twenty-third day after" my justification, I found a total change, together with a clear witness that the blood of Jesus cleanses from all unrighteousness. A pleasing thought passed through my mind, that I was saved from the remains of all sin. As yet I have felt no return thereof.

This is indeed an unequivocal testimony. Unfortunately the author cites no sources. Certainly Wesley's journal entry for June 16, 1738—which would have been the "twenty-third day after"— gives no indication of such experience. On the other hand, there is the journal entry of June 23, 1761, in which Wesley says:

After meeting the society I talked with a sensible woman, whose experience seemed peculiar. She said: "A few days before Easter last I was deeply convinced of sin; and in Easter week I knew my sins were forgiven. . . . But in about eighteen days I was convinced, in a dream, of the necessity of a higher salvation; and *I mourned day and night, in agony . . . to be thoroughly sanctified, till, on the twenty-third day after my justification, I found a total change, together with a clear witness that the blood of Jesus had cleansed me from all unrighteousness."* [1]

Wesley adds no comment. The similarity between this entry and the above article is too striking for mere coincidence. The latter sentences of the article beginning with "A pleasing thought passed through my mind" can be found in that exact form in Francis Asbury's journal entry of August 6, 1786. The article, therefore, can hardly be accepted as proving anything regarding Wesley's own testimony.

In a considerably earlier edition of that same *Christian Advocate*, Nathan Bangs had argued that Wesley had testified to instantaneous sanctification as having taken place in his own experience around 1740-42. Bangs reaches that conclusion from a letter which Wesley wrote to Thomas Maxfield in 1762, which he quotes as follows: "I have known and taught it [instantaneous sanctification] above these twenty years." This, said Bangs, is a "plain and direct" testimony to it. It is, of course, no such thing.

Maxfield's group had been asserting that they had "discovered" the idea that sanctification may be achieved by faith. Wesley is assuring them in explicit terms that they had not.

In 1744, however, Wesley does enjoy a remarkable period of spiritual uplift which he records as follows:

> In the evening, while I was reading prayers at Snowsfields, I found such light and strength as I never remember to have had before. I saw every thought, as well as action or words, just as it was rising in my heart; and whether it was right before God, or tainted with pride or selfishness. I never knew before (I mean not as at this time) what it was "to be still before God."
>
> I waked, by the grace of God, in the same spirit; and about eight, being with two or three that believed in Jesus, I felt such an awe and tender sense of the presence of God as greatly confirmed me therein: so that God was before me all the day long. I sought and found Him in every place; and could truly say, when I lay down at night, "Now I have *lived* a day." [2]

This for some (for example, Olin A. Curtis) indicates that Wesley did, in fact, enter into the "great salvation"; for others (Sugden, Bett, Flew, McConnell, Lindström) the inference is less obvious.

If this *was* such an experience for Wesley, there is no record that he testified to it as such. This may have been due, of course, to a reluctance at making himself an even greater target for the ridicule and misunderstanding that already was directed at him. Thus when in a discussion concerning Christian perfection he was asked, "Can you show one such example now?" Wesley replied:

> If I knew one here, I would not tell you; for you do not inquire out of love. . . . You are like Herod; you seek only the young child to slay it. . . . There are many reasons why there should be few, if any, indisputable examples. What inconveniences this would bring on the person himself, set as a mark for all to shoot at.[3]

It may be argued, then, that for such reasons he fails to testify to what he had nevertheless experienced.

But in 1748 he wrote a letter in which he said:

I no more imagine that I have already attained, that I love God with all my heart, soul, and strength, than that I am in the third heavens.[4]

This is not mere reluctance to testify; this is overt disavowal. It may be concluded that for himself Wesley did not consider that his blessing of 1744 was his attainment.

In January of 1749, however, Wesley spent twenty days answering what he considered to be an attack upon the Fathers by Conyers Middleton of Trinity College, Cambridge. In that lengthy answer Wesley makes his most decisive commitment on the question of his personal experience. He has been describing what "real, genuine Christianity" is and how through faith it may be realized. Following this he says:

So Christianity tells me; and So I find it, may every real Christian say. I now am assured that these things are so: I experience them in my own breast. What Christianity (considered as a doctrine) promised is accomplished in my soul. And Christianity, considered as an inward principle, is the completion of all those promises. It is holiness and happiness, the image of God impressed on a created spirit, a fountain of peace and love springing up into everlasting life.[5]

This is part of a general and lengthy defense of Wesley's concept of "true religion." Is it his testimony to entire sanctification? The answer would depend, of course, upon individual interpretation.

Wesley's comments upon his own spiritual state are exceedingly rare. But in 1756 he wrote:

In the sermon on Salvation by Faith I say, "He that is born of God sinneth not" . . . "by any sinful desire; for any unholy desire he stifleth in the birth." . . . "Nor doth he sin by infirmities; for his infirmities have no concurrence of his will, and without this they are not properly sins." Taking the words as they lie in connexion thus . . . , I must still aver they speak both my own experience and that of many hundred children of God whom I personally know.[6]

205

This is a high claim, a claim to a life above sin, "properly so called." Yet it was no more than Wesley maintained was characteristic of anyone who is "born of God." It cannot therefore be counted his personal testimony to anything beyond that.

In the *Plain Account,* Wesley explores a point of doctrine in the discussion of which he says, "And the difference is still plainer when I compare my present state with my past, wherein I felt temptation and corruption." [7] Now "corruption" is one of Wesley's favorite expressions for "inbred sin," and not to feel temptation is above his usual portrayal of perfection. But the context indicates that the *I* is used to assist in more graphic portrayal of the truth intended—a sort of editorial "we"—than of any particular personal testimony. Wesley frequently uses *I* in this sense in his sermons and defends such usage as not having personal reference. [8]

As the revival of 1759-63 grew in impetus and scope, Wesley's journal entries and writings reflect his deep interest in and identification with its phenomena. In October of 1762 he writes:

Many years ago my brother frequently said: "Your day of Pentecost is not fully come, but I doubt not it will, and you will then hear of persons sanctified as frequently as you do now of persons justified." Any unprejudiced reader may observe that it was now fully come. [9]

Some have held *this* to be Wesley's testimony to his personal Pentecost. It does not seem likely. In the first place Wesley did not consider, as many of his followers did, that Pentecost was a type of or parallel to entire sanctification. [10] In the second place Wesley goes on to say that it may be judged a Pentecost, not because of anything that has happened to him, but because "we did hear of persons sanctified, in London, . . . and in Dublin."

In the process of the revival a group of the more enthusiastic began to make the most extreme claims regarding the doctrine of Christian perfection and the most bigoted professions regarding themselves. The result was well-nigh disaster to the whole movement. A letter from John to Charles in 1764 not only reflects this situation but includes a statement which in my opinion is Wesley's most significant commentary on what he judged his personal testimony should be. In the letter he says:

The frightful stories wrote from London had made all our preachers in the North afraid even to mutter about perfection. . . . O let you and I hold fast whereunto we have attained, and let our yea be yea and our nay be nay! [11]

The picture in the societies was of extreme profession on the one hand and disavowal by complete silence on the other. Wesley counsels that they do not surrender that which they have attained (and certainly the inference here is that *some* degree of perfect love was attained—Charles would not have been tempted to surrender his justification), but that their claims concerning it shall be made with the most careful frugality—"let our yet be yea and our nay be nay."

Whatever John may have felt himself possessed of, it was not that degree of perfect love for which he was seeking. For a year later he writes discussing Christian perfection and concludes with the words:

Now, whether *you* desire and expect this blessing or not, is it not an astonishing thing that you or any man living should be disgusted at *me* for expecting it?

Not yet is Wesley ready to make a profession of attainment.

In 1767 John wrote to Charles a letter comparable in many ways to the letters from his "desertion" period of 1739-40. It is stronger, however, than anything that came out of that earlier period. To see it in its proper context, a brief account of the circumstances which preceded it will be helpful.

First of all, the revival years had brought their burdens as well as their blessings. At the close of the year 1762 Wesley wrote in his *Journal*:

I now stood and looked back on the past year: a year of uncommon trials and uncommon blessings. . . . Yet I have had more care and trouble in six months than in several years preceding. [13]

The Maxfield-Bell controversy had almost exhausted him. Members of his own societies had accused him of "pulling down perfection," had called him a "hypocrite," and had avowed that "Blind John is not capable of teaching us." A major schism was threatened.

Finally, by dint of much suasion, prayer, and sheer effort the division was largely healed. But in its wake there followed a wave of reaction, doubting the reality and value of a doctrine which would lead into such extremes. These were dark days for him who felt that Christian perfection was the "grand depositum which God has lodged with the people called Methodists."

Moreover, Wesley, busy as ever but now with tasks far from pleasing, found temporary impairment in that seemingly boundless energy of his. In mid-December of 1765 he suffered a serious fall from his horse, which left him "exceedingly sick." Even being "electrified" (one of his favorite treatments) aided him but little. He continued, however, to try to fill his always crowded schedule. And by the following April he is forced to write:

I know not to what it is owing that I have felt more weariness this spring than I had done before for many years; unless to my fall at Christmas, which perhaps weakened the springs of my whole machine more than I was sensible of.[14]

Nevertheless, next month he was in Scotland. And the reports of that tour indicate that Wesley was, as he said, "plowing sand." The following excerpts will explain the phrase:

May 23,—I spoke as plain as I possibly could, but very few appeared to be at all affected. . . .

24.— . . . they were mere stocks and stones—no more concerned than if I had talked Greek. . . .

28.—A few received the truth. . . .

June 1,—A few, I trust, closed with the invitation. . . .

10.—I spoke exceeding plain; yet the hearers did not appear to be any more affected than the stone walls.[15]

These were not the usual responses to sermons that had shaken a nation. The tired warrior was simply not striking fire. And nothing would have been more likely to depress John Wesley than the kind of responses reported above. As though to enforce a physical parallel, on the 24th of June, Wesley's horse flung him into a bog. He was covered with mud but managed after a few hours to find shelter.

Three days later he wrote the following letter to Charles, the portions in brackets being originally in the cryptic writing he and Charles had used since boyhood:

I do not feel the wrath of God abiding on me; nor can I believe it does. And yet (this is the mystery) [I do not love God. I never did]. Therefore [I never] believed in the Christian sense of the word. Therefore [I am only an] honest heathen, a proselyte of the Temple, one of the φοβούμενοι τὸν Θεόν. And yet to be so employed of God! and so hedged in that I can neither get forward nor backward! Surely there never was such an instance before, from the beginning of the world! If I [ever have had] *that faith,* it would not be so strange. But [I never had any] other ἔλεγχος of the eternal or invisible world than [I have] now; and that is [none at all], unless such as fairly shines from reason's glimmering ray. [I have no] direct witness, I do not say that [I am a child of God], but of anything invisible or eternal.

And yet I dare not preach otherwise than I do, either concerning faith, or love, or justification, or perfection. And yet I find rather an increase than a decrease of zeal for the whole work of God and every part of it. I am φερόμενος, I know not how, that I can't stand still. I want all the world to come to ὃν οὐκ οἶδα. Neither am I impelled to this by fear of any kind. I have no more fear than love. Or if I have [any fear, it is not that of falling] into hell but of falling into nothing.[16]

How is this letter to be understood? What criteria led Wesley to decide that he had never loved God? The statement evokes incredulity. It may be possible to look from a distance at Wesley's public career and assign some other motive to the drive that carried him forward. But it is impossible to study his private diaries, read his letters, and examine his *Journal* without coming to the conclusion that few men loved God more devotedly than did John Wesley. Why, then, did he deny it?

It is obvious that the events which led up to the letter were not without their effect upon it. It was a letter written out of physical exhaustion and psychological depression. As Francis J. McConnell says: "The physical resources of one who never rests finally run low. When the tides of bodily strength are out, the mind is like a stretch of barren sand." [17] Moreover, Wesley had been for some years in the midst of a revival marked by strong emotional manifestations. And for the most part he had accepted them as evidences of the power and approval of God. They were bestowed, he thought, in answer to the right degree of believing faith. They were testimonials to the reality of the recipient's love for God. Yet Wesley had not deeply shared these emotional certifications. In a sense he was psychologically incapacitated to share them. His was an ardent temperament, so disciplined as to be well-nigh inhibited—a warm zeal, constantly checked by a cool judgment. And sometimes, sensing this, he was self-deprecatory. A few years earlier he had written in his *Journal*:

> I was . . . not a little refreshed by the conversation of one lately come from London, notwithstanding an irregularity of thought, almost peculiar to herself. How much preferable is her irregular warmth to the cold wisdom of them that despise her! How gladly would I be as she is, taking her wildness and fervour together! [18]

But he could not. And so in these hours of complete exhaustion and deep discouragement he writes this harsh and condemnatory self-analysis. Yet it bespeaks a commitment more significant than would the emotional evidences whose absence wrung it from him.

Whatever the interpretation of this letter, it seems idle to speculate over whether or not Wesley felt he had attained unto Christian perfection—at least in 1766. He gives his own answer to that question in a letter which he wrote several months later to the editor of *Lloyd's Evening Post,* in which he said, "I have told all the world I am not perfect. . . . I have not attained the character I draw." [19]

An account of an incident in Wesley's life during the year 1777 sheds some light on our problem. The account is taken from *The Life and Times of Rev. George Lowe* and relates the following concerning Wesley:

During his . . . short stay at Macclesfield, he held a love-feast, at which Mr. Lowe and many others related their experience. A delightful spirit of lively and fervent devotion was breathed upon the people, and several spoke on the subject of entire sanctification. One of the stewards, who had just been invested with a little "brief authority," perceiving that there was much simplicity and enlargement of heart amongst the brethren, rose up, and addressing himself to Mr. Wesley, said, "Sir, I am persuaded that it would be very gratifying to the friends present to hear *your experience,* and especially *your views of entire sanctification.*" Mr. Wesley instantly stood up, and said, with great solemnity of manner and voice, "By the grace of God I am what I am!" He then sat down; and after a short pause the speaking was resumed, and the meeting closed with a baptism of the Holy Ghost.[20]

The new steward had much to learn, including the fact that Wesley felt no obligation to lay bare his soul in general testimony. He had previously written Mrs. Crosby, who was concerned because some of her friends thought his spirituality might be improved:

Your companions know nothing about it but by those *surmisings* with which God is not well pleased. . . . The wants I feel within are to God and my own soul; and to others, only so far as I *choose to tell them.*[21]

Yet this testimony at Macclesfield, "By the grace of God I am what I am," was neither boast nor evasion. Wesley had emphasized, and doubtless all present were familiar with his teaching, that it is the "power of Christ every moment resting upon us, whereby alone we are what we are." In his testimony Wesley does not profess entire sanctification, nor does he disavow it; he is, as he exhorted Charles, letting his yea be yea and his nay be nay.

There were other instances when point-blank questions regarding his experience were put to Wesley. One of them was related to the Second Ecumenical Methodist Conference (1891) by T. B. Stephenson, delegate to the conference from the Wesleyan Methodist (British) Church. He said:

> I was talking to Dr. Osborn a couple of years ago. You know that he was the last link between the present generation and early Methodism. . . . I said to him one day: "It has often been said that Mr. Wesley, although he wrote a great deal about perfect love, never professed to possess it. What is the fact of that?" He replied: "I was once talking to some old preachers, and they told me this story: 'Some of them were talking to John Wesley, and they ventured—for they were in considerable awe of the old gentleman and did not take liberties with him—to say: "Mr. Wesley, will you tell us what is your own feeling about this, and what are your own experiences?" He paused for a moment, and said: "This is my experience:
>
> > 'Jesus, confirm my heart's desire
> >   To work, and speak, and think for thee;
> > Still let me guard the holy fire,
> >   And still stir up thy gift in me.
> >
> > 'Ready for all thy perfect will,
> >   My acts of faith and love repeat,
> > Till death thy endless mercies seal,
> >   And make the sacrifice complete.' " [22]

Mr. Stephenson felt that this was Wesley's definite testimony to the attainment of perfect love.

In similar fashion Samuel Bradburn reports that Wesley

> told me that his experience might almost, at any time, be expressed in the following lines:
> > "O Thou, who camest from above,
> >   The pure, celestial fire to impart,
> > Kindle a flame of sacred love
> >   On the mean altar of my heart;
> > There let it for thy glory burn,
> >   With inextinguishable blaze;
> > And trembling to its source return
> >   In humble prayer and fervent praise." [23]

That these hymns bespeak high aspiration and unqualified commitment, none can doubt. That they constitute an unequivocal testimony to the attainment of entire sanctification is open to question.

It is sometimes assumed that deathbed testimonials reveal what may have been heretofore clouded. On Wesley's deathbed, however, his testimony does not illuminate the point in question. That testimony is reported in this fashion:

> There is no need for more than what I said at Bristol (where in 1783 he thought he was dying):
> > "I the chief of sinners am,
> > But Jesus died for me!"

He later added, "We must be justified by faith, and then go on to sanctification." And his last words include: "The best of all is, God is with us," and a prayer:

> We thank thee, O Lord, for these and all thy mercies: bless the Church and King; and grant us truth and peace, through Jesus Christ our Lord, for ever and ever! . . . The clouds drop fatness. . . . The Lord is with us, the God of Jacob is our refuge! . . . I'll praise—I'll praise! [an effort to repeat the words of a favorite hymn. And then], Farewell! [24]

This is the record of a glorious homegoing, an account hardly suited to the decision of points of mere doctrinal curiosity. Nevertheless it does not supply the answer to the question under consideration.

It is well-nigh impossible to read the public and private record of Wesley's life and thoughts without concluding that he had some inward knowledge of the doctrine he strenuously espoused during his mature ministerial career. *"Now* give yourself up to God," he wrote Peggy Dale. "This is all you have to do. And even while you are doing it light will spring up." "What you preach to others you have particular need to apply to your own soul," he said to Joseph Algar. ". . . Believe, and enter into rest!" "What a difference," he told Hester Ann Roe, "between the *first* love and the *pure* love!" Surely this sort of counsel comes not from merely hearsay evidence. Wesley undoubtedly knew experientially what in some measure was this perfect love the preaching of which he so earnestly urged.

Yet he never bore unequivocal testimony to its attainment. What prevented him? Was it modesty, or fastidiousness, or realism (all these have been adduced) that kept him from such profession? Could it not be that Wesley found himself upon the horns of a dilemma? He had drawn high his delineation of Christian perfection—and he believed his picture to be both scriptural and factual. For there were those who seemed by their lives and professions to measure up to his "exceedingly complex idea" of the sanctified life. In consequence he felt himself bound not to alter the description. He recognized that to set perfection too high was "effectually to renounce it," but on the other hand he feared that to set it too low was to "drive [men] into hell-fire." So he kept his doctrine of Christian perfection high. And there were those who even on those terms felt themselves able to profess it. In those testimonies for the most part Wesley rejoiced— decrying his own inability to join them. For in his own life he was keenly, almost morbidly, conscious of shortcomings which weighed mightily upon him. For instance, he tells of a time when with a certain group he "did not dare to be altogether singular, to be constantly, steadily serious before them." As a consequence he said:

This sin sets heavier upon my conscience at this time than almost all my crimes and all the transgressions of my youth. And one sin lying on the conscience is a load of misery. . . . O when shall we . . . repent of all our sins and all our backslidings? [25]

Feeling that his spiritual development was in some instances so much slower than that of others, he is deeply humiliated. Such considerations, therefore, keep him from laying claim to the perfection he preached.

From another point of consideration Wesley knew himself to be the cynosure of every critical eye. His domestic troubles had been exaggerated and widely advertised. His distinctive teachings had been perverted and lampooned. Any profession on his part would be interpreted in the most extreme fashion, while every personal shortcoming would be in refutation magnified. Therefore Wesley refrained. The portrait he had painted lay, he felt, still beyond him. He would neither change it nor claim it.

Yet, as J. S. Simon has said, "surely John Wesley has an exalted place on the roll of the saints." He lived higher than he testified, which is far better than the too frequent instance of him who testified higher than he lived.

B
John Fletcher: The Record of His Testimony

In the case of John Fletcher the only possible problem with regard to his testimony to the attainment of perfect love lies in the evaluation of a report concerning that testimony. For such a report is a matter of record.

In August of 1781 Fletcher had been in attendance at the conference held in Leeds. He was then in his fifty-first year and justly famed for his piety and wisdom. The conference ended on August 14, but Fletcher remained as the guest of Miss Mary Bosanquet, whom he was to marry in the succeeding November. During this stay on August 24 he attended a meeting of the Select Society at a "Mr. Smith's, in Park Row." Mrs. Hester Ann Rogers was at the meeting and describes it in considerable detail. Fletcher, it seems, was more or less in charge and at the request of Mrs. Rogers undertook to explain Acts 2, stressing in his explanation the *witnessing* of the disciples at Pentecost. After a hymn and a prayer for a "more abundant outpouring of the Spirit," Fletcher gave the following testimony, as reported by Mrs. Rogers:

My dear brethren and sisters, God is here! . . . but I would hide my face in the dust, because I have been ashamed to declare what He has done for *me*. For many years, I have grieved His Spirit; I am deeply humbled; and He has again restored my soul. Last Wednesday evening, He spoke to me by these words, *"Reckon yourselves, therefore, to be*

215

dead indeed unto sin; but alive unto God through Jesus Christ our Lord." I obeyed the voice of God: I now obey it; and tell you all, to the praise of His love,—*I am freed from sin.* . . . I received this blessing four or five times before; but I lost it, by not observing the order of God; who has told us, *With the heart man believeth unto righteousness, and with the mouth confession is made unto salvation.* . . . When I first received this grace, Satan bid me wait awhile, till I saw more of the *fruits*: I resolved to do so; but I soon began to doubt of the *witness*, which, before, I had felt in my heart; and, in a little time, I was sensible I had lost both. A second time, after receiving this salvation, I was kept from being a witness for my Lord, by the suggestion, "Thou art a public character—the eyes of *all* are upon thee—and if, as before, by *any* means thou lose the blessing, it will be a dishonour to the doctrine of *heart-holiness.*" I held my peace, and again forfeited the gift of God. At another time, I was prevailed upon to hide it, by reasoning, "How few, even of the *children of God,* will receive this testimony; many of them supposing every transgression of the Adamic law is sin; and, therefore, if I profess to be *free* from sin, *all* these will give my profession the lie; because I am *not* free in *their* sense: I am not free from ignorance, mistakes, and various infirmities; I will, therefore, enjoy what God has wrought in me; but I will not say, *I am perfect in love.* Alas! I soon found again, *He that hideth his Lord's talent, and improveth it not, from that unprofitable servant shall be taken away even that he hath.*" Now, my brethren, . . . I declare unto you, . . . I am now *dead indeed unto sin.*[1]

This report, given at such length and in such *verbatim* fashion, lays itself open to certain reservations regarding its complete accuracy. The tremendous significance of such an event for those who were present must, however, not be forgotten. Every word would be as far as possible treasured and remembered. At any rate the report has never been seriously challenged, and there is no good reason to believe that Fletcher did not testify substantially as recorded.

Other reports concerning Fletcher tend to corroborate the above. For instance, Joseph Benson, who knew him intimately, tells this about Fletcher concerning their days in Trevecca together:

Being convinced that to be *filled with the Holy Ghost* was a better qualification for the ministry of the Gospel than any classical learning, (although that too be useful in its place,) after speaking awhile in the school-room, he used frequently to say, "As many of you as are athirst for this fulness of the Spirit, follow me into my room." . . . And I have sometimes seen him, on these occasions, once in particular, so filled with love of God, that he could contain no more, but cried out, "O my God, withhold thy hand, or the vessel will burst." But he afterward told me . . . that he ought rather to have prayed, that the Lord would have enlarged the vessel.[2]

Whatever the judgment upon the fact of the personal testimony may be, Fletcher's life was of such quality as to be evaluated in the highest terms by those who had observed it at the closest range.

C
Francis Asbury: The Character of His Testimony

It has been flatly affirmed that Asbury testified to the attainment of perfect love, and it has been as dogmatically denied. The record favors the affirmation.

Asbury's references to his religious experience begin with an account of his conversion at about the fifteenth year of his life, after which, he says, he soon perceived the "excellency and necessity of holiness." And he relates that when he was sixteen he "experienced a marvellous display of the grace of God, which some might think was full sanctification, and was indeed very happy."[1] He neither affirms nor denies what "some might think." But shortly after his arrival in America he is saying: "I am still sensible of my deep insufficiency, and that mostly with regard to holiness." And a few years later, "I long to be made perfect in love."

In 1779 there appears what could certainly be pronounced a testimony to this experience. His journal entry for March 14 of that year states:

On Friday I was inclined to believe, that the night before the Lord had re-sanctified my soul. It afforded me much comfort; and I was ready to conclude it had been so for many years past, if I had maintained and believed it. . . . May the Lord help me from this time, to live free from outward and inward sin.[2]

Here Asbury implies a previous relationship once enjoyed, not maintained, and now again, he is "inclined to believe," recovered.

But the record does not end there. On June 28 of the following year he says, "O, my God! when shall I be established in purity!" And the following day, "I am still seeking full and final salvation." Thus the account continues with bursts of praise and assurance alternating with admissions of failure and need.

Perhaps the key to what appears to be the vacillation of this period is to be found in the fact that Asbury, depending in considerable measure on subjective criteria to determine his spiritual state, was at the same time constantly plagued with illness and always burdened with vast administrative responsibility. On July 14, 1774, he wrote: "I have now been sick near ten months; and many days closely confined. Yet I have preached about three hundred times, and rode near two thousand miles in that time."[3] He did not, could not, constantly enjoy the same high level of feeling that he tended for a while to regard as necessary to the possession of perfect love.

On the other hand, it was also true that Asbury, like Wesley and Fletcher, considered that Christian perfection was maintained on a moment-by-moment basis. When he said, "I am filled with love," he added, "from day to day." He never measured today's possession by yesterday's experience. In fact, the attainment of any specific height for Asbury was but to provide him with a new vantage point for the recognition of new and ever-widening vistas ahead. And thus he could say: "My soul was watered with the peaceful influence of divine grace. But what I enjoyed was a stimulus urging me to groan for more."[4] One day's profession, therefore, became the next day's petition. It was not vacillation but aspiration.

However, around 1803 the temper of this spiritual autobiography changes. And if Wesley's division of "little children, young men, and fathers" be allowed, here begins Asbury's period of maturity. He seems, in fact, to recognize this maturation; for he says:

I have felt deeply engaged, and much self-possession; indeed, age, grace, and the weight and responsibility of one of the greatest charges upon earth, ought to make me serious. In addition to this charge of superintendent, to preach, to feel, and to live perfect love! [5]

In spite of physical ills there is a continuity of assurance, a prevailing confidence. Now he speaks repeatedly of being kept "in perfect peace," of enjoying God in "pure and perfect love." The record is no longer interspersed with the cries of stormy conquest; it is now a calm and continuing testimony to established possession.

Thus the "father of American Methodism" ended his days. His deathbed remarks, like those of Wesley, indicate a victorious end but add no specific detail to the record already established.

Bibliography

Works by John Wesley

Wesley, John. *Explanatory Notes upon the New Testament.* 1st American ed. Philadelphia: Prichard and Hall, 1791.

——. *The Journal of the Rev. John Wesley, A.M.* Ed. Nehemiah Curnock. 8 vols. London: Robert Culley, 1910.

——. *The Letters of the Rev. John Wesley.* Ed. John Telford. 8 vols. London: Epworth Press, 1931.

——. *Minutes of Several Conversations between Rev. John Wesley, A.M., and the Preachers in Connection with him, containing the Form of Discipline established among the Preachers and People in the Methodist Societies.* London: G. Whitfield, 1779.

——, and others. *Original Letters by the Rev. John Wesley and His Friends Illustrative of His Early History.* Ed. Joseph Priestley. Birmingham: Thomas Pearson, 1791.

——. *Reasons against a Separation from the Church of England.* London: W. Strahan, 1760.

——. *Sermons on Several Occasions.* 2 vols. London: William Tegg, 1867.

——. *A Short Account of the Life and Death of the Rev. John Fletcher.* London: J. Paramore, 1786.

——. *A Survey of the Wisdom of God in the Creation; or, A Compendium of Natural Philosophy.* 2 vols. 3rd American ed. New York: N. Bangs and T. Mason, 1823.

——. *Wesley's Standard Sermons.* Ed. E. A. Sugden. 2 vols. Nashville: Lamar and Barton, *ca.* 1920.

——. *The Works of the Rev. John Wesley, A.M.* 14 vols. London: John Mason, 1856.

Works About John Wesley

Baines-Griffiths, David. *Wesley the Anglican.* London: Macmillan and Co., 1919.

Cannon, W. R. *The Theology of John Wesley.* New York and Nashville: Abingdon Press, 1946.

Cell, G. C. *The Rediscovery of John Wesley.* New York: Henry Holt & Co., 1935.

Coke, Thomas, and Moore, Henry. *The Life of the Rev. John Wesley, A.M.* London: G. Paramore, 1792.

Fitchett, W. H. *Wesley and His Century.* London: Smith, Elder & Co., 1906.

Green, Richard. *The Works of John and Charles Wesley—A Bibliography.* London: C. H. Kelly, 1896.

Hampson, John. *Memoirs of the Late Rev. John Wesley.* 3 vols. Sunderland: James Graham, 1791.

Hill, Richard. *A Review of All the Doctrines Taught by the Rev. Mr. J. Wesley.* London: E. and C. Dilly, 1772.

Lee, Umphrey. *John Wesley and Modern Religion.* Nashville: Cokesbury Press, 1936.

Léger, Augustin. *La Jeunesse de Wesley.* Paris: Librairie Hachette & Cie., 1910.

Lindström, Harald. *Wesley and Sanctification.* Stockholm: Nya Bokförlags Aktiebolaget, 1946.

McConnell, F. J. *John Wesley.* New York and Nashville: Abingon Press, 1939.

Meredith, W. H. *The Real John Wesley.* Cincinnati: Jennings and Pye, 1903.

More, Henry. *The Life of the Rev. John Wesley, A.M.* 2 vols. New York: Bangs and Emory, 1826.

Osborn, George. *Outlines of Wesleyan Bibliography.* London: Wesleyan Conference Office. 1869.

Parker, D. *A Letter to the Rev. Mr. John Wesley.* London: D. Hart, 1766.

Piette, Maximin. *John Wesley in the Evolution of Protestantism.* New York: Sheed and Ward, 1937.

Rattenbury, J. E. *The Conversion of the Wesleys.* London: Epworth Press, 1938.

———. *Wesley's Legacy to the World.* Nashville: Cokesbury Press, 1928.

———. *John Wesley, the Last Phase.* London: Epworth Press, 1934.

———. *John Wesley, the Master-Builder.* London: Epworth Press, 1927.

Simon, J. S. *John Wesley and the Religious Societies.* London: Epworth Press, 1921.

Southey, Robert. *The Life of Wesley and the Rise and Progress of Methodism.* 2 vols. New York: Harper & Brothers, 1847.

Telford, John. *The Life of John Wesley.* 3rd edition. London: Robert Culley, 1910.

Toplady, Augustus. *A Letter to the Rev. Mr. John Wesley, relative to his pretended Abridgment of Zanchius on Predestination.* London: Joseph Gurney, 1770.

Tyerman, Luke. *The Life and Times of the Rev. John Wesley, M.A.* 3 vols. New York: Harper & Brothers, 1872.

Vulliamy, C. E. *John Wesley.* New York: Chas. Scribner's Sons, 1932.

Watkinson, W. L., and others. *Wesley Studies.* London: Charles H. Kelly, 1903.

Watson, Richard. *The Life of the Rev. John Wesley, A.M.* (Watson's Library of Standard Biography and Theology, Vol. III.) 6th ed. London: John Mason, 1842.

Whitehead, John. *The Life of the Rev. John Wesley, M.A.* 2 vols. in one. Boston: Hill & Brodhead, 1846.

Works Relating to Christian Perfection

Ackerman, G. E. *Love Illumined.* Cincinnati: Curts & Jennings, 1900.

Arthur, William. *The Tongue of Fire.* Nashville: Stevenson and Owen, 1857.

Ball, E. *Review of a Sermon on Growth in Grace in Opposition to the Wesleyan Doctrine of Entire Sanctification.* Canton, Ohio: Hartzell and Saxton, 1871.

Brady, J. W. *Grace Magnified.* Bloomington, Ill.: Banner of Holiness Publishing Office, 1873.

Breeden, Henry. *A Call to Holiness and Usefulness.* 2nd ed. rev. Albany: Stowe and Hurly, 1846.

Brooks, J. R. *Scriptural Sanctification, an Attempted Solution of the Holiness Problem.* 3rd ed. Nashville: Publishing House of the Methodist Episcopal Church, South, 1899.

Brooks, Thomas. *The Crown & Glory of Christianity; or, Holiness the Only Way to Happiness.* London: Printed for H. Crips, J. Sims, and H. Mortlock, 1662.

Bryant, T. J. *Plain Things to Holiness People.* Nevada, Iowa: "The Highway" Press, *cir.* 1887.

Buckler, H. R. *The Perfection of Man by Charity.* London: Burns & Oates, 1894.

Caldwell, Merritt. *The Philosophy of Christian Perfection.* Philadelphia: Sorin and Ball, 1848.

Carradine, Beverly. *Sanctification.* Syracuse: A. W. Hall, 1896.

Clarke, Adam. *Entire Sanctification.* Philadelphia: Edward Jones, 1874.

Crane, J. T. *Holiness the Birthright of All God's Children.* New York: Nelson & Phillips, 1874.

Dunn, L. R. *Holiness to the Lord.* New York: Nelson & Phillips, 1874.

———. *A Manual of Holiness.* Cincinnati: Cranston & Curts, 1895.

———. *Sermons on the Higher Life.* Cincinnati: Walden and Stowe, 1882.

CHRISTIAN PERFECTION AND AMERICAN METHODISM

Flew, R. N. *The Idea of Perfection in Christian Theology.* London: Oxford University Press, 1934.

Foster, R. S. *Christian Purity; or, the Heritage of Faith.* Rev. ed. New York: Carlton & Lanahan, 1869.

———. *Nature and Blessedness of Christian Purity.* New York: Harper & Brothers, 1851.

Franklin, Samuel. *A Critical Review of Wesleyan Perfection.* Cincinnati: The Methodist Book Concern, 1866.

French, M. and A. M., eds. *Beauty of Holiness,* Vols. XI-XIII. New York: M. French, 1860-62.

Gaddis, M. E. "Christian Perfectionism in America." Unpublished Ph.D. dissertation, the Divinity School, University of Chicago, 1929.

Garrigou-Lagrange, Réginald. *The Three Ages of the Interior Life.* St. Louis: B. Herder, 1947. Vol. I.

Guide to Holiness, 1839-1900. A monthly periodical begun in 1839 under the title *Guide to Christian Perfection.* The name was changed after 1845. Timothy Merritt, first editor; Dr. and Mrs. W. C. Palmer editors for the longest period. Published first in Boston, later in New York.

Hughes, George, ed. *Holiness Year Book,* 1884-94. Published from 1844-88 as *Christian Holiness Almanac and Year Book.* New York: Palmer and Hughes.

———. *International Holinesss Directory and Year Book.* Philadelphia: International Holiness Publishing House, 1894.

Huntington, D. W. C. *Sin and Holiness; or What It Is to Be Holy.* Cincinnati: Curts & Jennings, 1898.

Keen, S. A. *Pentecostal Papers; or, The Gift of the Holy Ghost.* Cincinnati: Cranston & Curts, 1895.

Lowrey, Asbury. *Possibilities of Grace.* New York: Phillips & Hunt, 1884.

Lucas, Richard. *An Enquiry After Happiness.* 3 vols. 4th ed. rev. London: Printed for S. Smith and B. Walford, 1704.

Lummus, Aaron. *Essays on Holiness.* Boston: Timothy Ashley, 1826.

Mahan, Asa. *The True Believer, His Character, Duty, and Privileges.* New York: Harper & Brothers, 1847.

Mallalieu, W. F. *The Fullness of the Blessing of the Gospel of Christ.* Cincinnati: Jennings and Pye, 1903.

Mattison, Hiram. *An Answer to Dr. Perry's Reply to the Calm Review.* New York: n.p., 1856.

———. *A Calm Review of Dr. Perry's Late Article in the Christian Advocate and Journal.* New York: John A. Gray, 1856.

Merrill, S. M. *Sanctification, Right Views and Other Views.* Cincinnati: Jennings & Pye, 1901.

Merritt, Timothy. *The Christian's Manual, a Treatise on Christian Perfection.* New York: N. Bangs and J. Emory, 1825.

BIBLIOGRAPHY

Mudge, James. *Growth in Holiness Toward Perfection; or, Progressive Sanctification.* New York: Hunt & Eaton, 1895.

————. *The Perfect Life in Experience and Doctrine.* Cincinnati: Jennings and Graham, 1911.

Palmer, Phoebe, *Pioneer Experiences, or, The Gift of Power Received by Faith.* New York: W. C. Palmer, Jr., 1868.

————. *Promise of the Father; or, A Neglected Specialty of the Last Days.* Boston: Henry V. Degen, 1859.

————. *The Way of Holiness.* New York: Lane & Tippett, 1846.

Palmer, W. C., ed. *Tracts on Holiness.* New York: W. C. Palmer, n.d.

Parson, C. R. *Purity and Power.* London: T. Woolmer, 1886.

Peck, George. *The Scripture Doctrine of Christian Perfection Stated and Defended.* New York: Lane & Sandford, 1842.

Perkins, H. W. *The Doctrine of Christian or Evangelical Perfection.* London: Epworth Press, 1927.

Platt, Frederic. "Perfection," *Encyclopedia of Religion and Ethics.* Ed. James Hastings. New York: Chas. Scribner's Sons, 1917. Vol. IX.

Platt, S. H. *A Philosophy of Christian Holiness.* West Winstead, Conn.: Published by the author, 1865.

Proceedings of the Western Union Holiness Convention. Bloomington, Ill.: Western Holiness Association, 1882.

Sangster, W. E.: *The Path of Perfection.* New York and Nashville: Abingdon-Cokesbury Press, 1943.

Schwab, R. K. *The History of the Doctrine of Christian Perfection in the Evangelical Association.* Menasha, Wis.: George Banta Publishing Co., 1922.

Scott, Jane A. *Letters on Christian Holiness.* Philadelphia: Tract Depository, 1859.

Searles, J. E. *History of the Present Holiness Revival.* Boston: McDonald, Gill & Co., 1887.

Steele, Daniel. *Love Enthroned, Essays on Evangelical Perfection.* New York: Hunt & Eaton, 1875.

Summers, T. O. *Holiness, a Treatise on Sanctification.* Nashville: Publishing House of the Methodist Episcopal Church, South, 1911.

Treffry, Richard. *A Treatise on Christian Perfection.* Boston: McDonald, Gill & Co., 1888.

Vansant, M. *Entire Holiness, Is It a Gradual or an Instantaneous Work?* New York: W. C. Palmer, 1881.

Villars, I. *The Theory of the Second Blessing—Is It Either Wesleyan or Scriptural?* Printed by the author, 1898.

Warfield, B. B. *Perfectionism.* 2 vols. New York: Oxford University Press, 1931.

Watson, G. D. *Love Abounding, and Other Expositions on the Spiritual Life.* Boston: McDonald, Gill & Co., 1891.

W. G. W., ed. *True Method of Promoting Perfect Love. From Debates in the New-York Preachers' Meeting of the Methodist-Episcopal Church.* 3rd ed. rev. New York: Foster & Palmer, Jr., 1867.

Whedon, D. A. *Entire Sanctification, John Wesley's View.* New York: Hunt and Eaton, n.d.

Zink, M. P. *Review of Dr. Huntington on Sin and Holiness.* Hillsboro, O.: published by the author, n.d.

Works Concerning Methodism

A. DOCTRINE AND POLITY

Anderson, W. K., ed. *Methodism.* New York: The Methodist Publishing House, 1947.

Bangs, Nathan. *Letters to Young Ministers of the Gospel, on the Importance and Method of Study.* New York: N. Bangs and J. Emory, 1826.

———. *An Original Church of Christ; or, A Scriptural Vindication of the Orders and Powers of the Ministry of the Methodist Episcopal Church.* New York: Mason and Lane, 1837.

Benson, Joseph. *An Apology for the People Called Methodists.* London: G. Story, 1801.

Bett, Henry. *The Spirit of Methodism.* London: Epworth Press, 1937.

Bowne, Borden P. *The Christian Life, a Study.* Cincinnati: Curts and Jennings, 1899.

———. *Studies in Christianity.* Boston: Houghton Mifflin Co., 1909.

Carroll, H. K., Harrison, W. P., and Bayliss, J. H., eds. *Proceedings of the Centennial Methodist Conference Held in Baltimore, Md., December 9-17, 1884.* Cincinnati: Cranston and Stowe, 1885.

Clarke, Adam. *Christian Theology.* New York: Carlton and Porter, 1835.

———. "Clavis Biblica," *The Preacher's Manual.* New York: Mason and Lane, 1837.

———. *Detached Pieces.* 3 vols. London: Thomas Tegg, 1844.

———. *Discourses.* 2 vols. New York: Waugh and Mason, 1832.

Curtis, O. A. *The Christian Faith.* New York: Eaton and Mains, 1905.

Dimond, S. G. *The Psychology of the Methodist Revival.* London: Oxford University Press, 1926.

Discipline of the Methodist Episcopal Church, 1784 to 1900. New York. Reprints of the *Discipline* from 1784 to 1789 published by the Methodist Historical Society of Boston, Mass.

Doctrines and Discipline of the Methodist Episcopal Church, South, 1846-98. Richmond, Louisville, and Nashville.

Emory, John. *A Reply to the "Objections against the Position of a Personal*

226

BIBLIOGRAPHY

Assurance of the Pardon of Sin, by a Direct Communication of the Holy Spirit." Philadelphia: Jonathan Pounder, 1817.

Emory, Robert. *History of the Discipline of the Methodist Episcopal Church.* ("Revised and brought down to 1856 by W. P. Strickland") New York: Carlton & Porter, 1857.

Fletcher, John. *The Works of the Rev. John Fletcher.* 9 vols. London: T. Cordeux, 1815.

Foster, R. S. *Philosophy of Christian Experience.* New York: Hunt & Eaton, 1891.

Godbey, J. E. *The Methodist Church-Member's Manual.* Kansas City: South-Western Methodist Publishing Co., 1889.

Harmon, Nolan B. *Understanding the Methodist Church.* Nashville: Methodist Publishing House, 1955.

Hymnal of the Methodist Episcopal Church. New York: 1791-1880.

Kern, P. B. *Methodism Has a Message.* New York and Nashville: Abingdon Press, 1941.

Liggett, F. M., ed., *The Book of the Sesqui-Centennial of American Methodism.* Baltimore: Stockton Press, 1935.

Miley, John. *Systematic Theology.* 2 vols. New York: Hunt & Eaton, 1894.

Minutes of the Fifty-Sixth Session of the Illinois Annual Conference of the Methodist Episcopal Church. Jacksonville, Ill., 1879.

Minutes of the Methodist Conferences Annually Held in America from 1773-1831, Inclusive. New York: Daniel Hitt and Thomas Ware, 1813.

Minutes of the Methodist Conferences from the First, Held in London, by the Late Rev. John Wesley, M.A. London: The Conférence Office, 1812.

Minutes of the Missouri Annual Conference of the Methodist Episcopal Church, 1879-88. Kirksville, Mo.

Moxon, R. S. *The Doctrine of Sin.* New York: George H. Doran Co., 1922.

Neely, T. B. *Doctrinal Standards of Methodism.* New York: Fleming H. Revell Co., 1918.

————., ed. *Journal of the General Conference of the Methodist Episcopal Church,* 1792. Cincinnati: Curts & Jennings, 1899.

P., C. [Perronet, Charles?]. *A Summary View of the Doctrines of Methodism.* Bristol: Felix Farley, 1753.

Phoebus, William. *An Essay on the Doctrine and Order of the Evangelical Church of America as Constituted at Baltimore in 1784.* New York: Abraham Paul, 1817.

Pope, W. B. *A Compendium of Christian Theology.* 3 vols. New York: Phillips & Hunt, 1881.

————. *A Higher Catechism of Theology.* London: T. Woolmer, ca. 1883.

Proceedings of the Oecumenical Methodist Conference, Held in City Road Chapel, London, 1881. Cincinnati: Walden and Stowe, 1882.

Proceedings of the Second Ecumenical Methodist Conference, 1891. New York: Hunt & Eaton, 1892.

Raymond, Miner. *Systematic Theology.* 3 vols. Cincinnati: Hitchcock and Walden, 1877.

Stebbing, Henry. *An Earnest and Affectionate Address to the People Called Methodists.* 5th ed. London: J. Oliver, 1751.

Tigert, J. J. *A Constitutional History of American Episcopal Methodism.* Nashville: Publishing House of the Methodist Episcopal Church, South, 1916.

Tillett, W. F. *Personal Salvation, Studies in Christian Doctrine.* Nashville: Publishing House of the Methodist Episcopal Church, South, 1902. Rev. ed., 1907.

————. *A Statement of the Faith of World-Wide Methodism.* Nashville: Publishing House of the Methodist Episcopal Church, South, 1906.

Tillett, W. F., and Atkins, James. *The Doctrines and Polity of the Methodist Episcopal Church, South.* Nashville: Publishing House of the Methodist Episcopal Church, South, 1905.

Watson, Richard. *Conversations for the Young.* New York: Lane and Sandford, 1843.

————. *Theological Institutes.* 3 vols. New York: Emory and Waugh, 1828.

————. *The Works of the Rev. Richard Watson.* 11 vols. 2nd ed. London: John Mason, 1834.

Wheeler, Henry. *History and Exposition of the Twenty-five Articles of Religion of the Methodist Episcopal Church.* New York: Eaton and Mains, 1908.

Willson, S. W., and Ireson, Ebenezer, eds. *The Methodist Preacher, or, Monthly Sermons from Living Ministers.* Boston: John Putnam, 1830, 1831. Vols. I, II.

Wilson, G. W. *Methodist Theology Versus Methodist Theologians.* Cincinnati: Jennings and Pye, 1904.

B. HISTORY

Alexander, Gross. *A History of the Methodist Church, South.* Vol. XI in the American Church History Series. New York: The Christian Literature Co., 1894. Rev. ed., 1907.

Allen, R. W., and Wise, Daniel. *Methodism in Earnest.* Boston: Charles H. Pierce, 1850.

Allen, Stephen, and Pilsbury, W. H. *History of Methodism in Maine, 1793-1886.* 2 vols. in one. Augusta: C. E. Nash, 1887.

The Arminian Magazine, VI-XIII. London: 1783-90.

Asbury, Francis. *The Journal of the Rev. Francis Asbury.* 3 vols. New York: Bangs and Mason, 1821.

BIBLIOGRAPHY

Atkinson, John. *Centennial History of American Methodism.* New York: Phillips & Hunt, 1884.

———. *Memorials of Methodism in New Jersey.* 2nd edition. Philadelphia: Perkinpine and Higgins, 1860.

Baker, G. C., Jr. *An Introduction to the History of Early New England Methodism, 1789-1839.* Durham, N.C.: Duke University Press, 1941.

Bangs, Heman. *The Autobiography and Journal of Rev. Heman Bangs.* New York: N. Tibbals & Son, 1872.

Bangs, John. *Auto-biography of Rev. John Bangs.* New York: n.p., 1846.

Bangs, Nathan. *A History of the Methodist Episcopal Church, 1829-1840.* 4 vols. New York: G. Lane and C. B. Tippett, 1845.

———. *The Present State, Prospects and Responsibilities of the Methodist Episcopal Church.* New York: Lane and Scott, 1850.

Benson, Joseph. *The Life of the Rev. John W. de la Flechere.* 2nd American from the 2nd (enlarged) London ed. New York: N. Bangs and T. Mason, 1820.

Browning, W. G. *Beyond Fourscore.* Poughkeepsie, N.Y.: A. V. Haight, 1907.

Buckley, J. M. *A History of Methodism in the United States.* 2 vols. New York: The Christian Literature Co., 1897.

Clarke, J. B. B. *Life of Adam Clarke, LL.D., F.A.S.* 3 vols. London: T. S. Clarke, 1833.

Coles, George. *The Supernumerary; or, Lights and Shadows of Itinerancy, compiled from papers of Rev. Elijah Woolsey.* New York: Lane and Tippett, 1845.

Conable, F. W. *The History of the Genesee Annual Conference of the Methodist Episcopal Church, 1810-72.* New York: Nelson & Phillips, 1876.

Cooper, Ezekiel. *The Substance of a Funeral Discourse, . . . on the Death of the Rev. Francis Asbury.* Philadelphia: Jonathan Pounder, 1819.

Crawford, G. A., ed. *The Centennial of New England Methodism.* Boston: Crawford Brothers, 1891.

Crooks, G. R. *Life and Death of the Rev. John M'Clintock, D.D., LL.D.* New York: Nelson & Phillips, 1876.

———, ed. *The Present State of the Methodist Episcopal Church.* Syracuse: Northern Christian Advocate Office, 1891.

Crowther, Jonathan. *A True and Complete Portraiture of Methodism.* New York: Daniel Hitt and Thomas Ware, 1813.

Curts, Lewis. *The General Conferences of the Methodist Episcopal Church from 1792 to 1896, a History.* Cincinnati: Curts and Jennings, 1900.

Drew, Samuel. *The Life of the Rev. Thomas Coke, LL.D.* London: Thomas Cordeux, 1817.

229

CHRISTIAN PERFECTION AND AMERICAN METHODISM

Du Bose, H. M. *A History of Methodism.* Nashville: Publishing House of the Methodist Episcopal Church, South, 1916.

Edwards, Maldwyn. *Adam Clarke.* London: Epworth Press, 1942.

[Emory, Robert]. *The Life of the Rev. John Emory, D.D.* New-York: George Lane, 1841.

Etheridge, J. W. *The Life of the Rev. Adam Carke, LL.D.* New York: Carlton & Porter, 1859.

Extracts of Letters, Containing Some Account of the Work of God Since the Year 1800. Written by the Preachers and Members of the Methodist Episcopal Church, to Their Bishops. New York: Ezekiel Cooper and John Wilson, 1805.

Farish, H. D. *The Circuit Rider Dismounts, a Social History of Southern Methodism, 1865-1900.* Richmond, Va.: The Dietz Press, 1938.

Ffirth, John. *Experience and Gospel Labours of the Rev. Benjamin Abbott.* New York: B. Waugh and T. Mason, 1832.

Finley, J. B. *Autobiography of Rev. James B. Finley; or, Pioneer Life in the West.* Cincinnati: The Methodist Book Concern, 1872.

Fitzgerald, O. P. *Dr. Summers, a Life-Study.* Nashville: Southern Methodist Publishing House, 1885.

Flood, T. L., and Hamilton, J. W., eds. *Lives of Methodist Bishops.* New York: Phillips & Hunt, 1882.

Garrettson, Freeborn. *The Experience and Travels of Mr. Freeborn Garrettson, Minister of the Methodist-Episcopal Church in North-America.* Philadelphia: Parry Hall, 1791.

Goss, C. C. *Statistical History of the First Century of American Methodism.* New York: Carlton & Porter, 1866.

Hibbard, F. G. *Biography of Rev. Leonidas L. Hamline.* Cincinnati: Jennings and Pye, 1881.

Historical Register of Boston University, 1869-1911. 5th decennial issue. Boston: The Atlantis Press, 1911.

Holdich, Joseph. *The Life of Wilbur Fisk, D.D.* New York: Harper & Brothers, 1842.

Hughes, E. H. *I Was Made a Minister, an Autobiography.* New York and Nashville: Abingdon Press, 1943.

Hurst, J. F. *The History of Methodism,* 7 vols. New York: Eaton & Mains, 1902.

Jackson, Thomas. *Memoirs of the Life and Writings of the Rev. Richard Watson.* 2nd ed. London: John Mason, 1836.

Janes, E. S. *Sermon on the Death of Nathan Bangs.* New York: Carlton and Porter, 1862.

Jarratt, Devereux. *A Brief Narrative of the Revival of Religion in Virginia.* With a supplement by Thomas Rankin. 2nd ed. London: R. Hawes, 1778.

Journal of the General Conference of the Methodist Episcopal Church.

New York: Carlton and Phillips, 1855. Vols. I and II, 1796-1844.

Journal of the General Conference of the Methodist Episcopal Church, South, 1878-98. Nashville: Southern Methodist Publishing House.

Joy, James R., ed. *The Teachers of Drew, 1867-1942.* Madison, N.J.: Drew University, 1942.

Lee, Jesse. *A Short History of the Methodists in the United States of America, 1766-1809.* Baltimore: Magill and Clime, 1810.

Lockwood, J. P. *The Western Pioneers; or, Memoirs of the Rev. Richard Boardman and the Rev. Joseph Pilmoor.* London: Wesleyan Conference Office, 1881.

Luccock, Halford E., and Hutchinson, Paul. *The Story of Methodism.* New York: The Methodist Book Concern, 1926.

Marlay, John F. *The Life of Rev. Thomas A. Morris.* Cincinnati: Hitchcock and Walden, 1875.

Matlack, L. C. *The Antislavery Struggle and Triumph in the Methodist Episcopal Church.* New York: Phillips and Hunt, 1881.

McConnell, F. J. *Borden Parker Bowne, His Life and His Philosophy.* New York: Abingdon Press, 1929.

McTyeire, H. N. *A History of Methodism.* Nashville: Southern Methodist Publishing House, 1884.

The Methodist Quarterly Review. Vols. I to LXXXII, 1818-1900. From 1818-30 Called *The Methodist Magazine;* from 1830-40 called *The Methodist Magazine and Quarterly Review.*

Mims, Edwin. *History of Vanderbilt University.* Nashville: Vanderbilt University Press, 1946.

Mudge, James. *History of the New England Conference of the Methodist Episcopal Church, 1796-1910.* Boston: Published by the Conference, 1910.

[Olin, Stephen]. *The Life and Letters of Stephen Olin.* 2 vols. New York: Harper & Brothers, 1853.

Paine, Robert. *Life and Times of William M'Kendree.* 2 vols. Nashville: Southern Methodist Publishing House, 1869.

Palmer, W. C. *Life and Letters of Leonidas L. Hamline, D.D.* New York: Carlton & Porter, 1866.

Peck, George. *Early Methodism Within the Bounds of the Old Genesee Conference from 1788 to 1828.* New York: Carlton & Porter, 1860.

Pell, E. L., ed., *A Hundred Years of Richmond Methodism.* Richmond, Va.: The Idea Publishing Co., 1899.

Phoebus, G. A. *Beams of Light on Early Methodism in America, Chiefly Drawn from the Diary, Letters, Manuscripts, Documents, and Original Tracts of the Rev. Ezekiel Cooper.* New York: Phillips & Hunt, 1887.

The Quarterly Review of the Methodist Episcopal Church, South. 1847-1900. From 1847 to 1886, with publication suspended from 1862-1878, it was published under this title. From 1886 through July, 1888 it was called the *Southern Methodist Review*. From Oct., 1888 to 1894 it resumed the original title. After 1894 it appeared bimonthly as *The Methodist Review*.

Raybold, G. A. *Annals of Methodism, first series, Camden and Vicinity.* Philadelphia: T. Stokes, 1847.

Ridgaway, H. B. *The Life of Edmund S. Janes.* New York: Phillips & Hunt, 1882.

———. *The Life of the Rev. Alfred Cookman.* New York: Harper & Brothers, 1873.

Seaman, S. A. *Annals of New York Methodism, 1766-1890.* New York: Hunt & Eaton, 1892.

Simpson, Matthew. *Cyclopedia of Methodism.* 4th rev. ed. Philadelphia: Louis H. Everts, 1881.

Stephenson, T. B. *William Arthur, a Brief Biography.* New York: The Methodist Book Concern [1906].

Stevens, Abel. *The Centenary of American Methodism.* New York: Carlton & Porter, 1865.

———. *A Compendious History of American Methodism.* New York: Carlton & Porter, 1867.

———. *The History of the Religious Movement of the Eighteenth Century, Called Methodism.* 3 vols. New York: Carlton & Porter, 1859.

———. *The Life and Times of Nathan Bangs.* New York: Carlton & Porter, 1863.

Summers, T. O. *Biographical Sketches of Eminent Itinerant Ministers.* Nashville: Southern Methodist Publishing House, 1859.

Sweet, W. W. *Men of Zeal.* New York: Abingdon Press, 1935.

———. *Methodism in American History.* New York: The Methodist Book Concern, 1933.

———. *Religion on the American Frontier.* University of Chicago Press, 1946. Vol. IV (The Methodists).

Thrift, Minton. *Memoir of the Rev. Jesse Lee. With Extracts from his Journals.* New York: N. Bangs and T. Mason, 1823.

Townsend, W. J., Workman, H. B., and Eayrs, George, eds. *A New History of Methodism.* 2 vols. London: Hodder & Stoughton, 1909.

Tuttle, A. H. *Nathan Bangs.* New York: Eaton & Mains, 1909.

Tyerman, Luke. *Wesley's Designated Successor.* London: Hodder & Stoughton, 1882.

Vail, S. M. *Life in Earnest or Memoirs and Remains of Rev. Zenas Caldwell, A.B.* Boston: J. P. Magee, 1855.

Ware, Thomas. *Sketches of the Life and Travels of Rev. Thomas Ware.* New York: T. Mason and G. Lane, 1840.

Watters, William. *A Short Account of the Christian Experience and Min-*

isterial Labours of William Watters, drawn up by himself. Alexandria, Va.: S. Snowden, 1806.

Wheatley, Richard. *The Life and Letters of Mrs. Phoebe Palmer.* New York: W. C. Palmer, Jr., 1876.

Youngs, James. *A History of the Rise and Progress of Methodism.* New Haven: A. Daggett and Co., 1830.

General Works

Alivisatos, H. S., and others. *The Doctrine of Grace.* New York: The Macmillan Co., 1932.

Allison, W. H. *Inventory of Unpublished Material for American Religious History in Protestant Church Archives and other Repositories.* Washington, D.C.: Published by the Carnegie Institution of Washington, 1910.

Ante-Nicene Fathers. Ed. Alexander Roberts and James Donaldson. 10 vols. Buffalo, N.Y.: Christian Literature Publishing Co., 1885. Vols. I, II, IV.

Arminius, James. *The Works of James Arminius.* Tr. James Nichols. 3 vols. Auburn, N.Y.: Derby, Miller and Orton, 1853. Vols. I, II.

Aubrey, E. E. *Present Theological Tendencies.* New York: Harper & Brothers, 1936.

Bass, A. B. *Protestantism in the United States.* New York: Thomas Y. Crowell, 1929.

Bassett, A. H. *A Concise History of the Methodist Protestant Church.* Pittsburgh: James Robinson, 1877.

Beard, C. A. and Mary. *The Rise of American Civilization.* 2 vols. New York: The Macmillan Co., 1927.

Beardsley, F. G. *A History of American Revivals.* New York: American Tract Society, 1912.

Beer, Thomas. *Hanna, Crane, and the Mauve Decade.* New York: Alfred A. Knopf, 1941.

Bennett, W. W. *The Great Revival in the Southern Armies.* Philadelphia: Claxton, Remsen, and Heffelfinger, 1877.

Bowne, Borden P. *The Christian Life, a Study.* Cincinnati: Curts & Jennings, 1899.

Bready, J. W. *England: Before and After Wesley.* London: Hodder & Stoughton, 1938.

Campagnac, E. T. *The Cambridge Platonists.* Oxford: Clarendon Press, 1901.

The Canons and Decrees of the Sacred and Oecumenical Council of Trent. Tr. J. Waterworth. London: C. Dolman, 1848.

Carroll, H. K. *The Religious Forces of the United States.* Rev. ed. New York: Chas. Scribner's Sons, 1912.

Chapman, J. B. *A History of the Church of the Nazarene.* Kansas City: The Nazarene Publishing House, 1926.

Clark, E. T. *The Small Sects in America.* New York and Nashville: Abingdon Press, 1937.

Clark, G. N. *The Later Stuarts, 1660-1714.* Oxford: Clarendon Press, 1944.

Constitution and Discipline of the Methodist Protestant Church. Eds. of 1830 and 1877. Pittsburgh: James Robison, 1877.

Cross, W. L. *Connecticut Yankee.* New Haven, Conn.: Yale University Press, 1943.

Cudworth, Ralph. *A Sermon Preached Before the Honourable House of Commons at Westminster, March 31, 1647.* Cambridge: Roger Daniel, 1647. A facsimile reprint. New York: Columbia University Press, 1930.

Daniels, W. H., ed. *Moody, His Words, Work, and Workers.* New York: Nelson and Phillips, 1877.

Discipline of the Wesleyan Methodist Connection of America. 1843, 1854, and 1887 eds. Boston and Syracuse.

Doctrines and Discipline of the Evangelical Association of North America. 1890 ed. Cleveland, Ohio.

Doctrines and Discipline of the Free Methodist Church. 1866 and 1895 eds. Rochester and Chicago.

Ferré, Nels F. S. *Faith and Reason.* New York: Harper & Brothers, 1946.

Finney, C. G., *Memoirs of Rev. Charles G. Finney.* New York: A. S. Barnes & Co., 1876.

Forster, Chas., ed., *Thirty Years Correspondence between John Jebb, Bishop of Limerick . . . and Alexander Knox, Esq.* 2 vols. London: James Duncan, 1836.

Goodykoontz, C. B. *Home Missions on the American Frontier.* Caldwell, Ida.: The Caxton Printers, 1939.

Green, V. H. H. *The Hanoverians, 1714-1815.* London: Edward Arnold & Co., 1948.

Hamilton, Henry. *England, a History of the Homeland.* New York: W. W. Norton & Co., 1948.

Haroutunian, Joseph. *Piety Versus Moralism.* New York: Henry Holt & Co., 1932.

Hogue, W. T. *History of the Free Methodist Church of North America.* 2 vols. Chicago: Free Methodist Publishing House, 1918.

Hopkins, C. H. *The Rise of the Social Gospel in American Protestantism.* New Haven: Yale University Press, 1940.

Hough, Emerson. *The Passing of the Frontier.* New Haven: Yale University Press, 1918.

Howland, C. L. *The Story of Our Church; Free Methodism, some facts and some reasons.* Winona Lake, Ind.: Free Methodist Publishing House, 1939.

Hughes, George. *Days of Power in the Forest Temple*. Boston: John Bent & Co., 1873.

Jackson, Thomas. *The Life of the Rev. Charles Wesley, M.A.* 2 vols. London: John Mason, 1841.

James, William. *The Varieties of Religious Experience*. New York: Longmans, Green & Co., 1902.

Jennings, A. T. *History of the American Wesleyan Church*. Syracuse: Wesleyan Methodist Publishing Association, 1902.

John of the Cross. *Saint John of the Cross, the Complete Works*. Tr. and ed. E. A. Peers. 3 vols. London: Burns, Oates, & Washbourne, 1947. Vol. II.

Jones, R. M. *Studies in Mystical Religion*. London: Macmillan & Co., 1909.

Keen, Mary P. *Memorial Papers; or, the Record of a Spirit-Filled Life*. Cincinnati: Martin Wells Knapp, 1899.

Lackington, James. *Memoirs of the First Forty-Five Years of James Lackington*. London: n.p., 1792.

Lanphier, J. C. *Alone with Jesus*. New York: N. Tibbals & Sons, 1872.

Latourette, K. S. *A History of the Expansion of Christianity*, 7 vols. 4th ed. New York: Harper & Brothers, 1939. Vol. III.

Law, William. *The Works of the Rev. William Law, A.M.* 9 vols. London: J. Richardson, 1762. Vols. III, IV.

Mahan, Asa. *Autobiography, Intellectual, Moral, and Spiritual*. London: T. Woolmer, 1882.

Man's Disorder and God's Design. The Amsterdam Assembly Series. New York: Harper & Brothers, 1948.

Manual of the Church of the Nazarene. Kansas City: Nazarene Publishing House, 1936.

Manual of the Pilgrim Holiness Church. Indianapolis: Pilgrim Publishing House, 1946.

M'Clintock, John, and Strong, James. *Cyclopedia of Biblical, Theological, and Ecclesiastical Literature*. 12 vols. New York: Harper & Brothers, 1880. Vol. IX.

McDaniel, S. C. *The Origin and Early History of the Congregational Methodist Church*. Atlanta: James P. Harrison & Co., 1881.

M'Geary, J. S. *The Free Methodist Church*. 4th ed. Chicago: W. B. Rose, 1917.

McLeister, I. F. *History of the Wesleyan Methodist Church of America*. Syracuse: Wesleyan Methodist Publishing Association, 1934.

Mode, P. G. *Source Book and Bibliographical Guide for American Church History*. Menasha, Wis.: George Banta Publishing Co., 1921.

Nicene and Post-Nicene Fathers. Ed. Philip Schaff. 14 vols. New York: The Christian Literature Co., 1888. Vols. V, VI, IX.

Overton, J. H. *The Church in England*. 2 vols. London: Gardner, Dalton & Co., 1897.

Prime, S. I. *Prayer and Its Answer*. New York: Chas. Scribner's Sons, 1882.

Raven, C. E. *The Creator Spirit*. Cambridge: Harvard University Press, 1927.

Riegel, R. E. *America Moves West*. Rev. ed. New York: Henry Holt & Co., 1947.

Schaff, Philip. *The Creeds of Christendom*. 3 vols. New York: Harper & Brothers, 1878.

Sheldon, H. C. *History of Christian Doctrine*. 2 vols. 2nd ed. New York: Harper & Brothers, 1895.

Stephen, Leslie, and Lee, Sidney. *The Dictionary of National Biography*. 22 vols. London: Oxford University Press, 1938.

Stoughton, John. *Religion in England from 1800 to 1850*. 2 vols. London: Hodder & Stoughton, 1884.

Strickland, W. P., ed. *Addresses Delivered in New York by Rev. William Arthur, A.M.* New York: Carlton and Phillips, 1856.

Strong, James. *The Exhaustive Concordance of the Bible*. New York and Nashville: Abingdon Press, 1946.

Swete, H. B. *The Holy Spirit in the Ancient Church*. London: Macmillan & Co., 1912.

Taylor, Jeremy. *The Rule and Exercises of Holy Dying*. London: Miles Flesher, 1682.

————. *The Rule and Exercises of Holy Living*. London: Miles Flesher, 1682.

Teresa. *The Complete Works of St. Teresa of Jesus*. Tr. and ed. E. A. Peers. 3 vols. New York: Sheed and Ward, 1946. Vol. I.

Thomas à Kempis. *The Imitation of Christ*. New York: E. P. Dutton & Co., 1913.

Tillotson, John. *The Works of Dr. John Tillotson, late Archbishop of Canterbury*. 10 vols. London: Printed for Richard Priestley, 1820.

Trevelyan, G. M. *English Social History*. London: Longmans, Green & Co., 1942.

Underhill, Evelyn. *Worship*. New York: Harper & Brothers, 1937.

References

The following references because of the frequency of their citation appear in the abbreviated forms indicated:

JFA—*The Journal of the Rev. Francis Asbury.*
JJW—*The Journal of the Rev. John Wesley.*
LJW—*The Letters of the Rev. John Wesley.*
MQR—*The Methodist Quarterly Review.* This publication from 1818-30 had the title of *The Methodist Magazine;* from 1830-41 it was called *The Methodist Magazine and Quarterly Review.* The one abbreviation is used to refer to all periods of the publication.
SSO—Wesley's *Sermons on Several Occasions,* the two-volume edition of 1867.
WJF—*The Works of the Rev. John Fletcher.*
WJW—*The Works of the Rev. John Wesley.* This is the 1856 edition with the exception of Volume X, which is from the 1872 edition and so indicated in the citations.
WSS—*Wesley's Standard Sermons,* E. A. Sugden, editor.

Chapter 1

1. Josiah Woodward, *Account of the Rise and Progress of the Religious Societies,* p. 107. Quoted in J. S. Simon, *John Wesley and the Religious Societies,* 12
2. *Sermon Preached before the Honourable House of Commons,* 28, 46, 48-49
3. *The Crown and Glory of Christianity,* 2, 572-73
4. P. 94
5. *The Works of Dr. John Tillotson,* VI, 532
6. WJW, XI, 351
7. JJW, I, 467
8. LJW, IV, 299
9. *The Rediscovery of John Wesley,* 361
10. WSS, I, 267-68
11. WJW, XI, 354
12. LJW, I, 188, 190
13. JJW, I, 151
14. JJW, I, 454-55
15. JJW, I, 423
16. *Original Letters by the Rev. John Wesley and His Friends,* ed. Joseph Priestly, 73-74
17. *Ibid.,* 83
18. WJW, VIII, 272
19. *Original Letters,* Priestly, 85-86
20. JJW, II, 13-14
21. LJW, III, 308, 309

22. JJW, II, 13
23. LJW, I, 248
24. JJW, III, 154
25. WJW, VIII, 285
26. JJW, IV, 370
27. LJW, V, 102
28. JJW, IV, 532
29. WJW, VI, 465

Chapter 2

1. LJW, V, 325
2. WSS, II, 394-95
3. WJW, VII, 195
4. SSO, II, 200
5. SSO, II, 201
6. LJW, V, 243
7. LJW, V, 266
8. LJW, VI, 129
9. LJW, VIII, 272
10. LJW, IV, 330
11. WJW, XIV, 305
12. LJW, VI, 76
13. LJW, V, 322
14. *An Interpretation of Christian Ethics*, 77-78
15. *John Wesley and William Law*, 206
16. WJW, IX, 409
17. LJW, VI, 239
18. WSS, II, 224
19. WJW, XI, 384
20. WJW, VII, 350
21. *Explanatory Notes*, 641
22. SSO, II, 205
23. JJW, II, 86
24. LJW, III, 213
25. LJW, IV, 167
26. LJW, V, 188-89
27. WSS, I, 277-78
28. WJW, VII, 350
29. LJW, I, 256
30. *Minutes of the Methodist Conferences*, I, 10-11
31. WJW, XI, 372
32. LJW, III, 221
33. LJW, III, 213
34. LJW, VIII, 190
35. LJW: Nov. 22, 1758, IV, 46; June 1, 1760, IV, 97; Oct. 12, 1764, IV, 268-69; May 17, 1767, V, 48; Dec. 3, 1771, V, 291; Apr. 26, 1772, V, 316; Dec. 19, 1773, VI, 59; Oct. 8, 1774, VI, 116-17; Feb. 8, 1775, VI, 138; Oct. 25, 1776, VI, 238; Sept. 8, 1778, VI, 319-20; Jan. 30, 1780, VI, 378; Jan. 19, 1782, VII, 102-3; May 3, 1783, VII, 178; Apr. 25, 1784, VII, 216; Apr. 9, 1785, VII, 267-68; Aug. 7, 1785, VII, 283; Oct. 8, 1785, VII, 295; March 4, 1786, VII, 322; May 14, 1786, VII, 329

REFERENCES

36. LJW, VIII: Aug. 5, 1788, 80; Oct. 12, 1788, 97; Jan. 24, 1789, 111; Apr. 29, 1789, 134; July 29, 1789, 156; Oct. (?), 1789, 173; Oct. 12, 1789, 175; Nov. 16, 1789, 184; Dec. 5, 1789, 190; Jan. 29, 1791, 258
37. WJW, VI, 465
38. WJW, VII, 195-96
39. *Wesley and Sanctification*, 121
40. WJW, VII, 203
41. WJW, XI, 380
42. WSS, II, 393
43. WSS, II, 156
44. LJW, VIII, 184
45. LJW, VI, 266
46. WJW, XI, 413
47. LJW, IV, 71
48. *History of Christian Doctrine*, II, 376-77
49. LJW, IV, 269
50. LJW, VII, 298
51. WJW, XI, 385-86
52. WJW, XIV, 331
53. LJW, VII, 114
54. LJW, IV, 308
55. LJW, IV, 183
56. LJW, V, 204
57. WSS, II, 448, 457
58. JJW, V, 41
59. LJW, II, 187-88
60. LJW, IV, 10
61. SSO, II, 321
62. "Epistle of Ignatius to the Ephesians." xiv. I. 55
63. "Epistle of Polycarp to the Philippians." iii, xii. I. 33-34, 36
64. "Irenaeus Against Heresies." V, vi, i, xii, 3, 4. I. 531-32, 538
65. "The Stromata." VI, xii, and especially VII, xiii, xiv. II. 502-3, 547-48
66. "On Man's Perfection in Righteousness." IX, 20; XI, 24. *Nicene and Post-Nicene Fathers.* V, 165-66, 167. Also "Against Two Letters of the Pelagians." III, 15, 22. 409, 413
67. Teresa, *Life.* XI. *The Complete Works of St. Teresa of Jesus.* I. 63. John of the Cross, *Spiritual Canticle* (Second Redaction). Stanza XXVI, 3; XXX-VIII, 11. *St. John of the Cross, Complete Works.* II. 329-30, 430-31
68. "Concerning Original Sin." Session V, 5. "On the Increase of Justification Received." Session VI. x. can. xxv. *The Canons and Decrees of the Sacred and Oecumenical Council of Trent* (Waterworth trans.). 23-24, 37, 38, 47
69. *The Life and Times of the Rev. John Wesley*, I, v
70. SSO, II, 282-83
71. SSO, II, 203

Chapter 3

1. LJW, IV, 192, 193, 194
2. LJW, IV, 245
3. LJW, V, 47
4. LJW, V, 61
5. LJW, V, 88
6. LJW, V, 93

CHRISTIAN PERFECTION AND AMERICAN METHODISM

7. LJW, V, 102
8. LJW, V, 185
9. LJW, VI, 25-26
10. JJW, VI, 239-40
11. JJW, VI, 120
12. LJW, VIII, 249
13. *Memoirs of the Late Rev. John Wesley*, III, 197-98
14. WJF, VI, 127
15. WJF, VI, 127-28
16. WJF, VI, 177
17. WJF, VI, 128-29
18. WJF, VI, 317
19. WJF, II, 43
20. WJF, II, 147
21. WJF, VI, 145
22. WJF, VI, 154
23. WJF, VI, 164-65
24. WJF, VI, 364
25. WJF, VI, 373-74
26. WJF, VII, 305-6
27. WJF, VI, 128
28. WJF, VI, 372-95, *passim*
29. WJF, VI, 370
30. WJF, VI, 367-69
31. WJF, VI, 359-60
32. *Christian Perfection*, 4
33. Luke Tyerman, *Wesley's Designated Successor*, 465
34. WJF, VI, 128, 191
35. WJF, VI, 326
36. WJF, VI, 348
37. WJW (1810), VI, 389-90
38. J. M. Buckley, *A History of Methodists in the United States*, 106
39. LJW, VI, 103
40. J. F. Hurst, *The History of Methodism*, III, 1252
41. *Men of Zeal*, 136
42. *The Experience and Travels of Mr. Freeborn Garrettson*, 63
43. MQR, XI, 98.
44. *A Brief Narrative of the Revival of Religion in Virginia. In a Letter to a Friend*, 7-8
45. *Ibid.*, 12
46. *Ibid.*, 24
47. JFA, I, 88
48. JFA, I, 339
49. JFA, I, 235
50. *Centennial History of American Methodism*, 362
51. W. W. Sweet, *Religion on the American Frontier*, IV, 77, 121
52. Abel Stevens, *A Compendious History of American Methodism*, 512
53. WJW, VIII, 316
54. Jesse Lee, *A Short History of the Methodists in the United States of America*, 85

REFERENCES

Chapter 4

1. C. B. Goodykoontz, *Home Missions on the American Frontier*, 157
2. R. E. Riegel, *America Moves West*, 107
3. Sweet, *Religion on the American Frontier*, IV, 53
4. Goodykoontz, *op. cit.*, 140
5. *Ibid.*
6. *The Rise of American Civilization*, I, 450
7. John J. Tigert, *A Constitutional History of American Episcopal Methodism*, 188
8. LJW, VII, 276
9. John Atkinson, *Centennial History of American Methodism*, 234
10. G. A. Phoebus, *Beams of Light on Early Methodism in America*, 204
11. JFA, II, 47
12. JFA, II, 174
13. Phoebus, *op. cit.*, 96
14. *A Short Account of the Christian Experience and Ministerial Labours, of William Watters*, 67
15. Unpublished letter on file in the New England Methodist Historical Association Library
16. *The Centennial of New England Methodism*, 6
17. Unpublished letter to Timothy Merritt. On file at the New England Methodist Historical Association Library
18. JFA, III, 210
19. JFA, II, 96. For an even stronger statement see JFA, III, 360
20. Sweet, *Religion on the American Frontier*, IV, 249
21. MQR, II, 342
22. *The Methodist Preacher or Monthly Sermons from Living Ministers*, II, 95-96
23. MQR, XVII, 44
24. *Guide to Holiness*, XX, 2
25. Stevens, *A Compendious History of American Methodism*, 371
26. M. L. Edwards, *Adam Clarke*, 32
27. Unpublished letter to "J. Emory, B. Waugh, N. Bangs, F. Hall, and Geo. Sackley." On file at the New England Methodist Historical Association Library
28. WJW, XI, 390
29. *Christian Theology*, 184-85
30. *Ibid.*, 207-8
31. J. W. Etheridge, *The Life of the Rev. Adam Clarke, LL.D.* 448
32. *Institutes*, III, 188
33. *The Works of the Rev. Richard Watson*, III, 52-53
34. *Institutes*, III, 188
35. *Ibid.*, 187
36. Richard Wheatley, *The Life and Letters of Mrs. Phoebe Palmer*, 633
37. LJW, VI, 287
38. *Life and Times of Nathan Bangs, D.D.*, 13-15
39. *Memoirs of Charles G. Finney*, 340, 341
40. *Ibid.*, 350-51
41. *The Present State, Prospects, and Responsibilities of the Methodist Episcopal Church*, 58 ff.
42. *Guide to Holiness*, XX, 4-7
43. WJW, VIII, 273
44. MQR, XXXI, 484 ff.

45. MQR, XXXIII, 512
46. *The True Wesleyan*, quoted in Sweet, *Methodism in American History*, 242
47. Unpublished letter on file at the New England Methodist Historical Association Library
48. I. F. McLeister, *History of the Wesleyan Methodist Church of America*, 29. Used by permission of the Wesleyan Methodist Publishing Assn.
49. A. T. Jennings, *History of American Wesleyan Methodism*, 38
50. McLeister, *op. cit.*, 38
51. *Ibid.*, 42
52. C. L. Howland, *The Story of Our Church, Free Methodism*, 31-32. Used by permission of Light and Life Press
53. *Ibid.*, 75
54. Sweet, *Methodism in American History*, 296

Chapter 5

1. George Hughes, *Days of Power*, 10-26; with an introduction by Bishop Gilbert Haven
2. C. C. Goss, *Statistical History of the First Century of American Methodism*, 184-85
3. JGCS, 1874, 568
4. MQR, LV, 229
5. *Guide to Holiness*, new series, XLIII, 27-28
6. Quoted in H. D. Farish, *The Circuit Rider Dismounts*, 74
7. WJW, XI, 381-82; LJW, V, 6; VII, 357; VIII, 14
8. *The Small Sects in America*, 92
9. George Hughes, *Holiness Year Book*, *1893*, 31
10. MQR, LVI, 492
11. *History and Exposition of the Twenty-five Articles of Religion of the Methodist Episcopal Church*, 23
12. *The Southern Methodist Review*, Oct., 1888, 41-42
13. *Systematic Theology*, II, 379
14. *Ibid.*, 350
15. *A New History of Methodism*, I, 479
16. *Systematic Theology*, II, 371
17. A. M. Hills, *Scriptural Holiness and Keswick Teaching Compared*, 29
18. *Possibilities of Grace*, 452-53
19. Edwin Mims, *History of Vanderbilt University*, 60-61
20. *Quarterly Review of the Methodist Episcopal Church, South*, Jan., 1881, 88
21. *Connecticut Yankee; An Autobiography*, 70
22. *The Varieties of Religious Experience*, 502n., Longmans, Green & Co., Inc., publisher. Permission to reprint granted by Paul R. Reynolds & Son, 599 Fifth Avenue, New York 17, N.Y.
23. *Personal Salvation: Studies in Christian Doctrine Pertaining to the Spiritual Life*, 530
24. *Ibid.*, 528
25. Feb. 2, 1899, 10
26. *The Perfect Life in Experience and Doctrine*, 17
27. M. L. Haney, "Current Errors Among Teachers of Holiness," *Proceedings of the Western Union Holiness Convention*, 46
28. Unpublished letter in the files of the New England Methodist Historical Association Library
29. MQR, LXXI, 476

30. *The Methodist Review,* Sept.-Oct., 1895, 120
31. *The Journal of the General Conference of the Methodist Episcopal Church,* 1896, App. III, 497, 498
32. *Sanctification, Right Views and Other Views,* 95-96
33. *The Journal of the General Conference of the Methodist Episcopal Church,* XIV, 59-60

Chapter 6

1. *The Idea of Perfection in Christian Theology,* 397
2. LJW, V, 16
3. WSS, II, 393
4. *The Christian Life, a Study,* 41
5. The term is used in the sense established by Ernst Troeltsch in his *Social Teaching of the Christian Churches* and modified for application to the American scene by Liston Pope in his *Millhands and Preachers.*

Chapter 7

1. (Wesley) LJW, VIII, 238 (Stevens) *The History of the Religious Movement of the Eighteenth Century Called Methodism,* I, 406. (Schaff) *The Creeds of Christendom,* I, 900. (Platt) *Encyclopedia of Religion and Ethics,* IX, 730
2. LJW, VIII, 238
3. *Methodism Has a Message!* 186. Used by permission of Abingdon Press
4. *Ibid.,* 185
5. *Man's Disorder and God's Design,* II, 75
6. Quoted in Réginald Garrigou-Lagrange, *The Three Ages of the Interior Life,* I, 204
7. *Ibid.,* 203-4
8. *The Perfection of Man by Charity,* 408

Appendix A

1. JJW, IV, 466 (Italics not in the original)
2. JJW, III, 157
3. WJW, XI, 375
4. LJW, II, 140
5. LJW, II, 383
6. LJW, III, 168
7. WJW, XI, 403
8. Cf. letter of April 5, 1758, LJW, IV, 12
9. JJW, IV, 532
10. Cf. *Explanatory Notes,* 277-78
11. LJW, IV, 245
12. LJW, IV, 300
13. JJW, IV, 542
14. JJW, V, 166
15. JJW, V, 167-70
16. LJW, V, 16
17. *John Wesley,* 212
18. JJW, V, 30
19. LJW, V, 43

CHRISTIAN PERFECTION AND AMERICAN METHODISM

20. Quoted in the *New York Christian Advocate*, XXVII, 48
21. LJW, V, 26-27
22. *Proceedings of the Second Ecumenical Methodist Conference*, 46-47
23. W. H. Meredith, *The Real John Wesley*, 294
24. Thomas Coke and Harry Moore, *The Life of the Rev. John Wesley, A.M.*, 504 ff.
25. LJW, IV, 8, 9

Appendix B

1. Tyerman, *Wesley's Designated Successor*, 468-69
2. *The Life of the Rev. John W. de la Flechere*, 152-53

Appendix C

1. JFA, I, 88
2. JFA, I, 235
3. JFA, I, 86
4. JFA, I, 195
5. JFA, III, 100

Index

Abbott, Benjamin, 94
Abolitionism, 125, 127
Adams, John, 81
Agape, 65
Aldersgate experience, 24, 25-26, 48-49, 184, 202
Andrew, Bishop James O., 124, 125
Angels, 35-36
Anger, 37
Anti-Perfectionists, 71
Antinomianism, 27, 38, 53, 62, 73, 75, 76, 161
Apostolic Holiness Union, 149
Arminianism, 39, 61, 74
Arminius, James, 62
Arthur, William, 132
Asbury, Francis, 85-86, 92, 93, 94, 96, 97, 98, 134, 203, 217-19
Asceticism, 48
Association of Pentecostal Churches of America, 149
Assurance, doctrine of, 57, 95
Atonement, 95, 96, 137
Atwood, A., 112
Augustine, 20, 61, 73, 74, 156, 199

Band Societies, 94
Bangs, Heman, 99
Bangs, Nathan, 99, 100, 102, 111, 113-14, 118-19, 178, 203
Baptists, 91, 95, 136
Barth, 199
Beard, Charles and Mary, 91
Bell, George, 67-68, 168, 183, 185, 208
Benson, Joseph, 81, 102, 216
Berry, Bishop J. F., 176
Bett, Henry, 204
Bible
    influence of, on Wesley, 15, 20, 21
    support of perfection doctrine in, 33, 181

Blackman, Launer, 96
Boardman, Richard, 85
Böhler, Peter, 23, 26, 49, 201
Boland, J. M., 154-55, 156, 168, 176
Bosanquet, Mary, 215
Boston University, 166-67
Bourignon, Antoinette, 20
Bowne, Borden Parker, 166-67, 192
Bradburn, Samuel, 212
Bresee, Phineas F., 148
Brooks, John R., 165, 176
Brooks, Thomas, 17, 18
Buckler, H. R., 199
Buckley, J. M., 152
"Buffalo Regency," 128
Burning Bush movement, 148, 149

Caldwell, Merritt, 121-22
Calvin, John, 62
Calvinism, 29, 38, 39, 61, 79, 88, 95
Cambridge Platonists, 18, 20, 61
Camp meetings, 134, 136, 138, 178
Castanzia, Juan de, 20
Catholic tradition, Wesley's relation to, 48, 61
Caughey, James, 116, 117, 134
Cell, George Croft, 20-21, 48, 62
Checks to Antinomianism (Fletcher), 71, 80, 96
Christian Church, 136
Christian Perfection (Peck), 165
Christian Standard, 162, 165
Christian Witness, 165
Christian's Manual . . . (Merritt), 101
Church of England, 15-16, 184
Church of God, 136
Church, pursuit of holiness within, 66, 184, 188, 198
Circuit system, 90, 91, 94, 96, 98, 120, 188
Civil War, 132, 133

245